A Working People

The African American History Series

Series Editors:
Jacqueline M. Moore, Austin College
Nina Mjagkij, Ball State University

Traditionally, history books tend to fall into two categories: books academics write for each other, and books written for popular audiences. Historians often claim that many of the popular authors do not have the proper training to interpret and evaluate the historical evidence. Yet popular audiences complain that most historical monographs are inaccessible because they are too narrow in scope or lack an engaging style. This series, which will take both chronological and thematic approaches to topics and individuals crucial to an understanding of the African American experience, is an attempt to address that problem. The books in this series, written in lively prose by established scholars, are aimed primarily at nonspecialists. They focus on topics in African American history that have broad significance and place them in their historical context. While presenting sophisticated interpretations based on primary sources and the latest scholarship, the authors tell their stories in a succinct manner, avoiding jargon and obscure language. They include selected documents that allow readers to judge the evidence for themselves and to evaluate the authors' conclusions. Bridging the gap between popular and academic history, these books bring the African American story to life.

Volumes Published

Booker T. Washington, W.E.B. Du Bois, and the Struggle for Racial Uplift
   Jacqueline M. Moore
Slavery in Colonial America, 1619–1776
   Betty Wood
African Americans in the Jazz Age: A Decade of Struggle and Promise
   Mark Robert Schneider
A. Philip Randolph: A Life in the Vanguard
   Andrew E. Kersten
The African American Experience in Vietnam: Brothers in Arms
   James Westheider
Bayard Rustin: American Dreamer
   Jerald Podair
African Americans Confront Lynching: Strategies of Resistance
   Christopher Waldrep
Lift Every Voice: The History of African-American Music
   Burton W. Peretti
To Ask for an Equal Chance: African Americans in the Great Depression
   Cheryl Lynn Greenberg
The African American Experience During World War II
   Neil A. Wynn
Through the Storm, Through the Night: A History of African American Christianity
   Paul Harvey
A Working People: A History of African American Workers since Emancipation
   Steven A. Reich

A Working People

A History of African American Workers since Emancipation

Steven A. Reich

ROWMAN & LITTLEFIELD PUBLISHERS, INC.
Lanham • Boulder • New York • Toronto • Plymouth, UK

Published by Rowman & Littlefield Publishers, Inc.
A wholly owned subsidiary of The Rowman & Littlefield Publishing Group, Inc.
4501 Forbes Boulevard, Suite 200, Lanham, Maryland 20706
www.rowman.com

10 Thornbury Road, Plymouth PL6 7PP, United Kingdom

Copyright © 2013 by Rowman & Littlefield

British Library Cataloguing in Publication Information Available

Library of Congress Cataloging-in-Publication Data
Reich, Steven A. (Steven Andrew), 1965-
  Working people : a history of African American workers since emancipation / Steven A. Reich.
     pages cm. — (The African American history series)
  Includes bibliographical references and index.
  ISBN 978-1-4422-0332-7 (cloth : alk. paper) — ISBN 978-1-4422-0333-4 (ebook) 1. Working class African Americans—History. 2. African Americans—Employment—History. 3. African Americans—Civil rights—History. 4. Labor—United States—History. I. Title.
  HD8081.A65R45 2013
  331.6'396073—dc23
                                                          2013018733

♾️™ The paper used in this publication meets the minimum requirements of American National Standard for Information Sciences—Permanence of Paper for Printed Library Materials, ANSI/NISO Z39.48-1992.

Printed in the United States of America

Negroes are almost entirely a working people. There are pitifully few Negro millionaires and few Negro employers. Our needs are identical with labor's needs: decent wages, fair working conditions, livable housing, old-age security, health and welfare measures, conditions in which families can grow, have education for their children, and respect in the community.

—Martin Luther King Jr., AFL-CIO National Convention, Miami Beach, Florida, December 11, 1961

Contents

~

Chronology

1863 Emancipation Proclamation

1865 Confederate surrender, ending the Civil War; Thirteenth Amendment

1868 Fourteenth Amendment

1870 Fifteenth Amendment

1876 Strikes by black workers in the South Carolina rice fields; end of Reconstruction

1886 American Federation of Labor (AFL) founded

1887 Thibodaux Massacre and Louisiana Sugar War

1890 United Mine Workers of America (UMWA) founded; Mississippi State Constitutional Convention

1909 National Association for the Advancement of Colored People (NAACP) founded

1911–1913 Brotherhood of Timber Workers, campaign to organize black and white lumber workers in western Louisiana and southeastern Texas

1914 World War I begins in Europe; Marcus Garvey forms the Universal Negro Improvement Association (UNIA)

1916 Great Migration begins

1917 United States enters World War I

1918 End of World War I

1919 Red Summer of race riots; Great Steel Strike; 100 percent organizing drive Stockyards Labor Council

1920–1921 Postwar recession

1924 National Origins Quota Act, places heavy restrictions on European immigration

1925 Founding of the Brotherhood of Sleeping Car Porters (BSCP)

1929 Stock market crash; beginning of the Great Depression

1934 Founding of the Southern Tenant Farmers' Union (STFU)

1935 The Committee for Industrial Organization (CIO) founded at the AFL annual convention; Congress passes the National Labor Relations Act

1936 Founding of the National Negro Conference (NNC); Steel Workers Organizing Committee (SWOC) launches its campaign to organize steelworkers

1937 BSCP wins labor contract with Pullman Company

1938 CIO breaks with the AFL and establishes itself as an independent labor federation, renamed the Congress of Industrial Organizations (CIO); Congress passes the Fair Labor Standards Act

1939 World War II begins in Europe

1941 United Automobile Workers (UAW) strike at Ford Motor Company; President Franklin D. Roosevelt issues Executive Order 8802, creating the Fair Employment Practice Committee; United States enters World War II

1943 Race riots in Mobile, Beaumont, and Detroit

1946 CIO launches Operation Dixie, its failed attempt to organize southern workers

1947 Congress passes the Taft-Hartley Act

1954 U.S. Supreme Court rules in *Brown v. Board of Education*

1955 The AFL and CIO merge, creating the AFL-CIO; Montgomery bus boycott begins

1960   Negro American Labor Council (NALC) founded

1962   President John F. Kennedy issues Executive Order 10988

1963   Civil rights marches in Birmingham, Alabama (April); Demonstrations in Philadelphia against employment discrimination in public construction jobs (April–May); March in Washington for Jobs and Freedom (August)

1964   Congress passes the Civil Rights Act of 1964

1965   Congress passes the Voting Rights Act; black workers file first grievances with the EEOC under Title VII

1968   Memphis Sanitation Workers' Strike; Dodge Revolutionary Union Movement (DRUM) founded in Detroit

1977   Sanitation Strike in Atlanta

1992   Settlement of *Haynes v. Shoney's*

2008   Great Recession; election of Barack Obama

~

Introduction

A *Working People*

African Americans "are almost entirely a working people," declared Reverend Martin Luther King Jr., in his address to the 1961 national convention of the AFL-CIO, the nation's largest federation of labor unions. As workers, King explained, African Americans were most in need of those things common to all workers: good wages, fair working conditions, a secure retirement, affordable housing, access to modern medical care, and a quality education. King emphasized that organized labor and African Americans shared the same aspirations and hence should be natural political allies. Together, King insisted that they could fulfill the dream of a new democracy, founded upon racial and economic justice, that protected equality of opportunity for all, distributed widely the wealth and property it created, and enabled all people to prosper and live in comfort. He dreamed of a society in which the wealth of the nation served not the interests of the few but the needs of humanity. In such a world, all people lived and worked with dignity and respect.

A Working People tells the story of African Americans in struggle "to make racial and economic justice a reality." It emphasizes the importance of work to the black experience because most African Americans spent the majority of their adult lives at work, and work shaped their social, political, and cultural outlook. African Americans' efforts to win equality and secure the rights of citizenship rested on their recognition that these broader goals could not be met or secured without guarantees of dignity at work. African American men and women experienced considerable discrimination in American workplaces, which underscored the necessity of economic rights as well as

1

civil rights. Many black labor activists thus had a keen understanding of the economic foundations necessary for political equality and for meaningful participation in American society. The fight for citizenship—for basic social recognition—was thus intimately connected to African Americans' workplace experiences. A labor history of African Americans is thus essential to understand and come to terms with the larger story of the African American freedom movement.

The narrative in this book emphasizes three interconnected subplots. First, as working people, African Americans knew that they could not achieve racial equality in a society that denied them economic justice. Despite former slaves' hope for a general redistribution of land in the aftermath of slavery, no fundamental changes in land ownership ever materialized. The rural labor system that emerged in the South after Reconstruction, backed by a repressive legal system, betrayed black expectations of rural independence through hard work. Without political power, few blacks accumulated resources sufficient to prosper and achieve economic security. Hard work alone could not protect rural blacks from poverty, racial violence, and relentless toil. Outside of agriculture, black workers well into the twentieth century labored under conditions that confined them to the most disagreeable, demanding, and dangerous jobs, deprived them of equal pay for equal work, denied them opportunities for promotion, left them vulnerable to employers who manipulated racial divisions of labor, exposed them to hostile white workers, and lacked security from periods of unemployment. World Wars I and II opened employment opportunities for African Americans in Northern industries, which alleviated but did not eliminate racial discrimination in the labor market. After World War II, automation in industry eliminated thousands of unskilled jobs held by African Americans, leaving them less able to share in the bounty of postwar prosperity. In 1960, in the midst of the civil rights movement, black workers suffered unemployment at a rate twice as great as whites; those who worked remained overwhelmingly concentrated in the lowest-paying occupations that offered limited hope for upward mobility.

Second, African Americans not only struggled to find work that paid a decent wage, they searched for work that conferred dignity. African Americans hoped to escape dead-end labor that promised no occupational mobility and reduced them, in the eyes of white employers and white coworkers, to a state of perpetual childhood and servility. Many blacks had the freedom to change jobs; few could expect a career that earned them social standing and respect. One investigator of the working conditions of blacks in New York City in 1906 found a situation typical of many blacks. When he interviewed a boy just a few months shy of his high school graduation, he asked him what kind of work he aspired to. The boy answered that he would like to work as a door boy. The investigator reminded him that such a job would only pay $3.00 a week and would not be sufficient and asked him what he would do next. The boy replied that he would seek work as an office boy. When the investigator asked him what he thought he would do after that, the boy replied that he would become a bellboy and then perhaps one day he could work his way up to head bellboy. Few blacks, the investigator discovered, saw much hope for upward mobility in a labor market that regarded them as boys; they entered the world of work in which white employers regarded them as children. In 1968, when sanitation workers—inspired by the victories of the civil rights movement—went on strike in Memphis, Tennessee, they carried signs that declared "I Am a Man!" In doing so, they contested this long history of the indignities of black labor. By asserting their manhood, they demanded not just good wages and fair working conditions, but they insisted upon being treated as adults—as full and equal citizens deserving of dignity, respect, and justice—and not like children.

As the example of the sanitation workers underscores, African Americans were not just victims of racism in the workplace. Although employment discrimination narrowed the life chances of African Americans, many black workers neither waited for white people to help them nor remained patient until white attitudes about race changed. Thus, the third storyline that this book explores are the many ways in which black workers struggled to change the conditions that structured their working lives. Black workers made the greatest gains when labor markets were tight, when they worked under a union contract, and when the federal government and its agencies supported and protected the interests of African Americans in the workplace. Tight labor markets, unions, and antidiscrimination laws alone did not necessarily improve the lot of black workers. From the moment of emancipation, the ex-slave and abolitionist Frederick Douglass warned African Americans that the price of liberty was eternal vigilance. Heeding Douglass's call for vigilance over complacency, many black workers thus acted in their own interests to take advantage of new circumstances when they arose. They migrated to take advantage of tight labor markets, joined and built a labor movement that eventually became responsive to their interests, and pressured government agencies to fulfill their commitment to equality and fair employment. Black labor activism thus emerged as essential for ensuring that the conditions for change—tight labor markets, unionization, and government intervention—produced substantive change.

The wartime labor markets of World Wars I and II transformed the African American labor force from an industrial surplus reserve of casual laborers into a population integral to America's industrial workforce. Both wars inspired massive migrations of African Americans that transformed the racial composition of the nation's industrial labor force and enabled African Americans to secure the right to work in industries—steelmaking, meatpacking, automobile manufacturing, and shipbuilding—that had long excluded black workers. For black women, especially, industrial employment in the nation's defense industries opened high-paying jobs outside of agriculture and domestic service. But even if black workers had become integrated into the urban-industrial life of the nation, they continued to encounter obstacles to promotion and found themselves unable to escape the hardest, heaviest, lowest-paying, and most dangerous jobs in these industries. Breaking the barriers of exclusion to employment in the industrial sector was insufficient to secure economic justice.

Black workers thus debated whether to regard labor unions as allies or as obstacles in their fight against employment discrimination. In the late nineteenth and early twentieth century, most African Americans remained ambivalent about or hostile to the labor movement. Many white trade unionists excluded blacks from their unions; moreover, they established workplace rules that protected their claims to the best-paying skilled and semiskilled occupations. On the few occasions when black and white workers came together to build interracial unions, employers proved adept at exploiting racial divisions to defeat those alliances. Many black workers remained skeptical, believing that unions catered to the priorities of white workers and only sought black allies out of necessity rather than out of any genuine concern about promoting their interests.

Nonetheless, by the mid-twentieth century, African Americans had become the most committed unionists in the American labor force. A number of factors account for the creation of a new union consciousness among black workers. These included changes in federal labor law, the emergence of industrial unionism, and new forms of black political activism. By the late 1940s, African American workers had come to value the advantages of a union-negotiated contract. It provided higher wages, better benefits, grievances procedures, and job security. Union solidarity provided protections unavailable to individual workers. All combined to elevate the living standards of black workers.

Still, the relationship between blacks and organized labor remained tense and uneasy. Although most labor leaders came to regard civil rights as important by midcentury, they often saw them as secondary to their primary focus on wages, working conditions, and benefits. Black workers, on the other hand, saw no distinction between civil rights and the rights of work. Employment discrimination, especially if sustained by union practices, prevented African Americans from obtaining those benefits that King claimed were the aspirations common to all working people. Black workers thus turned to the federal government to force employers and unions to eliminate employment discrimination.

As in their relationship with organized labor, black workers could not count on government officials to create, let alone enforce, laws and executive orders designed to promote antidiscrimination. The 1863 Emancipation Proclamation ended slavery but did not grant citizenship; New Deal labor laws of the 1930s protected the labor rights of workers but excluded agricultural workers and domestic servants, many of whom were black. During World War II, the Fair Employment Practice Committee banned racial discrimination in defense industries but received limited support and funding, and it lacked the enforcement power to compel employers and unions to comply with its directives. The Civil Rights Act of 1964 prohibited racial employment discrimination but initially lacked effective enforcement powers. Black workers realized that they could not rely on government agencies and the bureaucrats who staffed them to protect, let alone identify, their interests. Although these federal policies were vital to the broader struggle for justice in the workplace and in the labor market, seldom did they go far enough to address the needs of black workers. Black workers again relied on vigilance, not complacency, to transform federal laws into effective instruments of public policy and to force the federal government to act on their behalf.

Throughout this history, many black workers fought back, determined to change the conditions of their work. They did not wait for others to improve their circumstances. Through their own initiative, many black workers helped to break the barriers of exclusion to employment, to force the labor movement to represent their interests as blacks and as workers, and to compel the government to enforce its own standards of fair and equal employment. This book emphasizes those efforts—often against great odds—that black laboring men and women undertook to improve the everyday working conditions of their lives. More often than not, they encountered stiff resistance and opposition, often violent, that thwarted the realization of their goals. That they eventually succeeded in creating a more open and inclusive workplace is testament to their commitment and sacrifice; that they did not succeed earlier nor achieve more is testament to the obstacles that they confronted and the endurance of racial economic inequality a century and a half after the end of the Civil War.

CHAPTER ONE

~

Emancipation and the Politics of Black Labor

Under cover of darkness on the evening of May 23, 1861, three slaves from Hampton, Virginia, escaped to the Union army stationed at nearby Fortress Monroe. The three field hands were about to be separated from their wives and sent to the Carolinas where they were to be forced into the service of the Confederate army to build fortifications for the rebel forces. The slaves' owner, a Confederate colonel, called upon the fort the next day and demanded the return of the slaves under the terms of the federal fugitive slave law of 1850. Claiming that Virginia's secession from the Union ended its white residents' recourse to relief under the federal statute, Union Major-General Benjamin Butler refused to comply. After interrogating the fugitives, Butler concluded that the slaves could be of great service to the Union forces, declared them "contraband of war," and put them to work around the fort. Once the slaves in the surrounding area learned that the Union army refused to return the runaways, they began to make their way to what they called freedom fort. Within the next several weeks, some nine hundred slaves—men, women, and children—had amassed behind Union lines, eager to work as contrabands for the Union rather than toil as slaves for the Confederacy.

Thus began what the African American scholar and civil rights activist W. E. B. Du Bois called the "general strike" against slavery.[1] From the beginning of the Civil War, a rising tide of fugitive slaves seeking refuge with the Union army deprived the Confederacy of the slave labor that was the lifeline of its war effort. Not all slaves had the means or the opportunity to

7

escape their bondage during the war. But the metaphor of a general strike against slavery captures how the thousands of slaves who did have the chance fled and in so doing undermined the Confederate war effort. Not only did slaves raise foodstuffs and cash crops on Southern plantations, they served the Confederate military by working in Southern mines, factories, and munitions plants, building army fortifications, hauling supplies for rebel armies, and acting as servants and cooks in military camps. "The very stomach of this rebellion," wrote the ex-slave and abolitionist Frederick Douglass, "is the negro in the form of a slave. Arrest that hoe in the hands of the negro, and you smite the rebellion in the very seat of its life."[2] Despite the military value of slaves to the Confederacy, federal officials initially refrained from interfering with Southern slavery, insisting that it waged war to preserve the Union, not to free the slaves. Yet wherever the Union army advanced, a stampede of fugitive slaves appeared, confounding the logic of the North's war aims. Many slaves appreciated from the beginning that the war heralded the end of bondage and quickly acted to hasten its demise. Union general William Tecumseh Sherman's encounter with an elderly black Georgian in November 1864 captures this expectant spirit among the slaves. "He had been looking for the 'angel of the lord' ever since he was knee-high," Sherman explained, "and though we professed to be fighting for the union, he supposed that slavery was the cause, and that our success was

Figure 1.1.   Fugitive slaves cross the Rappahannock River in Virginia for the promise of freedom behind Union lines, 1862. Civil War glass negative collection, Prints & Photographs Division, Library of Congress, LC-DIG-cwpb-0021.

to be his freedom."[3] When Sherman asked him if all slaves understood the war in those terms, the man assured him that they did.

As fugitives overwhelmed federal military camps, they forced the presidential administration of Abraham Lincoln to reconsider its policy. Military authorities responded to the refugee crisis by adopting the policy Major-General Butler had implemented in Virginia, neither returning nor emancipating fugitive slaves but organizing them into a workforce of laborers, servants, and spies. As the Union army advanced further into the South, it shifted its policies toward slaves yet again. Under the provisions of the Emancipation Proclamation, which President Lincoln issued on January 1, 1863, the military began to enlist blacks into the army and navy on a massive scale. Military service converted thousands of fugitives from laborers into soldiers of democracy and transformed the invaders from the North into an army of liberators. Through their own collective action, black workers helped turn the tide of the war and assure that emancipation would become a consequence of Northern victory.

The defeat of the Confederacy assured the collapse of slavery, but it left the meaning and security of black freedom far from settled. Few Americans, Northern or Southern, white or black, agreed upon a universal definition of freedom, let alone the social, economic, or political conditions necessary to preserve it. Is freedom "the bare privilege of not being chained," asked Congressman James A. Garfield in 1865. "If this is all, then freedom is a bitter mockery, a cruel delusion."[4] But did emancipation confer upon ex-slaves anything further, such as civil equality, the right to own property, or a share of political power? Or did it mean no more than a simple recognition of personal liberty? These were not just philosophical questions, but concrete issues that surfaced in the immediate aftermath of the war in day-to-day confrontations between former slaves and former slaveholders. Since slavery had always been a labor system that bound slaves to masters who held absolute power over their lives, the freedoms that African Americans could claim in the absence of slavery had much to do with the new configurations of work that would replace slavery. When blacks escaped slavery during the war, they contested the conditions of work that sustained the plantation economy and the political power of its ruling elite. Having forced emancipation upon a reluctant nation, blacks were determined to realize a broader vision of freedom. Blacks would not be content with an emancipation that did little more than recognize their personal liberty and failed to alter the conditions that sustained their economic subordination. Class as well as racial conflict, with the interests of former slaves pitted against those of former masters, would determine the boundaries of freedom in post–Civil War America.

Following the war, Southern white planters tried to retain as much control as possible over the labor of their former slaves. Indeed, the prosperity of the South, and the planters' own class survival, depended upon the ability of white planters to command the labor of their former slaves. Former slaveholders may have begrudgingly accepted the fact that they now had to pay African Americans for their labor, but they did not believe that emancipation changed the freedmen's status as a dependent plantation labor force. Slaves might be free, but they were only free to labor. To planters, that meant free to work on employers' terms. Thus as former slaveholders across the South reluctantly negotiated labor agreements with the former slaves, they tried to stipulate that ex-slaves had to work as they had during slavery. Under the terms of these first postwar labor contracts, planters required former slaves to labor in the fields from sunup to sundown in work gangs under the strict and direct supervision of an overseer. Planters also expected to retain authority over their former slaves' lives after work. Early contracts regulated the private lives of employees, constricting their rights to travel, entertain visitors, or assemble meetings. Some planters even tried to dictate whom their employees could marry. In asserting an unrestricted claim to the time and labor of their former slaves, planters expected blacks to obey their employers as slaves had their masters.

Instead of paying regular cash wages planters compensated their black field hands with a collective share of the crop, which usually ranged between one-eighth and one-fourth of the harvest. They deferred this payment to the end of the agricultural season, in effect forcing their black workers into granting them an interest-free loan that enabled cash-poor planters to operate their farms. This method of payment also forced black laborers to remain working on plantations until the end of the agricultural cycle, because if they left before the harvest, they would forfeit any claim to the crop that they had earned. The compensation that they did receive was pitifully low, barely providing the subsistence that ex-slaves needed to survive, let alone to prosper.

African Americans rejected this narrow definition of freedom. They expected to live free of the indignities and humiliations that they had endured as slaves. In countless ways, blacks asserted personal liberties denied to them under bondage: to move as they wished, to reunite with family and friends, to worship in congregations of their own choice, to learn to read and write, to claim and enjoy leisure time where and when they desired. In asserting control over their familial, religious, and social lives, they understood eman-

cipation to mean freedom from the white intrusions that had so dominated
their lives in bondage. To remain under the authority of whites struck many
freedmen as a condition akin to slavery.

Without some measure of economic independence, ex-slaves realized
that they would remain subject to the arbitrary authority of their former
masters. Only by taking command of their working lives and exercising
control over the fruits of their labor could they accumulate the resources
necessary to reunite their families, govern their domestic lives, educate
their children, worship as they wished, and build the institutions that
would stabilize their communities. Planters considered freedmen's hopes for
economic independence as further evidence of how freedom had corrupted
their capacity for work. Freedmen rejected these accusations, but in doing
so they distinguished between toiling as slaves and working for themselves.
An ex-slave in Tennessee acknowledged that he had to make his living by
hard labor, but he now expected to be treated with the same dignity and respect as any other human being. "If we could make our masters rich," asked
a former slave in Louisiana, "cannot we make ourselves rich?"[5] As he saw
it, freedom to work for themselves was the great promise of emancipation.
Former slaves expected to work fewer hours than under slavery, to do so on
their own time and at their own pace rather than in gangs under the direct
supervision of overseers, to receive a rightful share of the product of their labor, and to negotiate the terms of their employment. If working conditions
did not meet these expectations, they insisted upon the freedom to move to
pursue economic independence.

African Americans regarded the ownership of land as the securest foundation for economic autonomy. "Gib us our own land and we take care
ourselves," a freedman explained, "but without land, de ole masses can hire
us or starve us, as dey please."[6] Throughout the South in the autumn of
1865, stories circulated among former slaves that the federal government
planned to redistribute the land of former Confederates to the freedmen.
Such rumors kindled the freedmen's faith that federal officials shared their
conviction that they had a just claim to the land of their former masters. It
was, they believed, a just compensation for generations of unrequited toil
and as a reward for their loyalty to the Union during the Civil War. Owning land, freedmen claimed, would allow them not only to gain control over
their own work, but also enable them to cultivate food crops rather than
devote all of their energies to the production of cash crops such as cotton,
rice, or sugar. For many, the freedom to manage their own farms represented
the greatest contrast between the degradation of slave labor and the dignity
of free labor.

Beyond the individual aspiration for propertied independence, black landownership had broader economic and political implications. In some places, freedmen abandoned the plantations where they had lived as slaves in favor of squatting on little patches of unimproved land in the woods or in creek bottoms where they intended to farm for themselves. Citing such behavior, one former slaveholder feared that a great many of the richest plantations in the South might remain uncultivated because of the lack of black laborers. Access to land enabled former slaves to withdraw their labor from the command of former slave owners, thus jeopardizing the labor supply vital for the revival of the South's plantation economy. The emergence of a class of independent, small-scale black farmers could form the basis of an agrarian democracy in the postwar South that would supplant the old plantation economy and the social and political hierarchies upon which it was founded.

By demanding the right to assert control over their persons and the fruits of their labor, freedmen across the South contested former masters' claims on their time and labor. Ex-slaves harbored deep suspicions about the intent of their former masters. One aging ex-slave, because he could neither read nor understand the contract his former master offered him, feared that it would return him to slavery. Even if former slaves had to work under such labor agreements, as free people they refused to act or live like slaves. Many black field hands insisted upon setting their own pace of work. Others refused to plow ground that was too hard, pull weeds in the rain, tend to general repairs and maintenance work without extra compensation, or work on Saturdays and Sundays. Many no longer showed the same servile deference expected of them under slavery, preferring to address their employers as "mister" rather than "master." Some black workers acted collectively and drafted petitions to renegotiate contracts, attempted to set region-wide wage scales, and even organized strikes. African Americans were most insistent in their refusal to work under strict white supervision and in their resistance to planters who resorted to corporal punishment to discipline their workers. When planters hired overseers or reached for their whips, they risked provoking retaliation or a mass exodus of essential labor from their estates.

Although planters retained considerable power and authority over ex-slaves, they also discovered that it was far more difficult to manage an emancipated workforce than an enslaved one. One South Carolina rice planter fretted that plantation owners were now at a great disadvantage. Black workers, he lamented, did what they pleased and seemed unmoved by planters' attempts to discipline them. When planters threatened to fire and evict them, freedmen laughed, claiming that they would simply go live and work at any number of other places. Landlords in East Texas grumbled that blacks had become undependable, showed no disposition to labor, wandered the country without purpose, plundered and stole, and quit work and left plantations without any apparent cause. They insisted that unless they resorted "to the overseer, whip, and hounds" their estates would deteriorate and never recover.[7] The Georgia Agricultural Commissioner captured the frustration of many Southern planters when he remarked that emancipation had thrown labor conditions into chaos by breaking the planters' power to compel blacks to work in the rice swamps. Planters resented that emancipation not only challenged their sense of racial supremacy but also eroded their authority as employers of labor.

This resentment exploded into a campaign of violence against ex-slaves across much of the South. In the three years following the Civil War, whites in Texas killed nearly five hundred blacks, committed two hundred and fifty serious assaults, and were involved in fifty-five cases of extreme brutality aimed at African Americans. While whites may have assaulted blacks "for the pure love of killing," as one federal official explained it, the government's own records suggest that the attackers tended to be planters and property holders.[8] They were determined to prevent blacks from claiming the fruits of their labor and for attempting to control the pace of their work. Violence erupted most frequently at the end of the contract year around crop settlements and wage disputes, but it also threatened freedmen's everyday lives. Whites assaulted black workers for claiming to be too ill to work, for lingering too long over breakfast, or for working in a manner that they considered incompetent, lazy, or careless.

Former slaves were not at the total mercy of planters, and many appealed to agents of the federal government in their struggle to redefine the South's new system of labor. Northern victors had their own vision of postwar labor relations, one that challenged the authority of former planters but that did not always advance the interests of black workers. With the South under military occupation at the war's end, the federal government assumed an expansive role in establishing and implementing the transition from slavery to freedom and determining the legal boundaries that would define black labor and freedom in the wake of emancipation. By the summer of 1865, the Bureau of Refugees, Freedmen, and Abandoned Lands assumed the authority to supervise labor relations in the South. When Congress created the Freedman's Bureau in March of 1865, it gave the agency an expansive mandate that included providing for the education, medical care, welfare, and legal protections of former slaves. The bureau also had the authority to rent out and eventually sell plots of abandoned and confiscated land to freedmen.

Most importantly, the bureau oversaw the introduction of a new system of labor on Southern plantations. Envisioning the bureau as a temporary agency, Congress provided only limited resources and manpower, thus undermining the bureau's ability to meet the many needs of former slaves.

Most of the white Northerners who staffed the Freedmen's Bureau had long maintained a faith in the superiority of free labor over slave labor and envisioned reconstructing the South in the image of the North. Free labor, they believed, made Northern society distinct because it offered wage earners the opportunity, limited only by their talent and ambition, to rise to the status of independent farmer or craftsmen. As Abraham Lincoln explained in his annual message to Congress in 1861, hired laborers in the North, unlike slaves, were not bound to their condition for life. Men who began their working lives as penniless laborers saved their wages, and through prudence, industry, and planning soon accumulated enough money to purchase the tools or land that they needed to work for themselves. Under such a system, the great majority neither worked for others nor hired others to work for them. As one Republican congressman from Ohio boasted, in the free and open society of the North, the relationship between workers and employers wasnever fixed. Today's wage earner, he declared, became tomorrow's capitalist; while today's capitalist could become tomorrow's laborer. They regarded free labor—the right to work free of the fixed condition of slavery and with the promise of self-improvement through hard work, thrift, industry, and occupational mobility—as the foundation of freedom and a universal right.

As advocates of free labor and representatives of the federal government, bureau agents often intervened on behalf of ex-slaves in their struggle against planters who were determined to impose slave-like working conditions. Agents invalidated contracts that violated the basic principles of free labor. They challenged contracts that stipulated repressive regulations of blacks' private lives, curtailed labor mobility, or erected other barriers to black economic advancement. Many bureau agents found that they spent much of their time enforcing contracts at the end of the harvest season and settling wage disputes between freedmen and planters. Many others responded to counteract planter cruelty and to protect black victims of white violence. When federal agents prosecuted white employers who disregarded contracts or whipped their black employees, they tried to force planters to recognize that they no longer had the absolute authority over their workers that slavery had once conferred.

Although bureau agents often intervened to discipline cruel and resistant planters, they proved to be unreliable allies of former slaves. Although all agents were committed to enforcing emancipation in the South, few of them had been devoted abolitionists before the war, and even fewer advocated racial equality. Most of them were Northern white men who had accumulated modest amounts of property and had risen through the ranks of the military. Most bureau agents considered African Americans a downtrodden people unprepared for the responsibilities and obligations of freedom. They regarded former slaves as children who needed the guiding hand of educated white men to teach them the proper values of hard work, obedience to the law, and respect for private property. Agents saw them as vulnerable and defenseless people who needed protection from violence. While bureau officials rejoiced at the demise of slavery, they were less optimistic about the ex-slaves' capacity for industrious labor. Many bureau officials and Southern planters shared the conviction—though derived from different assumptions about the nature of slavery—that most African Americans embraced freedom as an escape from hard work. Whereas slaveholders assumed that blacks were inherently lazy and only worked under compulsion, many white Northerners believed that toiling under slavery for no wages had corrupted the black work ethic and left former slaves ill prepared for the challenges and responsibilities of free labor. No matter how much they expressed their horror at persistent planter cruelty, bureau agents often seemed more fearful of black idleness and the threat it might pose toward the South's recovery. In response, bureau agents tried to instruct ex-slaves about their responsibilities as dutiful employees. They tried to compel them to sign labor contracts that they believed would teach freedmen important lessons of frugality and thrift as well as encourage them to become self-sufficient and free of dependence upon the federal government or charity for support.

By repeating white Southern claims that blacks preferred largesse to labor, federal officials voiced what would become one of the most enduring explanations for persistent black poverty and unemployment. Fears of encouraging the growth of an idle black class led bureau officials to conclude that it was more socially responsible to put freedmen to work for their former masters than to provide them with relief, land, or other resources. To compel former slaves to return to the fields and prevent them from migrating to cities in search of work or roaming the countryside without employment, Bureau agents frequently urged, if not forced, them to sign unfavorable contracts with their former masters. Bureau agents then prosecuted blacks who broke those contracts, punished vagrants, and imposed other restrictions on black workers' physical mobility to discourage what they considered the wandering ways of former slaves.

Not all white Northerners were unsympathetic to black aspirations for land. Some, especially so-called Radical Republicans, believed that the federal government had a responsibility to assist blacks in acquiring land. The Radicals were a group of Northern legislators who had, for the most part, been uncompromising abolitionists before the war and embraced the Union victory in the Civil War as a historic moment to use the expanded powers of the federal government to establish and protect the equal rights of all Americans, regardless of race. They emerged during Reconstruction as the most committed advocates of granting civil and political rights to former slaves, of prohibiting former Confederates from holding political office, and of confiscating the land of former slaveholders and redistributing it to former slaves.

The prospects for land reform seemed especially promising at war's end. More than 850,000 acres of abandoned land fell under the jurisdiction of the Freedmen's Bureau, which was authorized to settle former slaves on forty-acre plots that they could rent for three years, with an option to purchase. The rental and sales of these lands would finance, in the absence of congressional funding, the bureau's extensive relief operations. Former slaves had already settled upon much of this confiscated land under federal control, including the so-called Sherman Reserve, an expanse of four hundred thousand acres of the Sea Islands and coastal low country of South Carolina and Georgia. In January 1865, Union general Sherman issued Special Field Order No. 15, which set aside this region of abandoned rice plantations for the exclusive settlement of slaves. Sherman issued the order to relieve his army of the burden of caring for the destitute slaves who had abandoned their plantations and followed the Union forces as they marched to the Atlantic Coast after capturing Atlanta in September 1864. Sherman later denied that the order conveyed permanent possession of the land to the slaves, insisting that it only supplied the freedmen and their families with temporary provisions for the duration of the war. Nonetheless, word of Field Order No. 15 quickly spread, and by June approximately forty thousand freedmen had settled upon the Sherman Reserve. That summer, the commissioner of the Freedmen's Bureau, General Oliver Otis Howard, kindled the hope that freedmen might secure legal title to the land when he issued a circular authorizing bureau officials to commence the process of allotting forty-acre plots of abandoned and confiscated land under federal control to loyal refugees and freedmen. Although the land under the bureau's control was less than 1 percent of all land in the former Confederacy, it was enough to provide the precedent for a broader policy of land reform, one that could challenge the power of the South's plantation elite.

Before the bureau had a chance to implement Howard's instructions, President Andrew Johnson intervened and forced the agency to reverse course. Johnson, who had assumed the presidency after Lincoln's assassination in April 1865, did not share any vision of a reconstructed South that allowed for the redistribution of land, however limited, to former slaves. Johnson, a Democrat from Tennessee and the only Southern senator who remained loyal to the Union during the Civil War, had been nominated to the vice presidency in 1864. Although Johnson had established a reputation as a bitter political foe of the Southern planter class, he firmly believed in states' rights and limiting the power of the federal government, and he envisioned no role for African Americans in postwar politics. Johnson despised African Americans as much as he hated slavery. In a speech before Congress in 1867, he declared that blacks had no capacity to serve in government and that granting them the right to vote would unleash a reign of tyranny. Under the terms of the proclamation of amnesty that he issued in May 1865, Johnson pardoned and restored the property rights of thousands of white Southerners, excluding only former Confederate leaders and the wealthiest planters. When Howard suggested that confiscated and abandoned lands set apart for refugees and freedmen could not be restored to their former owners by presidential pardon, Johnson overruled him, ordering Howard to withdraw his circular and issue a new one that restored all land under bureau control to pardoned insurgents. In October Howard traveled to the Sherman Reserve to inform the black settlers that the land they occupied would revert to its former white owners and that they either had to sign labor contracts with the planters or face eviction.

In eloquent letters to President Johnson and to Commissioner Howard, a committee of black settlers on Edisto Island, South Carolina, pleaded with the government to reconsider its position. They reminded Howard that the government had promised them homesteads because they were the only true and loyal people in the region. As they explained to the president, they regarded the land as their home: their labor had improved the land and made it productive. By taking away their right to the soil they occupied, the government not only broke its promise but took from them the very foundation of freedom. Restoring the property rights of those who had rebelled against the Union, the petitioners insisted, would bring back the power relations of slavery. Nor did the petitioners believe that the government appreciated the depth of the conflict of interest between former slaves and planters. Freedmen, they continued, simply could not forgive their former masters and agree to work for those who had once tied them to trees, whipped them, and flogged their mothers and sisters. The petitioners argued that planters had no desire or willingness to treat them with fairness or respect.

Most importantly, the loss of the Sherman Reserve underscored the political powerlessness of ex-slaves under Presidential Reconstruction. As the Edisto Island settlers recognized in their letter to Commissioner Howard, the government controlled their destiny, for without political representatives, they had no power to prevent the state from making laws that denied them the right to own land. Without land, homes, or votes, the freedmen had no other recourse but to pray to God for help and to petition the president for his influence. Prayers and petitions, however moving, were weak and ineffective instruments of persuasion with a president committed to a swift and limited reconstruction founded upon the pardon of former rebels and a restoration of their property rights. Johnson's vision of emancipation imagined no change of the civil or economic status for the country's 4 million former slaves.

Johnson's intervention transformed the function of the bureau. No longer would it have the authority to promote the emergence of a class of small-scale black farmers situated upon the estates of former masters. Those agents most committed to granting former slaves portions of confiscated land either resigned from the bureau or were relieved of their duties. Even if many white Northerners still believed that ex-slaves had rightful claims to land, most could not shake their faith in the sanctity of private property, another key belief of free labor ideology, to endorse a redistribution of land. Federal officials encouraged blacks to acquire property through the free market, not through redistribution or confiscation. As General Joseph Fullerton declared to ex-slaves in Louisiana when he explained why the government would not grant them land, the government had made them free and would protect them in that freedom. But it would do nothing more.

Johnson's amnesty policy was part of the president's broader plan for Reconstruction. With Congress not in session from April through November 1865, Johnson proceeded with his own plan for readmitting the former Confederate states into the Union. Under the terms of what came to be called Presidential Reconstruction, Johnson authorized Southern states to call new state constitutional conventions—delegates to which would be elected by whites only—to establish new loyal governments. To qualify for readmission, Johnson required Southern states to abolish slavery and renounce the principles of secession. Because he favored states' rights, Johnson granted

Southern lawmakers wide latitude in shaping the postwar South and issued no federal mandate regarding the rights of freedmen.

The Southern legislatures that organized under Presidential Reconstruction enacted a series of statutes designed to codify planters' vision for postemancipation labor relations. Although these so-called black codes granted nominal freedoms to former slaves, such as the right to marry, to own personal property, and to have limited access to the courts, in other ways they severely constrained their freedoms. First, in direct violation of free labor principles, they obligated blacks to enter into labor contracts. Under a Texas law, labor contracts, which were to be executed in the presence of a county official and filed with the court, bound the worker and his family to the employer for the duration of the contract. The contracts could only be severed with the employer's consent or if the employee could prove that the employer treated him with "inhumanity" or "cruelty," which the law failed to define. Yet the law specified at length the heavy fines and stiff penalties that employers could impose on workers for "habitual laziness" or disobedience, which the law defined as neglecting their duty, failing to obey "reasonable orders," leaving the plantation without permission, acting with impudence, fighting with other workers, or swearing in the presence of the employer or his family members.[9] Moreover, the contract labor law guaranteed employers an unrestricted claim to the time and labor of their workers. The law authorized employers to control the labor of all the members of the family, including all minors who were able to work. Finally, the law required all employees promptly to obey all commands of their employers, regardless of the time of day or the day of the week. Most Southern states passed similar measures as well as a host of other laws that restricted the labor rights of former slaves. Apprenticeship laws gave planters control over the unpaid labor of black orphans or black minors whose parents the local courts found either unfit or unable to support them. The law thus empowered the state to entrust thousands of young blacks into the care of planters, who put them to work on their estates, without the consent (or at times even knowledge) of their parents. Vagrancy laws empowered local law enforcement officials to arrest, detain, or hire out for work any person who had no visible means of support, lived in idleness, refused to work at the prevailing wage, or begged. Southern states also passed labor statutes that made it a crime to entice workers under contract to leave their employer by offering them higher wages. Taken together, the black codes ensured, as one Southern lawmaker openly admitted, that former slaves remained menial laborers.

Not content with the federal government's failure to protect their interests, African Americans mobilized on their own behalf to challenge the restoration of planter authority under Presidential Reconstruction. Black activists organized local assemblies, mass meetings, and statewide conventions where they proclaimed their right to the same social and political privileges as white citizens. They gathered to demand access to free public education, the rights to bear arms, serve on juries, assemble peacefully, and publish their own newspapers, and the repeal of all laws that discriminated against African Americans. Above all, they insisted upon the right to earn a living and the right to vote. As a meeting of "colored citizens" in Mississippi declared, since few white men were willing to pay fair wages, blacks needed laws that protected their property, labor, and right to collect the wages that they earned. Just as paid labor distinguished the free man from the slave, the ballot conferred a social dignity unavailable to those who did not have the right to vote. The state had no right to deny blacks, as loyal citizens, the right to vote, attendees of that gathering resolved. Blacks flooded state legislatures, governors' mansions, Congress, and the White House with petitions and communications demanding these rights as the key attributes of citizenship. As Frederick Douglass recognized, "slavery is not abolished until the black man has the ballot" because to deny blacks the vote was "to brand us with the stigma of inferiority."[10]

More than a stigma, exclusion from politics had real consequences. Without the vote, and hence without access to the machinery of government, African Americans would remain at the mercy of the whites who retained control of the legislative process. The latter would continue to use their political power in ways that would deprive African Americans of the dignity of labor and the right to earn a living. Here was the essence of black politics during Reconstruction. By connecting political rights with labor rights, freedmen underscored how the exclusion from politics sustained social and economic subordination. That is why so many black activists equated freedom without economic opportunity, civil rights, and the right to vote only as a partial emancipation.

The political mobilization of African Americans helped persuade federal officials to expand the political and civil rights of ex-slaves. Just as African Americans had mobilized against slavery during the Civil War—helping to create the conditions that enabled the federal government eventually to adopt emancipation as a war aim—black political mobilization in the early days of Reconstruction helped to usher in a more radical phase of Reconstruction under the authority of congressional Republicans. If most advocates of free labor in the North proved unwilling to redistribute land to ex-slaves, they did become convinced that the South under Presidential Reconstruction violated the basic principles of free labor. Developments in the South—the restoration of former Confederates to political power at the state and local level, the passing of the black codes, the unabated racial violence, and black political mobilization—convinced Republicans in the North of the necessity of granting freedmen civil and political rights. At the very least, they reasoned, former slaves needed legal protections to acquire land through the free market.

In late 1865, Republicans in Congress began to challenge the Johnson administration's handling of Reconstruction. In December they refused to seat the Southern congressional delegations elected under Presidential Reconstruction. During the ensuing congressional term, President Johnson vetoed two bills passed by Congress—a bill that would extend the life of the Freedmen's Bureau and a civil rights bill that defined all persons born in the United States as citizens and guaranteed them basic rights such as equality before the law, regardless of race. The president's bold move alienated moderate Republicans in Congress who had hoped to work with Johnson to modify, not overturn, Presidential Reconstruction. They now joined the Radical Republicans in calling for a dissolution of the Southern state governments and for Congress, not the president, to set federal Reconstruction policy. In June 1866 Congress passed the Fourteenth Amendment to the Constitution and sent it to the states for ratification. The amendment gave citizenship to all persons born in the United States, regardless of race, and guaranteed to them the rights of due process and equality before the law. In March 1867, Congress passed the Reconstruction Act over Johnson's veto. The law established new conditions that former Confederate states had to meet in order to gain readmission to the Union. Under the provisions of the legislation, Congress divided the South into five military districts, placed them under martial law, and sent troops into the region to maintain order and enforce federal authority. It also ordered Southern states to draft new state constitutions, ratify the Fourteenth Amendment, and grant African American men the right to vote.

Radical Reconstruction changed the fortunes of former slaves across the South. The Reconstruction Act of 1867 created overnight more than 1 million new voters in the former Confederate States. Armed with the ballot, black workers, many of them men of no property or education, now had the opportunity to channel their discontent into the formal political process and challenge the planters' monopoly on power. During Reconstruction, more than six hundred African Americans—many of them former slaves from the plantation districts—served as elected representatives in Southern state legislatures. At the local level, former slaves won election to positions of authority—mayors, aldermen, justices of the peace, tax commissioners—that had been dominated by local elites before the Civil War. But even if ex-slaves won important constitutional guarantees of civil and political rights, these did not necessarily translate into meaningful political power at the state and local level. Prospects for political success varied widely across the South. Despite the political resolve of former slaves, local conditions often constrained their ability to organize politically. In many places, former slaves could not challenge planter authority to the same degree and with the same effect as in others. Moreover, the Republican Party often lacked the power, the resources, and the resolve to advance the former slaves' interests as workers. A brief look at three different regions of the South—the cotton plantations of southwest Georgia, the sugarcane fields of southern Louisiana, and the rice swamps of coastal South Carolina—reveals the different ways that black workers adapted to local circumstances to assert their claim to an economic foundation of freedom.

Emancipation had arrived late to southwest Georgia, a remote region of the cotton South. Unlike Atlanta and the coast, it had escaped wartime occupation—federal troops did not enter the region until May 1865—and the Freedman's Bureau's staff had few resources to protect the material and political interests of former slaves. Free of any significant military or federal intervention, planters quickly reasserted their authority over former slaves. In 1865 when the Georgia legislature convened to rewrite the state's constitution under President Johnson's plan for Reconstruction, it strengthened planters' political power by adopting a series of black codes that subordinated African Americans by denying them the right to vote and access to most of the legal and legislative system.

Many black Georgians refused to accept this settlement without a challenge. In January 1866, black activists gathered in Augusta to found the Georgia Equal Rights Association (GERA) to promote an alternative vision of black freedom. Most of the delegates were propertied men who tried to reassure white lawmakers of their moderate views. They denounced idleness and vagrancy, rejected land redistribution, and insisted that former slaves were industrious and diligent laborers who were willing to work the fields for fair wages. In return, the delegates asked that white employers treat black workers with respect and that the state grant conditional voting rights for educated black men, guarantee the right of blacks to sit on juries in cases involving ex-slaves, and equal accommodations for passengers on the state's railroads. Determined to expand the organizational reach of the GERA across the state, organizers took their message into southwest Georgia. There they found thousands of willing recruits among the former slaves suffering under exploitative and abusive working conditions and the oppressive governance of their old masters. Adapting the GERA to their own needs, many freedmen in southwest Georgia transformed the organization's moderate approach into a more confrontational one. Black workers refused to renew labor contracts, staged strikes, left the region for the promise of higher wages elsewhere, and otherwise became more assertive in their everyday interactions with white employers.

In 1867 when Congress ordered Southern states to draft new state constitutions and granted African Americans the right to vote and participate in the political process, black activists in southwest Georgia intensified their organizational efforts. Black working-class men led the way, electrifying audiences with speeches that trumpeted the themes of good wages, land reform, and civil justice. Inspired to use the vote to redress the glaring inequities between black workers and white planters, more than 90 percent of the region's eligible black men registered to vote that summer. Black voters flocked to the polls in November, where they elected a slate of Republican delegates, most of them former slaves, to represent the region in the state's

Figure 1.2.   This illustration titled "Electioneering at the South," appeared in *Harper's* in 1868, depicting newly freed slaves engaged in impassioned discussion of political questions prior to the elections in which they would vote for the first time. The editors declared that the scene was eloquent evidence of former slaves' eagerness and readiness to participate in the political process as full and equal citizens. Prints & Photographs Division, Library of Congress, LC-USZ62-125422.

constitutional convention. When delegates campaigned for the April 1868 election to ratify the new constitution and elect a new legislature and slate of local officeholders, they kindled hopes that former slaves could now elect black men to political office. Once there, they would craft a new legal order that no longer favored the interests of the region's planters and that protected black workers.

Black workers soon learned that the path to political power would not be so easy. Economic collapse precipitated by a poor harvest at the end of 1867 left former slaves vulnerable to planter intimidation. In the winter of 1868, planters exploited their economic insecurity to pressure them into signing oppressive labor contracts and then threatened them with eviction if they voted for candidates who supported the policies of Presidential Reconstruction. White assaults against blacks intensified in the weeks preceding the April election. Intimidation, violence, fraud, and bribery reduced black voter turnout. Even as Georgians voted to adopt the new constitution and elected several African Americans to the state legislature, Republicans carried only seven of the twenty legislative seats in southwest Georgia, and only one of these was an African American. Black workers fared better in local elections, capturing key offices in some counties that would give them control of the local police force and the courts. But no Republican, black or white, ever occupied the office he won because they all lacked the money to pay the excessive bonds required to take their position. Then in September, Democrats in the Republican-controlled state legislature moved to expel black members of the legislature. Enough white Republicans—uncertain of their own political power and fearful of being accused of promoting racial equality—gave their support to enable the motion to carry. The Democratic maneuver not only enabled the conservative minority to impose its will upon the majority party, but it also exposed the indifference of white Republicans to the interests of the party's dedicated black supporters and their unwillingness to defend the principle of racial justice.

Violence tipped the balance of the scales in planters' favor. On September 19, 1868, ex-slave Philip Joiner, southwest Georgia's expelled black legislator, and his supporters organized a twenty-five-mile march of 150 freedmen and a few whites, from Albany to the town of Camilla, for a Republican Party rally to protest the action of the legislature and promote the candidacies of local Republicans in the November congressional election. When the marchers entered Camilla's town square, white assassins gunned them down. With the local police force and court system firmly controlled by planters, gangs of whites, without fear of reprisal, scoured the countryside for the next several days hunting down not only survivors of the massacre but any Republican leaders or their black supporters. Although Joiner escaped the manhunt, this wave of political terror disrupted the Republican fall election campaign. Local officials jailed Republican organizers on bogus charges, and those candidates who avoided prison suspended their campaigns in fear of their lives. Most black men stayed home on election day. As a result, conservative Democrats carried the region's congressional seats despite the substantial majority of black working-class voters in those districts. Not only did the violence restore white supremacy but it also enhanced the power of planters as employers of labor. Planters effectively used the weapons of terror to suppress black political mobilization, advance their class interests over the aspirations of ex-slaves, and block the possibility of a government committed to a vision of freedom on workers' terms.

In the Louisiana sugar parishes, by contrast, the peculiar demands of sugar cane production gave ex-slaves leverage that their counterparts in southwest Georgia lacked. Sugar production required a series of tasks that had to be completed on a tight time schedule in order to prevent the crop from ruin. Planters thus sought to centralize and coordinate operations of laborers by organizing them into groups of workers, or what contemporaries called labor gangs, who worked under the direct supervision of white overseers. Long familiar with the process of sugar cultivation, freedmen accepted the necessity of a centralized labor operation but insisted that planters must pay good wages as the price for the continuation of gang labor. Whereas freedmen in the cotton South fiercely resisted working for wages in gangs and coveted their own patch of land as the path to economic independence, former slaves in Louisiana considered wage labor, at fair compensation, as economic conditions conducive to freedom.

Although the daily work routine on sugar plantations changed little in the aftermath of the war, labor relations had been transformed. While many freedmen labored under conditions similar to those of slavery—even working for the same masters on the same land—they now related to those masters within a very different social, legal, and political context. Planters no longer held legal title to the people who cultivated their crops and had to negotiate with them in the open labor market. Former slaves seized upon the freedom to move in search of the highest bidder for their services, which forced planters to compete with each other for the labor that they once owned. Planters desperate for workers inadvertently drove up wages and gave sugar workers leverage in the labor market. Competition for labor also strengthened the freedmen's hand in wage disputes. Freedmen defeated planters' attempts to reduce wages and impose uniform wage rates. They also forced planters to revise, and in some cases abolish, the practice of withholding up to half

Figure 1.3. In the sugar plantations of Louisiana, former slaves continued to labor in the fields in work gangs under the supervision of overseers. Courtesy of the Collections of the Louisiana State Museum.

of their wages until they harvested the crop. By winning wage concessions, regular pay, and improvements in the conditions of work, freedmen in the sugar fields secured livelihoods that compared favorably to what white workers earned in the nonagricultural North. Sugar workers used these rewards of wage labor to accumulate property and to build the foundations of black community institutions.

Access to politics strengthened the ability of Louisiana's black sugar workers to curb the power that planters could exercise over their lives. Working and living in the centralized labor system of sugar plantations enabled black labor activists to coordinate effectively grassroots political activity. Black voters, who held substantial majorities in the sugar parishes, used their new political rights to elect Radical Republican majorities to the state government. As part of the Radical Republican coalition, black lawmakers helped to defeat planter-sponsored legislative initiatives—vagrancy, anti-enticement, and contract-enforcement laws—designed to stack the labor market in favor of white employers. Moreover, African Americans had won local electoral contests that gave them control of the police and courts in several sugar parishes. Finally, the state's Republican governors were reluctant to order the Louisiana militia to intervene in labor conflicts. As a result, white planters could not rely on the coercive power of the state to exploit black workers.

Despite making important political gains and winning concessions from white employers, freedmen in Louisiana found economic independence as elusive in the sugar parishes as it was in the cotton South. Louisiana's freedmen had conceded to sugar planters their exclusive claims to the land in exchange for better working conditions and wages. Although throughout the 1870s, black sugar workers earned relatively good wages, paid in cash on a monthly basis, they had become a landless, rural working class who had nothing but their own labor to sell to secure a living. Moreover, black workers had only exerted limited influence on state politics by preventing the passage of planter initiatives rather than securing legislative protections for labor rights. Consequently, they had little economic, legal, or political security to fall back upon should favorable circumstances suddenly change. And change they did. Democrats swept back into power in the election of 1876, bringing an end to the rule of Radical Republicans in the state. Even though African Americans in the sugar parishes continued to vote, they no longer exerted the same influence over state politics. Once in control of the state government, Democrats not only repealed the reform agenda of the Radical Republicans, but they also did not hesitate to use the militia to discipline labor.

The consequences of these political changes became all too evident in the so-called sugar war of 1887. Planters began to reassert their control over labor by reducing wages and replacing payment in cash with payment in plantation scrip, a certificate redeemable only at the plantation store. In the absence of state regulations governing wages for plantation laborers, sugar workers had no choice but to rely upon their own resources to resist the new wage scheme. In 1887, on the eve of the sugar harvest, ten thousand workers organized a massive strike. In response, the Democratic governor of Louisiana mobilized the state militia to force the eviction of all striking workers who remained in their planter-owned houses. Tensions came to a head in Thibodaux where guardsmen and white vigilantes fired upon black strikers. Violence carried on for several days, killing as many as one hundred sugar workers. With their strike crushed under the weight of organized violence, black workers had no choice but to return to the fields to harvest the sugar crop on planters' terms.

Prospects for a government responsive to the needs of black workers were perhaps strongest in South Carolina. Planters in the state's valuable rice fields complained that emancipation had transformed the former slaves into people with a keen interest in politics who no longer seemed willing to work, unless forced to by starvation. Planters had good reason to worry. Not only did black political mobilization undermine their notion of proper labor discipline, it also delivered substantial Republican majorities to state and local office during Radical Reconstruction. In 1868 African Americans captured a majority of the seats in the state's House of Representatives, giving them control of the legislative body's key committees and leadership positions. In 1874 South Carolina became the only Southern state during Reconstruction in which blacks won a majority in the state senate. And in Beaufort, the heart of state's rice district, where former slave Robert Smalls had ascended to local political power, blacks controlled several local political offices.

South Carolina's black legislative majority advanced an economic agenda that addressed some of the needs of the state's rural black workers. Not only did the Republican-majority legislature repeal the dehumanizing black codes passed during Presidential Reconstruction, it passed measures that gave farm tenants legal protections against planters who tried to cheat them out of wages or their just portion of crop settlements. South Carolina was the lone state to pass an ambitious land reform program. The law established a state land commission, which was authorized to purchase land and resell it to state residents on long-term credit, enabling some fourteen thousand black families to acquire homesteads by 1876. Still, the Reconstruction government stopped far short of what it might have done to strengthen the bargaining power of black labor. In 1869, a South Carolina labor convention proposed a series of new laws to improve the working conditions of the state's laboring classes. The more than three hundred, mostly African American, delegates advocated such things as the appointment of county supervisors to oversee labor contracts and ensure that they incorporated adequate protections for workers, a nine-hour work day for manufacturing and skilled labor, and public funding for lawsuits brought by workers against their employers. But when the legislature took these measures up for consideration, white and black conservative voices carried the day, arguing that the state had no authority to intervene in the private labor market. Consequently, the state's general assembly rejected most of them, although the votes of freedmen in the legislature enabled watered-down versions of some to become law.

Dissatisfied with the failure of the state's Radical Republicans to use its political leverage to improve the working conditions of its substantial black working-class constituency, black laborers took matters into their own hands. In May 1876, day laborers in the low country rice fields staged a strike to protest wage reductions and payment in scrip. Over the next several months the strike expanded and intensified as bands of largely illiterate and impoverished rice workers fanned out across the low country broadening their support among the black, rural working class. Fearful of the low country becoming overrun by what they considered the anarchy of mob rule, planters pleaded with Republican governor Daniel H. Chamberlain to mobilize federal troops to put down the strikes. Aware of how his own political future hung in the balance between placating the interests of the state's propertied elites and responding to the needs of black voters, Chamberlain refused to send troops. Planters had no choice but to make wage concessions to the workers. Emboldened by their own success and radicalized by impending fears of the devastating consequences should Democrats capture control of state government in the November elections, black workers intensified their militancy in preparation for the fall elections.

Chamberlain's refusal to call in troops to defend planter interests notwithstanding, the state's Republican leadership responded to black working-class militancy in the rice districts with ambivalence. As governor, Chamberlain showed no disposition to support labor. He dedicated much of his time to building white support for the Republican Party. He curried favor with Charleston's propertied elite and reduced the influence of blacks within local government by removing them from office and appointing white Democrats to take their place. Even some black elected officials greeted the politicization of the working class with considerable reservation. Thomas Hamilton, a prominent black Republican from Beaufort who opposed the strike from the outset, used the authority of his position to lecture rice workers that they shared the same interests with the planters and that labor organizers stoked black discontent to advance their own selfish ambitions rather than to improve the conditions of work in the rice fields.

The tepid response of South Carolina Republicans exposed the broader limits of the party as a vehicle for advancing the interests of black workers. Chamberlain's policies had won praise from Northern Republicans, who by the mid-1870s had started to retreat from Radical Reconstruction. The political activism of black workers in the low country caused Northern Republicans to fear the African Americans would corrupt the political system by seizing the reins of government in order to confiscate property, redistribute wealth, and erode the promise of social mobility through hard work. Faced with growing white working-class unrest in the North and politically mobilized former slaves in the South, Northern Republicans abandoned their working-class allies, fearful that they would sow the seeds of political and economic disorder by strengthening the rights of labor at the expense of the rights of property. Instead, they advised former slaves to respect the rights of property, recognize the harmony of interests between labor and capital, reconcile their differences with former Confederates, and accumulate their fair share of wealth through patience and hard work rather than through the redistributive power of government.

Republican ambivalence strengthened planters' hopes for a counterrevolution in the 1876 election. The entrenched strike and the governor's failure to use state power to defend their class interests convinced planters of the necessity of a regime change in order to reclaim command over plantation labor. They found their man in Wade Hampton, one of the state's wealthiest planters and former Confederate cavalryman, whom they convinced to run for governor. While Hampton portrayed himself as a "friend of the Negro," his supporters organized a vicious paramilitary campaign to intimidate the black vote into submission and deliver the election to Hampton. Such tactics, however, did not entirely derail black working-class political mobilization in the low country. Many black workers fought against Democratic rifle clubs and fiercely defended their right to vote. Consequently, black Republicans won key local victories in the low country, but the state-wide triumph of the Democrats delivered the counterrevolution that planters had hoped for, bringing to an end Republican governance in the South and with it the nation's uneven experiment with Reconstruction.

Whether at Camilla in Georgia, Thibodaux in Louisiana, or in the rice swamps of South Carolina, underlying the overthrow of Reconstruction were men eager to reassert the authority of property in Southern politics. The election of 1876 completed the return of Democrats to power in the South, who subsequently used their authority to further subordinate the political interests of African Americans and of workers of both races, ensuring the class survival of the region's propertied elite. As so many Southern white commentators observed, the reorganization of labor in the aftermath of slavery was the critical issue of Reconstruction and the one issue that would not only define the boundaries of freedom but also the distribution of resources and power in post–Civil War America.

The activism of many African Americans, both during the Civil War and Reconstruction, helped to create the political conditions that forever transformed the place of African Americans in the United States. Union victory in the Civil War not only preserved the union but also abolished slavery. Former slaves not only won their freedom but also secured an emancipation that guaranteed their civil and political rights. Former slaves responded by the thousands, ready to use the power of the vote to transform Southern politics. Nevertheless, black working-class agitation could not achieve a fundamental redistribution of the region's economic resources and hence break the political power of the ruling white elite. Just as in the industrializing North, political equality could not ensure economic equality. The Republican Party, the former slaves' powerful ally in the struggle for emancipation and civil and political rights, ultimately failed to advance an economic agenda that would secure the labor rights of Southern workers. Many Republicans, who valued property rights over labor rights, grew fearful of encouraging a class politics from below. More and more, they became convinced that it was safer and wiser to come to terms with former Confederates than to promote and protect the interests of their black working-class constituents. In so doing, they enabled the white propertied elites of the South to survive the trials of Reconstruction.

With the region's ruling class securing the command of black labor, the stage was set for the emergence of a new South. In coming decades, Southern planters and industrialists sustained the economic subordination of African Americans through several methods. They controlled and later suppressed the votes of black workers, divided the working class by stoking racial discord between black and white workers, and used the police power of the state to break labor militancy. In the wake of the political failures of Reconstruction, new apostles of black freedom emerged who would counsel black workers to cast their fortunes with employers rather than with labor unions, to heed the advice of a new class of black elites rather than forge alliances with white workers, and forgo political solutions to class problems. Without political power, meaningful political representation, or command of significant productive resources, former slaves had to rely upon their own initiative to secure the economic conditions of freedom.

CHAPTER TWO

~

Jim Crow's Black Workers

Without meaningful political power or political representation in the aftermath of Reconstruction, former slaves relied upon their own initiative and resources to achieve a modest prosperity and build the social and community institutions that enabled them to claim some measure of economic freedom. As early as 1873, a convention of African Americans reported from Brenham, Texas, that blacks in twenty-one counties in their state had already accumulated more than $2 million in real estate. The *New York Times* applauded the news as evidence that blacks did not need the federal government to grant them land. The free labor system, argued the editors, would empower former slaves to accumulate property through their own diligent efforts and enterprise. Despite some remarkable successes, blacks' attempts to lift themselves through hard work, thrift, and frugality underscored the limitations of securing economic advancement without political power. Nate Shaw, the son of a former slave who came of age in post-Reconstruction Alabama, encountered these very obstacles. Shaw started farming for himself as a sharecropper in 1906, and slowly accumulated the resources—wagons, mules, and livestock—that enabled him to improve his circumstances and eventually buy his own eighty-acre farm on credit in 1923. Nonetheless, economic security remained elusive. Shaw forever lacked what he called "political pull," which placed him at the mercy of moneylenders and landlords who used their access to financial and political institutions to defraud him out of the little that he worked so hard to accumulate. The daily lives of black workers such as Shaw, who labored on the farms and factories of the South, revealed the limitations of advancement through individual effort and the obstacles to economic empowerment without political pull.

In the absence of land redistribution, sharecropping spread across the Cotton South as the predominant form of agricultural labor in the region. Although long associated with black poverty, sharecropping first emerged as a concession to the freedmen's demand for land. Planters had hoped to maintain full authority over the management of their plantations, organizing their operations into centralized gangs of laborers under the direct supervision of overseers. Former slaves, who aspired to landownership and greater freedom over their day-to-day working lives, refused to sign contracts that submitted them to such labor arrangements. In the face of blacks' determined resistance to gang labor, planters began to subdivide their plantations into small tracts, ranging between ten and fifty acres, which they rented to black farming families. In addition to providing land, planters furnished these croppers with a house, food, clothing, and other necessities and supplied them with the tools, draft animals, seeds, and fertilizer that they needed to raise crops. In exchange, croppers and their families worked their plots, receiving a share of the harvest as compensation for their labor. They did not, technically, rent the land. Blacks who had the means to furnish their own tools, supplies, and food either received a greater share of the crop or negotiated a tenancy arrangement in which they rented the land for a fixed price, usually a share of the crop. But even as sharecropping broke up plantations into decentralized family farms, it did not break up landownership patterns. By 1880, 80 percent of southern farms were fewer than fifty acres in size, but 10 percent of the region's landowners still owned 60 percent of the land. Sharecropping may have reshaped the spatial geography of the southern countryside, but it left the power of the planter class unchanged.

Although sharecropping failed to provide blacks with land of their own, it did provide freedmen with a welcome, if imperfect, alternative to wage labor. Sharecropping enabled black farmers to gain access to productive property and to manage independently the cultivation of their plots. Physical distance minimized the intrusions that white landlords could exert over their daily lives. With their croppers scattered about the plantation, planters found it impractical to hire riding bosses to supervise black labor. Since croppers occupied and were directly responsible for a specific parcel of land, they had a direct claim upon a share of the agricultural output, giving them a stake in the land that wage hands did not have. Because they shared, along with the landlords, the risks of raising the crop, sharecroppers were sensitive to (and deeply worried about) the environmental and economic hazards of growing cash crops. The quality of the soil, droughts, floods, insect infestations, and falling commodity prices preoccupied croppers and nurtured an emotional attachment to the land and the livestock they worked. Although their entitlement to the fruits of their labor was more theoretical than real, croppers saw themselves as small-scale producers.

The decentralized family-farm system also enabled black farmers to control—to an extent—their household economies. For former slaves, exerting control over their family relationships was an act of political and economic self-assertion. In the wake of emancipation, ex-slaves strove to reunite with relatives who had been scattered under slavery, demanded legal recognition of their marriage rights, challenged former slaveholders for custody of their children, and asserted the authority to discipline and control family dependents without the intrusion of their white employers. Having wrested control over family labor from their landlords, black farming families could deploy the labor of family members to any number of productive activities without the knowledge of white landlords. Housebound enterprises such as making baskets, axe handles, hats, and clothes for use or sale, or peddling, hauling, hunting, and foraging generated important surpluses for the household economy. The fruits of household production, though small, flowed to blacks directly rather than to their landlords. Blacks applied surplus cash from household production to the purchase of farms and the building of community institutions, including schools, churches, benevolent associations, and fraternal orders.

The burdens of producing for the household economy were not evenly distributed among family members, and women and children often bore the brunt of the labor. As a family-based labor system, sharecropping and tenant farming relied heavily upon unpaid, largely female, agricultural labor. Under the terms of sharecropping and tenancy contracts, landowners recognized the black men with whom they executed contracts as heads of household. If landlords were legally forbidden from disciplining sharecroppers with force, husbands and fathers retained that authority over dependent family members. Contracts often obligated fathers to raise their children strictly and to make sure that children obeyed the commands of their employer. Through the patriarchal authority of male sharecroppers, landlords thus ensured that women and children worked for the interests of the landlord as unpaid dependents of the male head of household. Even as they worked in the fields, women remained exclusively responsible for household chores, which meant that they worked the longest hours of any member of the household. Still, many black men strove to create a sexual division of labor in their households, granting black women a respite from fieldwork they could not have claimed under slavery. As Nate Shaw explained, he did not want his wife to work as a field hand, especially after she began to bear children. He preferred instead to work his children in the fields once they were old enough.

As heads of household, rural black patriarchs also controlled the wages that dependent family members earned off the farm. Men retained decision-making power in the rural black household economy, especially over the allocation of income and the distribution of property. These patriarchs seldom invested extra earnings into labor-saving devices that benefitted their wives, preferring instead to use them to purchase farm equipment, livestock, and other productive resources. Many family conflicts erupted over control of wages that dependent family members earned. When Nate Shaw was a teenager, he accused his father of profiting from his own hard work. His father had hired him out but collected his wages as fast as he earned them. Even though Shaw considered submitting to his father's will akin to slavery, he swallowed his pride and remained in his father's household until he turned twenty-one. Many other young black men, Shaw observed, did not share his patience and simply ran away when they reached their late teens.

Still, under sharecropping, unlike slavery, black rural patriarchs could divide the labor time of family dependents between fieldwork, housework, and off-farm labor that met the needs of the household rather than those of the landlord. And blacks translated the fruits of their household economies into some impressive material gains. If few African Americans worked their own land in 1865, more than two hundred thousand had acquired some form of real property by 1910, constituting one out of every four black farm families in the South. Black landownership was not evenly distributed across the South. It was highest in the Upper South, where nearly half of all black farmers owned the land that they cultivated, and lowest in the Deep South. In Georgia, for example, only 13 percent of African American farmers owned their land in 1910. Black landowning predominated in regions of the South with limited cotton production, cheap land, less fertile soil, white population majorities, and plentiful wage-paying jobs. Still, even in the black-majority counties of the plantation belt, blacks forged paths to landownership that challenge persistent images of the rural South as an economic desert for African Americans.

Hard work and forbearance were not the only conditions that enabled black landownership in the South. Acquiring property was often the fruit of cooperative energies such as extended networks of kith and kin who pooled their resources to purchase land. However, black landownership only expanded in tandem with white goodwill. Most blacks made their real estate purchases through personal connections with white people of influence— former landlords and masters, or merchants and moneylenders with whom they had conducted business as renters—who helped them to negotiate the many formal and informal barriers to black landownership. Powerful whites who acted as sponsors to aspiring black owners thus retained significant say in determining which blacks ascended to landownership and which lands were available for their purchase.

Even if most black landowners only acquired marginal lands that demanded relentless effort to yield a productive crop, landownership had tangible advantages over renting and working on shares. Not under contract to grow exclusively a cash crop, landowners had far greater freedom to determine what they raised on their land. Black owners grew far more corn, wheat, oats, vegetables, and fruits and set aside land for pasture on which they raised livestock, all of which enabled them to eat a far more varied diet than renters who relied upon the provisions that landlords furnished. They enjoyed greater leverage in marketing their crops and in forging relationships with local mill operators, smiths, and merchants. Owners exercised greater control over the pace and rhythm of work on their farms and thus had the ability to determine when to withdraw their children from labor on the homestead and send them to school. The advance of black landownership thus signaled the emergence of economic differentiation among rural blacks, with independent black southern farmers constituting perhaps the largest group of African Americans to achieve some measure of economic security before World War I.

Despite the significance of property ownership, rural blacks could not convert their hard-won economic security into political power or influence. When Democrats regained control of southern state and local governments in the 1870s, they rewrote a series of laws on credit, labor mobility, and property rights that strengthened planter control over agricultural labor. During Reconstruction, Republican–controlled state legislatures had passed laws that gave workers a lien superior to all other claims upon a planters' crop. This meant that the planter had to satisfy the laborer's claim to his share of the crop for wages before the planter could pay the laborer his share or use the share to satisfy other debts. Under such a legal regime, croppers considered themselves partners in the crop with property rights in the harvest. But after Reconstruction, planters gained legal authority over the crop through a series of court decisions and new legislation. In 1872, for example, the Georgia Supreme Court ruled that title to the crop resided exclusively with the owner of the land and that a cropper had no claim to his share until he fulfilled the terms of his contract and paid for the supplies that the planter had furnished him.

States resurrected repressive features of the black codes to restrict the ability of rural blacks to move in search of more favorable economic conditions. Although the new laws adopted race-neutral language, they created a legal apparatus that enabled planters to weaken the labor rights of African Americans and strengthen their control over their agricultural workforce. Local authorities enforced vagrancy laws, arresting blacks who could not show evidence of employment. Anti-enticement statutes penalized employers who attempted to lure black workers away from their place of employment with promises of higher pay and better working conditions. Other laws regulated and restrained the activities of out-of-state labor recruiters. Contract enforcement statutes made tenants criminally liable for breaking a contract with a landlord. Despite this dense body of law dedicated to restricting the mobility of blacks, southern whites did not consistently enforce these statutes. Consequently, as many as one-third of African American sharecropping families moved at the end of each agricultural year, most often to a neighboring plantation where they would sign a new contract for the coming year.

Other laws undermined the black household economy. Sunset laws, for example, prohibited farm tenants from selling agricultural products after dark. Although the statute's architects claimed that the law's intent was to prevent the trafficking in stolen produce, the law actually strengthened planters' control over black households. Croppers and tenants, under command to work from dawn to dusk, had little choice but to sell their own garden produce after dark. The law, in effect, made no distinction between produce that farmers raised on their own garden plot and that which some white landlords claimed they had allegedly stolen from them. State legislatures also passed a series of laws to enclose the open range and eliminate access to other common resources of the rural South. Under the laws of many southern states, farmers could allow their livestock to roam and feed upon any unfenced lands. New fence laws, however, closed access to this open range by requiring farmers to raise cattle and hogs in enclosed pastures, which many sharecroppers and tenant farmers did not have. New restrictions that curtailed hunting, fishing, foraging, and squatting on vacant, unfenced land also cut off the lifelines of many rural black households.

Legal changes were more than mere abstractions but had real and devastating human consequences. Many black farmers failed to raise crops that were sufficient enough to cover their debts after the harvest. According to Nate Shaw, this was not for lack of effort on the part of black farmers but because they had no influence or voice in the cotton market, which was controlled by the landlords, merchants, and storekeepers. Throughout his farming career in the 1910s and 1920s, Shaw discovered that every year he earned less for his cotton than his white neighbors did. Likewise, educator and civil rights activist William Pickens, who grew up on a farm in Arkansas in the 1880s and 1890s, remembered that when his father returned from settling with their landlord, he informed the family that they had fallen deeper into debt. But Pickens had no way to challenge the terms of the settlement because the landlord and merchant did all the calculating, while he and his family did all the work. Most black farmers had no choice but to sign a contract for another year in the hopes of clearing their accumulated debts. Shaw never questioned the landlord's right to collect rent. He resented, however, having no control over the amount of rent that he paid. Because those who owned the land, rather than those who worked it, had exclusive authority to determine the rent, landlords prevented most rural blacks from being able to get ahead.

If renting on shares left blacks constantly vulnerable to indebtedness, landownership proved less secure or as profitable as rural blacks had hoped. Although they had an easier time of it than croppers and tenants, landowners still lacked access to reliable credit, capital, and other necessary resources that remained in the control of propertied whites. Because black material success often rested on white goodwill, blacks took great care not to appear too successful or to transgress racial boundaries. One black teacher in the rural South related the story of a successful black farmer who built a nice house but had received a warning from local whites not to paint it. Fearful for his personal safety and security, he continued to live in his unpainted house. As Shaw explained, white folks hated to see African Americans living like people; they were afraid that if an African American accumulated too much wealth, he would act too much like his own man.

In the absence of just law enforcement, whites who coveted black property had wide latitude in resorting to vigilante violence to dispossess African American landowners. Organized groups of white farmers, often referred to as "whitecaps," terrorized propertied blacks, often forcing them to abandon their homesteads. One of the most heinous transfers of property by racial violence happened in 1910 in the Blackland Prairie of east-central Texas. An argument between an independent black farmer and a white neighbor escalated into a massive riot in which more than five hundred whites mobilized against the residents of a prosperous black farming community. Over the course of three days, roving bands of whites killed at least eight unarmed blacks and wounded two others. Many observers put the death toll much higher. Although a grand jury indicted five white men for murder, justice did not prevail. The white men eventually secured their release on bail and were never tried for their crimes. Black residents, in fear for their lives, abandoned their settlement, leaving the substantial amount of desirable farmland that they owned for the region's white farmers to purchase at tax sale.

The rural labor system of the New South, backed by its elaborate legal framework and pervasive racial violence, betrayed many blacks' expectations of rural independence through hard work. Few worked the land harder than Nate Shaw, but the rewards he reaped were small. No matter how much he raised as a farmer, he forever failed to collect what he considered the just reward for his labor. To Shaw, it came down to politics. Without political rights, he recognized that he had no power to demand what he produced on his farms. "What good for me to work myself to death," Shaw asked, when "somebody else get the benefit of my labor?" Shaw never doubted his ability to prosper from the Alabama soil. "It's the people here," he concluded, who were forever the source of his troubles.[1] The work ethic alone failed to deliver Shaw, and so many like him, from poverty, insecurity, violence, and relentless toil.

Many black farmers looked beyond the land to supplement their livelihoods. When Nate Shaw was a young tenant farmer who held fast to the dream of one day owning his own farm, he began hauling timber for a local lumber company. Tempted by the possibility to earn cash, he reasoned that the mules and wagon that he had purchased for farming could be used to haul lumber for wages. Shaw drew as much as $225 a month, income that he used to purchase new farming equipment, household goods, and even some luxuries. Despite the lure of good wages, farming always came first. Shaw never considered lumbering permanent work, and he intended only to earn what he could and returned to his farm. Many rural southern blacks shifted between farms and factories in this manner, working for wages at temporary jobs in rhythm with the planting cycle of their farms. Throughout the rural South, a pattern of seasonal labor migration emerged in which rural blacks, who remained contributing members of agricultural households, provided much of the labor for the South's expanding industries.

Southern black workers who remained committed to farming but entered the wage labor market sporadically generated a profusion of complaints among southern industrialists. Bosses, foremen, and supervisors bemoaned that black workers routinely deserted their jobs on a whim for religious revivals, funerals, marriages, Emancipation Day celebrations, fishing excursions, or simply to return to their farms. Bewildered by the seemingly undisciplined work habits of southern blacks, employers made a host of racial assumptions. They regarded blacks as a degenerate race, with a natural predisposition to wander in search of cheap amusements on which to trifle away their wages. The work habits of African Americans that so frustrated employers had nothing to do with any racial characteristics but derived from two sources. First, they were shaped by the working environment that blacks encountered in southern industry—dangerous work, low pay, persistent employment discrimination, and barriers to occupational mobility—that offered them few incentives to become steady employees. Second, many blacks—like Nate Shaw—had options outside of wage labor that gave them the freedom to engage the labor market, at least partially, on their own terms.

Unskilled African Americans provided much of the brawn that fueled southern industrial development in the decades after Reconstruction. Between 1890 and 1910, the number of African Americans employed in manufacturing in the United States nearly tripled; whereas 6.8 percent of the black population worked industrial jobs in 1890, approximately 10.6 percent were so employed by 1910. Nearly all of these workers lived in the South. But those numbers do not account for the many thousands of African Americans who were farmers and only occasionally worked jobs in factories. The southern lumber industry, which rapidly expanded after Congress passed a tariff in 1897 that raised the price of foreign lumber, accounted for much of the growth in the number of black industrial workers. By 1910, more than 20 percent of African Americans employed in industry worked in the logging camps and sawmills that dotted across the vast pine forests of the South (see Table 2.1). Blacks found plentiful work in the South's other extractive industries such as phosphate mines, coal mines, and turpentine orchards. They also worked in manufacturing plants such as iron foundries, steel mills, brickyards, and cotton gins. Black southerners also found wage work in the region's growing transportation sector. Blacks constructed many of the railroads that provided the transportation network upon which southern industrial development relied. Crews of black longshoremen, freight handlers, and teamsters loaded and unloaded the heavy cargo that came in and out of the port cities of the Gulf and Atlantic coasts.

Table 2.1. African Americans, Ten Years of Age and Older, Employed in Manufacturing and in the Lumber Industry, 1890–1910

Year	No. of Working-Age Blacks	No. of Working-Age Blacks Employed in Manufacturing	No. of Working-Age Blacks Employed in Lumber Industry
1890	3,073,164	208,374 (6.8)	22,285 (10.7)
1900	3,992,337	275,116 (6.9)	39,375 (14.3)
1910	5,192,535	552,815 (10.6)	122,216 (22.1)

Note: Numbers in parentheses in second column indicate percentage of all employed blacks; numbers in parentheses in third column indicate percentage of all blacks employed in manufacturing.

Source: U.S. Bureau of the Census, Negro Population in the United States, 1790–1915 (Washington, DC: Government Printing Office, 1918), 526–27.

Figure 2.1. Two African American log sawyers cut pine logs in the forests of East Texas, circa 1900. At the turn of the century, more black industrial workers labored for the lumber industry than any other industry. The East Texas Research Center, R. W. Steen Library, Stephen F. Austin State University, Nacogdoches, Texas.

Whether they mined for coal in the Alabama coalfields, tapped for turpentine in the Georgia pine woods, or hauled lumber in a Louisiana sawmill, southern black workers were more likely to be found toiling at the heaviest unskilled jobs or consigned to work gangs under the direct supervision of white foremen. Four-fifths of black workers on southern railroads endured the South's extreme heat maintaining roadbeds and laying track, labor that required strength, stamina, and little skill. In the steel mills of Birmingham, blacks outnumbered whites ten to one working the various jobs amidst the blast furnaces. Top fillers, who worked atop the furnaces some eighty feet above ground, shoveled iron ore into the hopper while risking death from asphyxiation, explosions, and falls. One in five black industrial laborers worked in the lumber industry, which ranked as one of the most dangerous industries in early twentieth-century American manufacturing. On a logging operation or in a sawmill imminent dangers lurked everywhere, from bursting saws to falling timbers. State safety regulations did little to improve working conditions because most lumber operators routinely violated state labor laws.

Employers resorted to a host of racial assumptions when they assigned jobs to their black laborers. Many hiring bosses considered blacks peculiarly well suited for the rough and heavy work of common labor and believed that whites would not accept jobs that required arduous toil. Not only did employers believe that blacks excelled over whites at the heaviest and most strenuous work, they also assumed that blacks lacked the mental faculties required to learn a skill or trade. The physiology of black men, they argued, qualified them for tasks that required strong muscles and physical exertion, while whites were allegedly better suited for jobs that demanded judgment and intellect. In explaining the absence of blacks in skilled and supervisory positions, industrial spokesmen maintained that blacks lacked the enterprise and ambition of white workers. Most blacks, they insisted, took little interest in their work or had the capacity to become more proficient. Employers thus justified their conscious managerial decisions to organize work crews along racial lines as in keeping with what they regarded as the natural order of society.

Blacks did not lack aptitude but opportunities. Even in occupations in which blacks worked in more skilled trades, they seldom could use those positions to advance to higher-skilled work. Most southern railroads employed blacks as firemen and brakemen, jobs that required skill and training and that outside of the South often led to promotion to engineer or conductor. Before the Civil War, southern railroads often rented slaves as firemen and brakemen, and after emancipation, railroads continued to hire them. Blacks, however, found themselves excluded from promotions. Rather than treating their black firemen as apprentices in training, white engineers in the South expected black firemen to wait on them like servants. The railroad brotherhoods also used the power of their unions to exclude blacks from occupational mobility, effectively preventing black firemen from becoming engineers. Elsewhere, such as in logging camps where crews of men cut and made railroad ties out of sawlogs, most woods bosses refused to employ blacks in apprentice positions in which they could learn the skills to advance to higher-paying jobs. As one experienced tie maker explained, he hired blacks to load ties but never encouraged them to wield a broadax.

As helpers and haulers in service to whites, most black workers never received the training necessary for job advancement. Black novelist Richard Wright learned this lesson in 1925, during the summer after he graduated from junior high school as the class valedictorian, when he worked for an optical shop in Jackson, Mississippi. The shop owner offered the seventeen-year-old Wright a position in hopes of teaching him the optical trade. He placed Wright under the supervision of two experienced white mechanics. They never taught Wright the art of grinding and polishing lenses, confining his duties to sweeping, mopping, dusting, and running errands. When Wright politely asked to learn the trade, they accused him of insolence and of trying to act white. Over the next several days, they subjected him to crude and vulgar insults. One day when the owner was out of the shop, they trapped him and forced him to quit or suffer violent reprisal. Wright left, realizing that no matter how humble he had acted, he had learned no skills and had reaped only the "wages of humility."[2]

When employers confined blacks to the hardest and lowest-paying jobs, they also placed them in work with the least job security. Volatile markets proved the most significant cause of intermittent employment among the unskilled. As markets weakened, mill and mine operators curtailed work schedules, cut wages, postponed pay days, and reduced the workforce and only rehired when the market strengthened. Supervisors at the Gulf Refining Company of Port Arthur, Texas, preferred to recruit wage hands from among the legions of displaced black transients who sought work in the city's industries. The company favored transients because it guaranteed a crew of workers who were always on the move. Not only did this prevent workers from organizing unions, it kept a reserve of surplus workers at the gates of the plant, which increased competition among workers for jobs, empowering the company to keep wages low. Intermittent employment was yet another check on job advancement and further ensured that blacks did not consider themselves long-term employees.

White working-class racism also contributed to the institutional racism that blocked black occupational mobility. As Richard Wright experienced, white workers used a variety of informal but potent tactics to intimidate blacks who threatened their occupational status. White craftsmen and skilled workers barred blacks from joining their unions and fought for workplace rules that excluded blacks from ascending the ranks of the skilled trades. When employers did not comply with white trade unionists' demands in drawing the color line in employment, white union members sometimes organized strikes and boycotts. Between 1882 and 1900, some fifty so-called hate strikes disrupted southern workplaces as white workers protested employers' plans to hire or promote black workers. In May 1909, one of the most dramatic hate strikes of the period began when eighty white unionized railroad firemen in Georgia walked off the job to protest the railroad's hiring of black firemen. The Georgia Race Strike captured national attention when white residents who lived along the railroad attacked trains operated by black firemen. The railroad eventually defeated the strike, but white workers in many workplaces continued to use their unions to defend their access to jobs and to preserve their advantages in job promotion.

Southern industrial development also drew black women into the region's wage labor market. African American women moved to the towns and growing cities of the New South in search of work to support themselves and their families. Excluded from employment in most industries, black women performed labor vital to the South's urban and industrial growth by working in the homes of white families as maids, cooks, and child-nurses. Because they earned such low pay, many black household workers supplemented their wages by helping themselves to leftovers, table scraps, and staples from the kitchen pantry in a practice known as pan-toting. Many private household employers tolerated pan-toting to justify the low wages that they paid. Some employers even reduced the cash wages that they paid by compensating their domestic servants instead with secondhand clothes, used household goods, or other payments in kind. Private employers frequently deducted wages from servants who broke or misplaced household goods or committed alleged infractions such as acting insolent. Many white families had such little regard for the welfare of their black servants that they spent more of their annual household budget on items such as chewing gum or liquor than they paid in wages. Because black women commanded such meager wages in the southern labor market, even white wage earners could afford to hire the services of washerwomen.

In exchange for low pay, black women worked long hours for employers who placed few limits on the kinds of tasks that they expected domestic servants to perform. They dusted furniture, polished silver, scrubbed floors, changed linens, emptied chamber pots, ran errands, cared for pets, and tended gardens. Cooking duties went beyond preparing meals and might include washing dishes, canning foodstuffs, and cleaning the kitchen. Laundry work required not only cleaning the clothes, but ironing, mending, and folding. Employers also enlisted black servants as the primary caretakers of their children. They expected them to feed, wash, entertain, put to bed, and otherwise act as governess to the children over the age of two as well as

Figure 2.2. African American wet nurse caring for a small white child in Georgia in 1907. Courtesy, Georgia Archives, Vanishing Georgia Collection, lau172.

nurse and tend to the round-the-clock needs of infants. Household workers described child care as the most exhausting and emotionally draining work that they performed. It required them to perform the most intimate of domestic chores even as employers, by requiring domestic servants to live on their premises, denied the right of domesticity to the women who worked for them. Most black women tried to avoid jobs that required them to live in the homes of their employers. Such arrangements separated them from friends and families, placed them at their employers' constant beck and call, and left them more vulnerable to sexual assault and abuse.

Restricted to dangerous and demanding unskilled tasks, denied prospects for promotion, and forced to endure racist coworkers and bosses, many blacks chose short-term work. Rather than endure endless toil at dead-end jobs under often intolerable working conditions, some black workers concentrated on satisfying their cash needs as quickly as possible and then moved on. Some black workers, for example, demanded work by the task—receiving pay for completing a particular amount of work rather than for a defined period. Such an arrangement enabled workers to control both the pace of their work and the time that they devoted to wage earning. Black workers in the phosphate mines of South Carolina threatened to return to their farms unless operators implemented a task system and made other concessions such as steady wages paid in cash. Sawmill operators in Louisiana often paid black workers by the amount of lumber they stacked rather than by how long they worked. Although some black lumber stackers worked long days at a feverish pace in order to maximize their earnings, many more worked diligently until they reached their personal quota for the day, causing employers to complain when their workers quit at midafternoon to go fishing.

In defining their own work goals, black workers strove to maximize the amount of time that they could claim as their own. Like the phosphate miners in South Carolina, many considered wage-paying jobs as temporary work that supplemented their rural household economies. Cash income from wage earning could help to meet living expenses, cover losses from a bad harvest, pay taxes, make mortgage payments, or be reinvested in farms. Black workers also sustained close ties to families and friends in the countryside through social and cultural rituals. African American workers forced the sawmills of East Texas to shut down every June 19 when they celebrated Juneteenth, the day black Texans observed as Emancipation Day. Black workers left for home to join friends and relatives for festivities that often included parades, marching bands, picnics, and barbecues. These affairs were something of a homecoming that offered those who had been working away from home the chance to take a few days leave from heavy labor and reunite with family members. The holiday coincided with the end of the spring planting season, and the long-awaited break from fieldwork enlivened the celebration. Although employers conceded the nineteenth as a holiday, the celebrations often exceeded one day, forcing operators to recognize Juneteenth as a holiday lasting three to four days.

Whatever their motives for seeking employment in southern industry, African Americans' work objectives clashed with employers' attempts to maintain a steady labor force. Like employers in other rapidly developing rural settings who were unable to recruit a labor force from a resilient peasantry, southern industrialists turned to state and local governments rather than to the labor market to secure the workers they needed. Most southern states adopted a system of convict leasing in which state prisoners served their sentences by working for private employers who, after paying the state a fixed sum, assumed responsibility for clothing, feeding, housing, and guarding convicts in their custody. The system enabled state governments to reduce the costs of operating penitentiaries and raise revenues for depleted state treasuries. At the same time, it provided employers with a disciplined labor force capable of developing the region's resources. The New South's railroads, forest industries, and coal mines, in particular, relied heavily on prison labor crews. Convict leasing thus distorted the criminal justice system into serving the labor needs of employers. Mississippi's infamous pig law, for example, classified hog theft as grand larceny punishable with up to five years in the state penitentiary. By aggressively enforcing such statutes, local sheriffs, deputies, and constables acted as de facto labor recruiters who disproportionately targeted poor, young black men, just the kind of workers southern industrialists demanded.

Black convicts labored under deplorable conditions. In Florida's turpentine orchards, convicts performed constant, heavy work extracting gum and pitch from the pines to be distilled into turpentine spirits. Each evening, the convicts returned to camp packed into transport vans that were nothing more than cages that had sat in the hot sun all day. Crude barracks housed the convicts. They slept on iron beds that supported filthy mattresses in rooms that reeked of a mix of unpleasant odors. Only once a week did camp officials permit convicts to bathe and have a fresh change of clothes. Convicts survived on a diet of salt pork, cornbread, biscuits, and beans. Prison laborers contracted a host of diseases, including chills, fever, pneumonia, skin maladies, dysentery, and scurvy. One state inspector found that employers did not even supply shoes, leaving the men's feet gouged, blistered, and swollen. Employers justified the brutality of convict leasing, rationalizing that should one convict die, they could simply get another.

In the early decades of the twentieth century, a diverse and vocal group of reformers exposed the cruel barbarism of convict leasing, creating a groundswell of support for its abolition. The termination of the system, however, did not signal the dawn of humanitarian reform or the end of the New South's reliance on black convict labor. While advocates of reform targeted the use of forced labor for private profit, they did not necessarily disagree with exploiting such labor for the public good. Instead, they criticized convict leasing as an unwarranted state subsidy to private corporations. When southern states abolished the leasing of convicts to private employers, they put inmates to work on state and county chain gangs. Laboring under the authority of the state, predominantly African American prisoners paved roads and built other public works vital to the region's economic progress. Thus, well into the twentieth century, long after southern states ended the practice of leasing convicts to private industries, the New South still depended upon forced black labor for economic development.

Industrial employers had also looked beyond the state for alternative methods of recruiting black workers and reducing labor turnover. As early as the 1890s a few industrialists began programs of welfare capitalism designed not only to attract reliable workers but to reform the work habits of those who came. Not only did employers promise regular payment in cash wages, they offered black recruits a range of nonwage benefits that they claimed would promote the welfare of workers. Company towns were central to these initiatives. As sawmill managers in western Louisiana discovered, black men with ties to the land were reluctant to take jobs in the mills and logging woods. To lure rural black men out of the countryside to work for wages and remain on the job, sawmill operators promised prospective employees the foundations of a stable family life: four- or five-room single-family dwellings, garden plots, permission to raise livestock, quiet neighborhoods anchored by schools, churches, fraternal orders, community centers, and recreational facilities such as swimming pools, athletic fields, and theaters. In recruiting African Americans, employers often made explicit appeals to black racial pride. Operators of the Blue Creek coal mines in Alabama, for example, described their workplace as a "Negro Eden." By assembling an all-black workforce, operators promised black workers a safe haven from the racial violence and poverty of the countryside as well as from the discrimination and exclusions that black workers encountered in racially mixed workplaces. Operators beckoned blacks to demonstrate their ability and to seize the chance to govern their own affairs in the safety of an all-black industrial community.

Although these industrialists saw themselves as guardians of black welfare, economic self-interest motivated employers to invest in welfare programs.

The Yellow Pine Manufacturers' Association, for example, advised member mills to sponsor educational training for workers and their families. Not only did such classes attract what industrialists referred to as a better class of workers who were less likely to leave, they enhanced employers' power to regulate the family and social lives of their workers. Regular sermons on sobriety, thrift, and home economics also taught workers how to survive on, as well as accept, low wages. Most importantly, employers invested in welfare capitalism because they believed that by making modest improvements in the living and working conditions of black workers, they could cultivate black loyalty, curb black working-class activism, and undermine the appeal of joining labor unions.

Employers found reliable allies among the region's emergent black middle class. Claiming to speak for the racial interests of southern black workers, black clergymen, educators, and other professionals encouraged black workers to avoid unions and argued that they had more to gain from white employers than from white labor organizers. Booker T. Washington, the nation's preeminent black civic leader and tireless advocate of black self-help through industrial education, emerged as the leading voice of this philosophy of black economic advancement. Washington even encouraged black workers to break strikes, arguing that labor disputes between white trade unionists and employers gave black workers an unprecedented opportunity to gain access to jobs from which they had been excluded. Local black ministers, newspaper editors, and community leaders across the South echoed that advice. An interracial alliance of southern industrialists and black elites thus worked in concert to create a reliable, efficient, and nonunion industrial labor force of black workers. Corporate executives provided Washington's Tuskegee Normal and Industrial Institute and other black trade schools across the South with significant financial support. Industrialists, in turn, hired graduates of these schools to implement welfare programs that taught black workers the virtues of individual effort and company loyalty and warned of the perils of organized labor.

Many black workers had good reason to heed such advice. Firsthand experience convinced many black workers to consider employers more trustworthy than white trade unionists. Although the American Federation of Labor (AFL), a national association of craft unions founded in 1886, adopted an official policy against racial discrimination, its affiliated trade unions often excluded black workers from membership and discriminated against them in the workplace. Many white trade unionists built a labor movement dedicated to protecting the privileges of white workers from competition with African Americans. When black workers crossed the picket lines of white unionists, they justified their actions as an economic necessity to which they were driven by the inequities of the labor market and the racial hostility of organized labor. African Americans were not strikebreakers, black labor activists explained, but workers who had no other option but to seize opportunities for work where they emerged. Although white trade unionists denounced black workers as a race of scabs—a slang term for strikebreakers—they failed to comprehend how strikebreaking was a form of labor activism that enabled African Americans to advance their economic interests and gain access to jobs from which they had been excluded.

As black workers encountered racism in the industrial workplace, many supported a race-conscious alliance with black elites. Black workers encountered African American race leaders through their membership and participation in a variety of religious, fraternal, and civic organizations. Fraternal orders, especially, appealed to black workers. They offered members tangible material benefits such as sickness and death benefits, but they also attracted working-class adherents because they promoted racial pride and opportunities for self-governance of their own organizations. Some black elites used their influence with employers to advocate for black workers. In West Virginia, for example, T. Edward Hill, the anti-union director of the state's Bureau of Negro Welfare and Statistics, negotiated with coalmine operators to secure long-term job security for black workers who crossed picket lines. Employers often dismissed strikebreakers once they resolved labor disputes, but because of Hill's intervention, the operators agreed to retain the black workers they recruited to break the strikes of the early 1920s. Civil rights activities also drew black elites and workers together. Race-based organizations that championed anti-lynching legislation, exposed racial discrimination in public accommodations, denounced police brutality, and lobbied for improved public resources for black communities resonated with black workers. These race-based institutions along with the local black press formed the associational foundation of many black working-class communities across the South.

Although black workers at times saw strikebreaking as an opportunity to crack the color barrier in employment, they did not oppose organized labor out of principle, as many white trade unionists (and black elites) assumed. Black workers always inhabited two worlds, one profoundly shaped by their experiences as African Americans in the racially oppressive post–Reconstruction South but also as workers in a region in which the labor movement had shallow roots. For all the benefits that race-based institutions offered black workers, they seldom addressed their specific concerns as workers, including low pay, dangerous working conditions, and intermittent employment. Nor did company-sponsored social welfare programs deliver on their promise to alleviate poverty, insecurity, and racism. Company officials limited their expenditures on the infrastructure of company towns, employee benefits remained meager and uneven, and welfare capitalism did little to alter the brutality of industrial labor relations. Federal investigators, for example, discovered in 1914 that black workers in the sawmill towns of western Louisiana lived and worked in a state of fear. Employers hired private detectives to maintain tight surveillance on black workers, company timekeepers cheated black workers out of wages, foremen commanded blacks to patronize company stores where they paid excessive prices for basic necessities, and company doctors seldom provided the medical care workers and their families needed, despite having the expense deducted from their wages. Conditions there were not unique.

Black workers in the South experimented with trade unionism to combat conditions specific to their experience as workers. Faced with exclusion from white unions, some blacks organized their own independent labor organizations. Black labor activists discovered that despite the white racism that prevailed in organized labor, southern affiliates of the AFL were not uniformly hostile to organizing or cooperating with black workers. Consequently, black trade unionists found opportunities to cooperate with white workers in biracial ventures in which workers of the same trade joined segregated locals. And in some instances, union activists of both races joined together in interracial unions. Although most southern black workers in the late nineteenth and early twentieth century never joined the labor movement, black trade unionism attracted tens of thousands of adherents between the 1880s and the 1920s. Black trade unionists at times played a decisive, even leading role, in a series of bold initiatives to organize workers across the color line.

In the 1890s a group of black organizers for the United Mine Workers of America (UMWA) emerged as some of the most energetic and eloquent black proponents of trade unionism. Richard L. Davis was among the union's early black leaders and pioneer organizers. Born in Roanoke, Virginia, in 1865, Davis moved to the mining community of Rendville in Ohio's Hocking Valley in the 1880s where he first learned the value of organized labor. He quickly became a devoted unionist who ascended the leadership ranks of the UMWA, first as a member of the executive board of one of the district offices in Ohio and then to the union's national executive board in 1896. Davis was not the only African American miner to hold positions of leadership in the union. Across the mining districts of the eastern United States in the 1890s, black miners won elective posts to the union's local, state, and regional offices. Through the efforts of organizers such as Davis, the UMWA experienced an upsurge of black membership in the 1890s. By 1902 some twenty thousand black miners had joined the union; ten years later the number of black unionists in the UMWA had doubled, constituting more than 70 percent of all black workers in the labor movement. Black and white miners had collaborated and established locals in which blacks held leadership posts. Despite the existence of racial tensions, the dangerous working conditions had forced them to recognize that they shared common interests.

Whether in the coalfields of Alabama and southern West Virginia, the wharves of the Gulf Coast, or the forest industries of western Louisiana and southeast Texas, black and white unionists built their coalition on pragmatism. Because these industries employed large numbers of unskilled and semiskilled workers, many of whom were African American, white unionists concluded that they had little choice but to organize their black coworkers. Activists appealed to the narrow economic interests of whites to bring them into the union's fold. Organizers exposed white supremacy as a ruse that denied all workers the power to control the terms of their employment. They told white workers, for example, that they did not possess the power to apply the color line and that they lacked the leverage to exclude blacks from working in these industries. White workers confronted a choice: either cooperate with blacks or watch employers use black workers to break white unions. Leading unionists thus tried to refocus the animosity of white workers, shifting it away from blacks and onto the abuses of employers. Blacks were not the problem, they argued, but part of the solution; if whites allied with them, they could relieve their common misery.

Union organizers not only directed their pragmatic appeals to white miners, they also appealed to black miners, many of whom harbored deep suspicions about the wisdom of joining a predominantly white union such as the UMWA. Davis, for example, criticized those black miners who supported mine owners' plans to operate some mines with an exclusively black labor force. Although such plans appeared to offer black workers employment security, Davis argued that they left black miners vulnerable to exclusion from work at other mines. The mine operators, he argued, showed no special concern for the welfare of black miners and sought only to create devastating racial divisions that enabled them to keep wages low for all miners. William Riley, a Tennessee minister and black miner, used his pulpit to criticize black miners who were reluctant to join the union. The union's battle against the coal operators, he insisted, was a continuation of the broader struggle for equality. W. E. Clark, a neighbor of Davis's in the Hocking Valley coalfields, warned black miners that race-based organizations delivered few benefits and only reinforced the racial prejudices that they all hoped to eradicate. When these black activists openly challenged the anti-union views of Booker T. Washington, black ministers, newspapers editors, and other prominent blacks used their positions of authority to denounce black workers who joined unions or went on strike as lazy vagabonds who were a disgrace to their race. Nevertheless, many black miners remained committed to the pursuit of working-class, rather than race-based, solutions to their problems.

Pragmatism alone does not explain the upsurge of interracial unionism in the late nineteenth and early twentieth century. Organizers mobilized workers around an alternative set of values and an egalitarian vision of working-class community grounded in class experience rather than racial or ethnic identity. In doing so, they developed a language of working-class solidarity that they hoped would transcend race. Black and white unionists urged workers to recognize that, despite racial differences, they all shared common interests. Organizers urged white workers to refrain from acts of bigotry and prejudice, insisted that there was no color line in their fight, and censured those who referred to unionists by race rather than as fellow workers. Stories of white miners who came to the aid of black unionists or who refused to patronize hotels and restaurants that discriminated against African Americans gave credibility to the UMWA's commitment to racial cooperation. Likewise, white miners frequently reported how the efforts of black organizers helped to dispel racial animosity among white workers and inspired some to rethink their racial assumptions. Although these organizations never overcame racial prejudice, they did succeed in limiting the ability of opponents to use it against their members.

This pragmatic interracialism, which appealed to workers' economic self-interest and built solidarity based on common grievances, nevertheless accommodated to the prevailing segregationist sentiments of late nineteenth-century America. Although the union press at times showcased the courage and militancy of black unionists, it continued to reproduce racist stereotypes of African Americans. It published derogatory images, referring to blacks in degrading terms such as "darkies," "coons," and "brutes," printed sensationalized stories of black criminality, and advertised minstrel shows that featured white actors performing in black face. White workers never translated biracial cooperation in the workplace into a broader agenda that embraced civic equality for African Americans, an issue that white unionists considered a destructive diversion from the all-important "labor question." But the color line in organized labor remained most evident in the organizational structure of unions. Union locals were more often segregated than racially integrated, with some unions even requiring the officers of black locals to send dues and membership fees to the nearest white local for what they called safekeeping. The UMWA's District 20 in Alabama adhered to an elaborate electoral formula that preserved racial hierarchy in its leadership. The union reserved the presidency for white members while the vice presidency was filled by blacks and the position of secretary and treasurer for whites. The union also observed strict racial quotas in selecting delegates to district conventions.

Whatever the limitations of the UMWA's pragmatic interracial unionism, it offered black workers a viable alternative to the prevailing pattern of black exclusion within the labor movement. Racial cooperation was far less successful, for example, in the iron foundries and steel industries of Birmingham, Alabama. There, white workers used the power of their unions to shore up control of skilled craft positions in the furnaces and foundries, and white craft unionists were among the city's strongest proponents of building the New South's segregationist order. The building trades adopted similar positions toward the organization of black workers, and the railroad brotherhoods remained steadfast in their exclusion of African Americans.

Rather than remain aloof from labor struggles, black working-class activists found that establishing their own separate or independent labor organizations offered distinct advantages. On the railroads, blacks responded to white exclusion by organizing independent black railway men's associations. Within these brotherhoods of color, they set their own course in which they agitated for goals shared by all workers—higher wages, better working conditions, and the rights of collective bargaining—but they also pursued an agenda shaped by their peculiar interests as black workers. Black trade unionists fought against racial barriers to promotion, and they used their independent organizations to advocate for black rights within the broader labor movement. Working from within their own locals, black unionists avoided the condescending, humiliating, and often patronizing demeanor of whites who frequently regarded blacks as subordinate allies. In all-black unions, members elected their own leaders, controlled their own resources, governed their own internal affairs, and defined an agenda reflecting their needs as blacks and as workers. Black trade unionists did not so much as express a demand for integrated locals as they agitated for access to employment and for inclusion and equality within the labor movement.

This biracial formula, which allowed workers belonging to the same union to organize into racially separate locals, provided black and white workers with space to collaborate for the material benefits of all workers in a society that was fast becoming racially polarized. The UMWA's District 20 in Alabama, for example, conducted an aggressive organizing drive in the spring of 1898 that succeeded in winning recognition of the union from the coal operators. For the next six years, the UMWA and the operators negotiated annual contracts that increased wages, including those of day laborers. These annual contracts also explicitly rejected racial discrimination in work assignments. Such provisions, along with other measures that curtailed employers' power to fire unionists, freed workers from shopping at company stores, and eliminated the hated practice of subcontracting, enhanced the union's reputation and broadened the base of its support.

Biracial cooperation also delivered tangible results on the New Orleans waterfront. There black and white waterfront unions of the International Longshoremen's Association (ILA) cooperated in an effort to prevent the city's long history of racial hostility from affecting working conditions. In the late nineteenth and early twentieth century, black and white unionists reached agreements that stipulated an equitable racial division of work on the wharves and assured close collaboration within the union hall. Because of their organizational strength, black unionists won seats to the New Orleans Dock and Cotton Council, the city's powerful labor federation, the right to participate on all ILA negotiating committees, and representation on the ILA's Executive Committee. Still, the ILA never challenged the logic of segregation. Labor solidarity on the wharves rested on separate but equal locals. Under ILA work-sharing agreements, crews remained racially divided and worked different sides of ships. Despite persistent objections by black unionists, unionized foremen on the docks were all white. Under this arrangement, the alliance among black and white workers secured increased wages, improved working conditions, and gave greater control over the work process while preventing shipowners from imposing a racially segmented labor market.

Black longshoremen along the Gulf Coast remained steadfast in their commitment to the union. African Americans endorsed the union's demands, which promised them tangible solutions to the problems that they confronted in the workplace. The union recognized the dignity of black workers and defended their interests as workers. Blacks assumed leadership positions, served as organizers, and challenged racial customs when they spoke before mixed-race audiences. Regardless of the racial dispositions of individual white workers and the pragmatic self-interest of white union officials, the ILA, like the UMWA and other biracial unions, remained one of the most progressive institutions in the lives of southern black workers after Reconstruction, enabling them to make demands for racial justice at work and equal recognition within the union at large. They left an important legacy that later generations of activists could draw upon.

Figure 2.3. Longshoremen break for dinner on the docks in Jacksonville, Florida, 1912. Courtesy of the State Archives of Florida.

Biracial working-class cooperation could only deliver so much and proved difficult to sustain. Biracial coalitions, however, succumbed not so much to the resurgence of white working-class racism but to employer counteroffensives, which often drew upon racial themes to promote dissension among the ranks of the working class. In 1911, the Brotherhood of Timber Workers (BTW), for example, built a broad but fragile interracial alliance of sawmill workers, loggers, and farmers in western Louisiana and southeast Texas. The union demanded land reform, a union-sanctioned wage scale, biweekly pay days, a ten-hour workday, and reduced doctor and hospital fees. In response, employers launched an aggressive crusade to weaken public support for the BTW. Lumber operators aroused white racial fears, using the regional press to claim that the union's real objective was to impose racial equality. To break the resolve of black unionists, employers hired black ministers and teachers who preached the gospel of anti-unionism and company loyalty. Lumber operators also took more direct action. The Southern Lumber Operators' Association (SLOA), an organization of lumbermen dedicated to preventing the unionization of the industry, agreed to close their plants rather than operate them with union labor. Sawmill operators pledged to reopen only after they could establish that they could do so with a nonunion labor force. Employers harassed stump speakers, deputized loyal workers, and infiltrated BTW locals with spies. Within six months, SLOA had compiled a blacklist of some twenty-five thousand union members and sympathizers that operators then used to screen those they hired when they reopened their sawmills. Although the BTW survived in places for another two years, employer intimidation defeated the struggle to unionize southern lumber workers.

Ultimately, the political conditions of the South doomed the workplace struggles of black workers in these years. Beginning in Mississippi in 1890, southern states revised their state constitutions or adopted new laws designed to prevent African Americans—and many poor whites—from voting. States imposed poll taxes, property qualifications, complicated residency requirements, literacy tests, and the infamous understanding clause in which a prospective registrant, in order to qualify to vote, had to convince a local registrar that he understood a randomly selected passage from the state constitution or some other legal text. By the early twentieth century, all southern states had adopted some voting restrictions, which had a dramatic and immediate impact on the composition of the southern electorate. In 1896, more than 130,000 African Americans were registered to vote in the state of Louisiana; eight years later only 1,300 remained registered. In 1906, five years after Alabama adopted a state constitution that imposed new barriers to voter registration, only 2 percent of the state's eligible black voters were registered.

The removal of African Americans from southern politics hastened the advance of legalized segregation in the South. The new legislatures passed a series of laws that transformed informal social customs of racial segregation into a legal, formal, and elaborate system of segregation. New ordinances established racially segregated public restrooms, drinking fountains, waiting rooms in train and bus stations, and sitting areas in theaters and on public transportation. Other laws barred blacks from access to public libraries, swimming pools, golf courses, tennis courts, and many public parks. Not only did these laws transform the social geography of the urban-industrial South, they made interracial working-class interaction increasingly difficult. A Birmingham ordinance, for example, made it illegal for whites and blacks to play games of cards, dice, billiards, and dominoes together. The legal advance of Jim Crow—the combined system of voting restrictions and segregation—further ensured that black and white workers would continue to inhabit separate worlds that made labor organizing across the color line more socially disreputable, dangerous, and unlikely. Voting restrictions ensured that the working class, white and black, exerted no influence in politics and largely forced unions to withdraw from or remain silent about proposing political solutions to labor conflicts. Jim Crow created deep racial divisions that favored the economic interests of the region's planters and industrialists.

These conditions left black workers with few options. No one persuasion dominated or characterized African Americans' strategy for economic gain in this environment. They shifted between the racial separatism of independent unions, the race-based strategies favored by many black elites, pledging loyalty to company employers, and biracial and interracial alliances with white workers. They weighed their strategies and tactics based on prevailing circumstances and their assessment of what they most stood to gain from any particular situation. Few black workers trusted white employers, broke strikes out of an inherent hatred of unions, or entered the labor movement under the illusion that class solidarity with white workers would dissolve racial antipathy in the South. None of these approaches could empower them to overcome their limited occupational mobility or strengthen their economic security.

The political and economic order of Jim Crow confined African Americans to farming on marginal land or toiling in low-wage labor. Despite the fact that by 1910, more than twenty thousand African Americans had managed to purchase some 15 million acres of southern land, a huge pool of underemployed southern black laborers had emerged who had few prospects of inheriting or prospering on the small farms and properties that their ancestors had accumulated since emancipation. Many African Americans who came of age in the first two decades of the twentieth century did not aspire, as their parents had, to economic independence through land ownership. Instead, this new generation of African American working people turned their eyes to emerging opportunities in the urban and industrial North opened by the outbreak of World War I. They imagined a Land of Hope that lay beyond the confines of the Jim Crow South and which promised a new foundation, rooted in steady employment at good wages in America's industries, for claiming the economic rights of citizenship.

CHAPTER THREE

~

The Great Black Labor Migration

By the time the United States entered World War I in April 1917, a mass movement of black southerners to the urban, industrial North was well underway. The war, which had started in Europe three years earlier, precipitated a restructuring of the American labor market. Northern industries, which had relied upon millions of European immigrants as their principal source of labor, suddenly confronted a labor shortage. The number of European immigrants declined sharply after the outbreak of the war, from 1.3 million in 1914 to fewer than two hundred thousand a year between 1915 and 1919. The supply of available workers needed to meet the increased demands of wartime industrial expansion shrank even further when millions of Americans entered the army in 1917 and 1918. American industrialists thus began to recruit new sources of labor, including African Americans from the South. Between 1915 and 1918, some five hundred thousand black southerners relocated to industrial cities such as Chicago, Cleveland, Detroit, New York City, and Pittsburgh. After a short but sharp postwar recession ended in 1921, the exodus of southern blacks resumed, with another 750,000 relocating to the North by the end of the decade.

The so-called Great Migration set in motion a dramatic redistribution of the nation's black population. Before World War I, the major cities of the American North were home to a small and diffuse black population. By 1930 these cities had absorbed tens of thousands of black newcomers. Whereas only 6,000 blacks lived in Detroit in 1910, some 120,000 called the Motor City home in 1930. Cleveland, which saw a tenfold increase in its black population between 1910 and 1930, had become such a magnet for migrants from the Deep South that black residents referred to the city as "Alabama North." Even places that had few, if any, black residents at the dawn of the century—Milwaukee, Wisconsin; Gary, Indiana; Toledo, Ohio—had now become home to substantial numbers of blacks. The influx of southern blacks into the urban North also transformed the composition of America's industrial labor force. Northern industries, such as steelmaking, meatpacking, and automobile manufacturing, that had long excluded or hired very few blacks, now employed African Americans by the thousands. By 1930 it was clear that the center of African American social, economic, political, and cultural life had taken a decisive shift away from the rural South and toward the urban, industrial North.

Although migrants cited a variety of reasons for leaving the region of their birth—racial segregation, disfranchisement, employment discrimination, mob violence, indebtedness, and persistent poverty—most did so in search of economic and political freedom. The northern black press, especially the *Chicago Defender*, increased its circulation in the South during the war years and encouraged southern blacks to move North with editorials, advertisements of employment opportunities, and offers of assistance to black southerners willing to relocate. African Americans responded by the thousands. Desperate to seek better lives elsewhere, prospective migrants expressed their hope to secure steady work at good wages and make a living with all of the privileges that whites enjoyed.

The Great Migration was thus a grassroots movement of the black masses. It had no central organization, discernible direction, or visible leader. Still, individual migrants saw themselves as part of a larger, collective enterprise. James Weldon Johnson, the first black field secretary of the National Association for the Advancement of Colored People (NAACP), the nation's leading civil rights organization, declared in 1917 that the migration of black workers to the North created the greatest opportunity for African Americans since the end of the Civil War. Not only did the move North enable southern blacks to earn lucrative wages, it also restored to them the right to vote. Armed with the ballot, black migrants had a powerful new weapon with which to demand social and political change. With 800,000 to 1 million new black working-class voters spread from New York to California, African Americans could amass the financial power and political influence that would enable them to demand their rights. New conditions also gave black activists in the South an unprecedented opportunity to use the threat of migration as leverage in wresting improved working conditions from southern planters and industrialists desperate to stem the exodus of black labor from the region. By describing the wartime exodus as a form of black labor activism capable of delivering both political power and economic opportunity, Johnson gave voice to the hope that the Great Migration would enable blacks to at last fulfill the promise of emancipation.

Black migration was not a new phenomenon. Ever since the days of slavery, African American runaway slaves had fled to the North to escape bondage in the South. After the Civil War, ex-slaves had embraced the freedom to move as essential to their quest for self-determination. Freedmen moved to reunite with loved ones who had been scattered by the slave trade and the war. They flocked to the region's cities and towns to seek work for cash wages. Despite the many laws southern legislatures passed to restrict black labor mobility in the years after Reconstruction, African Americans found plenty of ways to move in search of economic opportunity. At the end of each agricultural season, anywhere from 30 to 40 percent of black sharecroppers and tenant farmers left one plantation and moved to another. Many black farmers established patterns of seasonal labor migration in which they moved between farm and factory, in rhythm with the planting cycle, to earn wages that supplemented rural household incomes.

The failure of Reconstruction left southern blacks with few options for dissent other than migration. As early as 1870, Philip Joiner, a black Radical Republican from Georgia, predicted that unless whites recognized black rights, African Americans would leave the plantations and drain the region of black agricultural workers. Robert Smalls, one of six black delegates to South Carolina's 1895 constitutional convention, challenged a series of provisions designed to deprive African Americans of the right to vote by declaring that blacks would migrate, leaving the state's cotton fields, rice swamps, and phosphate mines devoid of labor.

Black workers in the decades between the Civil War and World War I at times made good on such threats. Henry Adams of Louisiana, a black veteran of the Union Army, organized a committee of some five hundred blacks to investigate the working conditions among rural blacks in the wake of Reconstruction's collapse. Finding conditions deplorable, they promoted a mass migration to Kansas where they believed blacks stood a better chance of buying land and enjoying political freedom. Calling themselves Exodusters, approximately twenty thousand black migrants left the South and made their way to Kansas in 1879 and 1880 where they established several all-black settlements. In subsequent years, other southern blacks escaped the repressive labor system of the New South by organizing various campaigns to relocate to places such as Africa, South America, Mexico, and the western territories of the United States. Although planters at times recognized that oppressive working conditions and the loss of political rights motivated migrants, they made no effort to make substantive changes.

America's entry into World War I created unprecedented conditions that expanded economic opportunities and improved the bargaining position of many black workers. Migration and the military draft caused labor shortages throughout the South, forcing planters and industrialists into a bidding war for workers that elevated wages and gave blacks greater freedoms to decide where and for whom they worked. Planters complained that blacks refused to work in cotton fields unless they paid "fancy wages," employers marveled that blacks preferred to pay fines for loafing rather than toil in factories, and managers despaired that blacks no longer showed a disposition to work at the low wages that they were willing to pay. Southern white women griped that black women had organized to demand better wages and working conditions. Cotton prices soared during the war years, freeing sharecroppers and tenant farmers to payoff long-term debts and purchase farms of their own. Planters made dire predictions that in the absence of tighter restrictions on black labor mobility, the cotton belt would become unproductive and never recover.

A newly responsive federal government strengthened—to a degree—the bargaining position of black workers. Recognizing the necessity of labor to the war effort, wartime federal agencies at times intervened to resolve labor disputes to maintain industrial production schedules critical for the war effort. The administration of President Woodrow Wilson gave these federal agencies the power to regulate wages and working conditions to promote labor stability, not racial equality. Nevertheless, black workers could still benefit from federal intervention. Black women in Little Rock, Arkansas, for example, won a case before the National War Labor Board that secured them equal pay with white women employed in commercial laundries that serviced nearby military camps. Despite the limited reach of the federal government as an agency of labor reform during the war, its presence in the field, advocacy of wage increases to low-paid workers, and commitment to the principle of equal pay for equal work gave black workers hope that the war might improve southern labor relations.

Fearful that an interventionist federal government would disrupt their authority in the workplace, southern employers vowed not to cooperate. They especially objected to the Division of Negro Economics (DNE), a bureau created within the Department of Labor in 1918. Lacking any enforcement power, the DNE's small African American staff primarily encouraged the efficient use of black workers in meeting the demands of wartime production, studied the impact of black migration on labor conditions, and promoted the welfare of black workers throughout the country. As the DNE pursued its moderate agenda on a tight budget with limited authority, it encountered intense hostility from southern employers. Planters and industrialists denounced the DNE as a dangerous reincarnation of the Reconstruction era's Freedmen's Bureau, claiming that they were under no obligation to recognize the authority of its agents. Yet even as they denounced the DNE's intrusion into southern labor relations, planters and industrialists demanded that the federal government act to restrict black migration from the South, claiming that black mobility undermined wartime production.

Wartime mobilization sparked violent racial conflicts throughout the South. The war may have presented blacks with new opportunities, but blacks assumed grave risks when they sought to take advantage of wartime labor conditions. In Vicksburg, Mississippi, white men had apparently disguised themselves in black face and then raped white women, inciting violence against black men earning good wages in local factories. When black cooks and nurses organized a union in Macon, Mississippi, to demand higher wages and an eight-hour work day, local whites retaliated by killing one organizer and arresting fifteen others whom they accused of plotting an uprising against the town's white population. Black iron miners in Alabama encountered similar hostility when they sought the intervention of the National War Labor Board in their struggle to win higher pay, shorter working hours, and the right to organize. The company deputized white workers to intimidate and harass the black unionists. They ambushed the AFL's black organizer, threw him into a car, and drove off into the woods where they brutally beat him. Southern whites often blamed racial conflicts such as these on blacks who refused to stay in their place and act, work, and talk as whites expected.

The intensity of white opposition to black aspirations inspired more African Americans to leave the South. As Robert Abbott, the *Chicago Defender*'s crusading editor claimed in one of his many editorials promoting black migration, the South wanted blacks to remain but only as "serfs and vassals," not as "men and citizens."[1] If propertied white southerners continued to subjugate, humiliate, and brutalize black workers, African Americans had no choice, he argued, but to leave the South. But Abbott and many others had begun to lose hope that migration could spur meaningful reform. The *Defender* despaired that race relations had worsened since the war and worried that black workers remained unprotected and vulnerable to violent assault. Although some leading white editors and clergy expressed sympathy with the demands of black migrants and advocated paying black workers higher wages and protecting African Americans' basic legal rights, most white southerners rejected their proposals and refused to make even minimal, let alone substantive, reforms that might encourage blacks to remain in the South.

Several factors had thus come together during the war to both push African American workers out of the South and to pull them North. But if push and pull factors constituted the broader economic and political context in which the Great Migration unfolded, they do not reveal who actually migrated or capture how blacks responded to these conditions. Like migrants of other mass population movements in world history, black southerners who relocated during these years tended to be young adults of prime working age who were more ambitious, less risk-averse, and better educated than those who remained behind. Although most migrants had been born and raised on farms, about half of them had lived in urban areas and worked for wages before coming North. Coming of age after 1900, they did not share their parents' faith in the promise of the New South. These young men and women concluded that there was no future for them in farming. They had seen their parents and other adult relatives struggle with erratic cotton markets, insect infestations, floods, droughts, debts, crop liens, and other legal restrictions. Even the children of those who had become landowners had no assurances of inheriting land because many parents were either unwilling to turn over control of their farms to their maturing children, or they had subdivided them into plots too small to farm profitably. Many of these younger black men and women had long labored in the South's casual labor market. Even though they endured many hardships toiling in the region's timber camps, mines, and waterfronts, or laboring in the homes of white people, this younger generation of black southerners gained a taste of freedom unavailable to them in the rural communities of their youth. These young adults were among the first to seize upon economic opportunity in the North opened by wartime mobilization.

Migrants may have moved North for economic opportunity, but their moves happened within the context of a dense web of kinship ties and social bonds. Oftentimes the oldest male member of a family made the first venture North. Once he established himself in a job, found adequate housing, and accumulated the means to assist others, he would write and send for his wife or other dependent family members. One relative would follow another until an entire extended family gradually transplanted itself North. Through letters and word of mouth, initial migrants spread information about housing, employment opportunities, wages, and the excitement of urban living. When these friends and relatives returned home for visits, they shared their success stories about life in the North and provided concrete proof of the possibilities for prosperity outside the South. By sustaining social and familial relationships over long distances, migrants pulled other black southerners North who were eager to rejoin loved ones. Having come North to rekindle personal and familial ties, they now had the opportunity to pursue new economic futures.

Not only did kin and friendship networks facilitate migration, the social links in the migration chain eased newcomers' transition to the North. Migrants often settled into neighborhoods populated with people from their hometowns, placing a greater emphasis on finding housing close to friends and relatives over proximity to workplaces. In doing so, migrants adopted flexible housing arrangements that reflected the importance of balancing economic and noneconomic needs. In many ways, migrants recreated the household economy of the rural South in the urban North, adopting the same values of mutual aid and familial obligation to convert tight budgets and scarce resources into economically viable households. Working-age adults depended on family members to care for young children and aging parents. African Americans who remained in the South often sent their children North to take advantage of better educational facilities and relied upon extended social networks to arrange for housing with siblings, relatives, or trusted friends. Single migrants often rented rooms from black families eager not only for extra income but also for the sociability, companionship, and emotional connections to the South that boarders provided. Because of these patterns, the average number of people per household and the number of unrelated persons living within households remained much higher among black migrants in the urban North than among other immigrant groups.

However they came and wherever they settled, black migrants found greater economic opportunity in northern cities than they had in either the rural or urban South. Through the Great Migration, African Americans secured work in the major sectors of American industry from which they had long been excluded. Northern cities had a diverse and varied industrial base that expanded job opportunities for black migrants not only in the nation's core industries—steelmaking, meatpacking, and automobile manufacturing—but also in secondary industries such as metals processing, machine-tool manufacturing, and in plants that specialized in producing automobile parts, paints, varnishes, and chemicals. The demand for southern black workers did not subside with the end of the war. After a brief postwar recession, the American industrial economy resumed its rapid expansion in the 1920s. At the same time, the United States revised its immigration policy with new laws in 1921 and 1924 that set strict quotas on the number of immigrants who could enter the United States each year. Immigration restrictions sharply reduced the European labor supply of American manufacturers. Consequently, northern employers continued to welcome southern blacks into the industrial labor force. By 1930 African Americans had not only become an integral and permanent part of the industrial labor force of the United

States, but they had achieved some measure of the occupational mobility, job security, and financial gain that eluded them in the South.

Black employment in the northern steel and meatpacking industries reveals how the Great Migration enabled African Americans to establish a permanent foothold in America's industrial sector. Before the Great Migration, blacks had only been able to enter these industries as strikebreakers in industrial disputes. Yet few blacks were able to translate strikebreaking into long-term employment. Among the first to be hired to break strikes, they were the first to be fired once labor conflicts ceased, and while they worked in these factories, black strikebreakers incurred the wrath of many white workers. According to one estimate, the number of black workers in the Chicago stockyards fell from more than ten thousand during a 1904 strike to less than one hundred six years later.

The labor shortage of the war years, however, opened lasting gains in black industrial employment. Whereas fewer than one hundred blacks worked in the Allegheny steel district of Pennsylvania in 1910, more than eight thousand black migrants worked there by 1916. By 1923 some sixteen thousand blacks worked in the Allegheny steel mills, constituting 21 percent of the steelworkers in the region. By 1918, African Americans constituted more than 20 percent of all workers in the nation's meatpacking industry, and by 1930, more than one-third of all black laborers in the cities of Chicago, St. Louis, Omaha, and St. Paul worked in the meatpacking industry. At the same time, the Great Migration and the decline in European immigration transformed the racial and ethnic composition of the northern industrial workforce. In 1909, for example, Polish and Lithuanian immigrants constituted nearly 40 percent of the workforce in Chicago's two largest packing plants, and only 3 percent of those who worked there were African American. By the end of the 1920s those ratios had been reversed. In 1928, less than 20 percent of the workers in these plants were Polish or Lithuanian immigrants, whereas almost 30 percent were African Americans. Likewise, in the automobile industry, fewer than six hundred African Americans worked in the automobile industry in 1910, constituting less than 1 percent of the nation's automobile labor force. But by 1930, more than twenty-five thousand blacks worked in the industry, which constituted more than 4 percent of automobile workers. In Michigan, African Americans constituted nearly 9 percent of the state's automobile labor force.

The Great Migration also drew working-age black women out of the South. Many of these newcomers for the first time secured employment outside of domestic service, especially in wartime industries. Factories that had never hired black women prior to the war, including manufacturers of muni-

Table 3.1. African American Industrial Employment during the Era of the Great Migration, 1910–1930

Year	Automobile Industry		Steel Industry		Meatpacking Industry	
	Total No. of Workers	No. of Black Workers (percentage)	Total No. of Workers	No. of Black Workers (percentage)	Total No. of Workers	No. of Black Workers (percentage)
1910	105,758	569 (0.5)	317,608	17,432 (5.5)	94,400	5,800 (6.2)
1920	204,405	8,156 (4.0)	352,457	47,797 (13.6)	132,400	28,300 (21.4)
1930	640,474	25,895 (4.0)	342,390	45,472 (13.3)	173,600	20,400 (11.8)

Sources: Herbert R. Northrup, *The Negro in the Automobile Industry* (Philadelphia: University of Pennsylvania Press, 1968), 8; U.S. Bureau of the Census, *Thirteenth Census of the United States, 1910: Population,* vol. *4, Occupation Statistics* (Washington, DC: Government Printing Office, 1914), 338–41; U.S. Bureau of the Census, *Fourteenth Census of the United States, 1920: Population,* vol. *4, Occupations* (Washington, DC: Government Printing Office, 1923), 346–48; *Fifteenth Census of the United States, 1930. Occupation Statistics, United States Summary* (Washington, DC: Government Printing Office, 1932), 29, 31; Walter A. Fogel, *The Negro in the Meat Industry* (Philadelphia: University of Pennsylvania Press, 1970), 28.

tions, paper products, tobacco goods, candy, glass, and especially garments, opened their doors to black women. Still, most black female migrants continued to work in domestic service. Many of those who did pushed for better conditions and for working arrangements that met their social and familial priorities. For example, migrant women objected to many of the indignities of domestic employment. They eagerly took advantage of organizations that offered classes that trained women to become hairdressers, manicurists, and beauticians. Many of those who continued to work as domestic servants transformed domestic service from a living-in occupation to a living-out one. In doing so, they escaped the stigma of the master-servant relationship that governed their labors when they lived in the homes of their employers. By demanding to live in their own homes, they now worked within an employer-employee relationship under a standardized scale of wages, hours, and working conditions. But most importantly, living-out arrangements enabled them to live with their families, raise their children, and take advantage of the varied leisure and recreational activities.

Northern jobs offered significantly higher wages than blacks could earn in the South. Farm laborers in the South on the eve of the First World War might earn a daily wage of about $0.75 and those who labored as unskilled workers in southern manufacturing earned about $1.50 to $1.75 a day. By contrast, African Americans who worked as unskilled laborers in the Chicago stockyards during the war earned more than $3.00 a day. Most occupations showed similar wage differentials between what blacks could earn in the North than in the South. Although black factory workers earned less than whites in both the North and the South, the racial wage disparity in the South far exceeded that in the North. Blacks in the northern steel industry earned only an average of $0.10 an hour less than white steelworkers, whereas blacks in the South earned nearly $0.25 an hour less than their white coworkers. Southern steel mills also employed far fewer higher-wage black workers. In 1935, about 13 percent of all black employees in northern steel mills earned more than $0.75 an hour; in the steel mills of the South fewer than 7 percent did so.

Black wage earners formed the basis of a new dynamic, black, urban, working-class culture. Because of housing discrimination, migrants congregated into distinctive, racially cohesive neighborhoods. Black migrants transformed these working-class neighborhoods into migrant communities. Newcomers not only rejoined family and friends, they readily detected the sights, sounds, and smells of the South in these expanding black ghettos. Flush with cash from good wages, migrants flocked to black-owned restaurants that served a taste of home such as barbecue short ribs, yams, and grits. A new commercial world of popular arts, athletics, motion pictures, street parades, and nightclubs that featured jazz, blues, and swing broadened African American culture. Migrants opened a range of businesses that catered to the growing needs and demands of black urban residents, and an emergent black consumer market expanded to reflect the widening tastes and sophistication of urban blacks. Migrant entrepreneurs expanded older media such as newspapers but also launched new ventures—such as radio programming that catered to black audiences—that cultivated a national African American cultural and political consciousness. The migrants' success, as industrial workers and as builders of communities, served as powerful evidence that contradicted white racists who claimed that blacks were unprepared for the demands, rigors, and challenges of life in the urban, industrial North.

Although black migrants found greater economic opportunity in the North than they had in the South, many, if not most, struggled to attain financial security, let alone prosperity. For one thing, employment discrimination depressed their wages and limited their occupational mobility. Even though occupational segregation was less severe in the North than in the South, it persisted in northern cities. In 1940, twenty-five years after the Great Migration had begun, African Americans continued to confront substantial barriers to occupational mobility. In the major northern cities, blacks remained considerably overrepresented in the labor force as service workers, domestic servants, and common laborers and were significantly underrepresented in skilled, clerical, and professional occupations. Blacks found themselves excluded from most managerial jobs in manufacturing and only gained access to supervisory positions when they worked in black-owned enterprises or in factories when they managed all-black work crews. Because most employers did not promote black workers into semiskilled and skilled positions, blacks could not ascend the job ladder. Many black migrants came North with varied work experiences, skills, and education and anticipated greater freedom to pursue their talent and ambition in the North. Yet whatever their background, most toiled as common laborers or held menial service jobs such as porters, chauffeurs, or waiters.

In the major manufacturing plants of the North, African Americans endured work that confined them to the heaviest, hottest, and most dangerous jobs. In the steel industry, for example, employers justified putting blacks to work on the coke ovens and other hot and dangerous places because they believed that blacks had the capacity to withstand the heat better than white workers and hence did the job better and more efficiently. Black workers knew that they had no special talent for enduring intense heat. Exposure to extreme heat quickened their heart beat, changed the pitch of their voice, gave them headaches and stomach cramps, and often left them unconscious and in need of hospitalization. Days in which six of seven crew members

Figure 3.1. Black worker tapping a blast furnace in a Pittsburgh steel mill, 1938. Farm Security Administration/Office of War Information Photograph Collection, Prints & Photographs Division, Library of Congress, LC-USF34-026562-D.

passed out from heat exhaustion and asphyxiation from toxic fumes were not unusual. Fires burned their clothes, and acid spills scarred their skin. Those who worked in the soaking pit came into continuous contact with water, leaving them susceptible to pneumonia. Black workers complained that foremen pushed the tempo of work and threatened to fire any who failed to keep pace because there were plenty of men outside the factory gates anxious to take their place. Such jobs also paid the lowest wages, forcing many black workers, according to a team of investigators studying the working and living conditions among Chicago blacks in the 1920s, to live hand to mouth.

Likewise, many of the employment gains that black women had made during the war did not persist into the postwar years. Once wartime labor shortages had subsided, many industrial employers began to replace the black women they hired during the war with returning servicemen or white women. Most employers admitted that they had hired black female migrants only as an experiment necessitated by the wartime emergency. One survey of 150 manufacturing plants in the urban North found that shortly after the war twenty had dismissed the black women they had hired during the war, forty had demoted black women to lesser-killed work than they held during the war, and others acknowledged that they had begun to phase out black female workers. By the early postwar years, most black women in northern cities toiled, like they did in the South, as domestic servants. During the 1920s, a time when large numbers of white women began working outside the home in clerical, retail, and professional positions, black women were virtually excluded from these occupations outside of black-owned enterprises.

Black workers confronted higher rates of unemployment than whites did after the war. The recession of 1920–1921 threw blacks out of work at a rate three times higher than white workers. Once the recession ended, migrants resumed flocking to northern cities in numbers that local labor markets could not absorb, overwhelming private social welfare agencies and shelters for the destitute. By the mid-1920s, the Chicago Urban League, an organization that among other things helped African American migrants with job placements, reported that it received 238 applicants for every one hundred job openings. African American workers were also far more susceptible to seasonal unemployment than white workers. Food industries such as meatpacking slowed in the winter after the holidays and also for several weeks during the summer. One meatpacking plant reported in 1926 that the number of black workers in its labor force declined from 15.3 to 8.3 percent during that year's slack periods.

Employment in northern factories did not insulate black migrants from racial hostility at the workplace. Black migrants often labored under abusive white foremen, many of whom were also recent migrants from the South.

They often represented themselves to northern manufacturers as experts in managing black workers. Not only did employers hire southern whites to supervise crews of black migrants but also they adopted other southern industrial labor practices. The *Iron and Trade Review*, a steel industry trade journal, advised northern plant operators with large numbers of southern black workers to build company stores and barracks for housing; employers could then deduct rent and store debts from paychecks, saving companies from having to pay their black workers their full wages in cash. Other plants segregated their lunchrooms and built company recreational facilities financed by deductions from the wages of all workers, even though companies excluded blacks from using the facilities. Employers justified the policy by insisting that blacks had no interest in socializing with whites and preferred to congregate among themselves.

Conditions beyond the workplace did not provide black migrants with appreciably better living conditions than in the South. A slowdown in housing construction during the war and postwar recession created severe shortages of housing for black migrants in all northern cities. To meet the demand for living quarters, landlords converted attics, cellars, and storerooms into rental spaces and subdivided apartments into single-room accommodations into which whole families moved. Migrants paid high rents to live in makeshift quarters that lacked basic amenities such as running water, toilets, and heat. Infestations of rodents and insects, crumbling plaster, standing water, and leaking roofs were all too common in these apartments. Discrimination in the real estate market compounded the problem of overcrowding in substandard housing. White realtors, bankers, insurers, landlords, and homeowners adopted policies that restricted black migrants' housing choices to segregated neighborhoods. Successful and ambitious blacks who sought to move beyond the confines of the ghetto to purchase property in all-white neighborhoods risked becoming targets of mobs of angry whites intent on preserving the racial exclusivity of their communities.

Intermittent employment, low wages, and limited housing options tested familial relationships and strained community cohesion. Even if many migrant households adapted to new conditions by working together, new experiences and new demands could just as easily draw family members apart, not just physically but emotionally. Outside their homes, black migrants lived in communities of stark contrasts. Black businesses thrived amidst poverty; a diverse nightlife offered entertainment in high-class, stylish clubs on the one hand and vice in disreputable dives on the other; and churches competed with gambling stations as the predominant community institution. The black novelist Richard Wright, who migrated from Memphis to Chicago in

1927, captured in his fiction how the cities of the urban North teased black migrants with a sense of possibility and achievement but left them feeling dispossessed and disinherited amid a world of elusive abundance.

Black migrants found the labor movement an unreliable ally in their pursuit of a share of that elusive abundance. Labor unions in the North were often as indifferent to the economic aspirations of black workers as they were in the South. Although the AFL maintained its commitment to a policy of nondiscrimination, it never challenged affiliated local trade unions that excluded blacks from membership. Regarding migrants as unfit for both skilled labor and union membership, labor leaders put little pressure on trade unions to admit black workers. Consequently, unions that represented skilled workers such as machinists, electricians, plumbers, and painters excluded black workers. Skilled black migrants thus confronted a choice of either accepting nonunion employment in their own craft at wages far below the union wage rate or finding work, usually unskilled, in another trade or industry. Unskilled black construction workers found the labor movement more welcoming. For example, one of Pittsburgh's strongest labor organizations, the Hod Carriers Union, counted more than four hundred blacks among its six hundred members, nearly half of whom were recent migrants from the South. Still, such evidence did little to persuade white unionists in the skilled building trades that blacks, when organized, were as committed to the labor movement as anyone.

Black migrants found similar attitudes among white unionists in the major industrial plants. Since its founding in 1876, the Amalgamated Association of Iron, Steel, and Tin Workers—the nation's largest union of steelworkers—had made few genuine attempts to organize black workers in the industry. Once one of the most powerful unions in the country, the Amalgamated Association had suffered a series of defeats at the hands of powerful steel operators. Consequently, employers ran their steel mills largely with nonunion labor in the first decade and a half of the twentieth century. When black migrants from the South began working in the steel works during the war, the Amalgamated Association made little effort to recruit them or to see them as a potential force that might help to revitalize the union. The Amalgamated Association thus gained little credibility among black migrants. As one black labor official lamented, most black workers in the region had come to believe in the merits, indeed the necessity, of doing what they could to disrupt the labor movement.

The consequences of organized labor's indifference to the interests and welfare of recent black migrants came home to roost in the Great Steel Strike of 1919. In 1918 the AFL launched an ambitious campaign to reorganize the steelworkers of America. Labor activists recognized the need to build an industry-wide organization not only to protect steelworkers from wage cuts and layoffs that employers planned to impose with the end of wartime production but also to win the right of collective bargaining, an eight-hour work day, and higher wages. Although organizers quickly enlisted more than one hundred thousand new recruits, most of whom were Eastern European immigrants, they won few black converts. Organizers failed to develop a specific plan or campaign to enlist the support of black steelworkers. They did not recruit in black communities, hire black organizers, or cultivate the cooperation of black community leaders. Most black workers did not see the new campaign as a significant departure from the Amalgamated Association's past racism.

When the steelworkers walked off the job on September 22, 1919, few African Americans heeded the call to join what quickly became a nation-wide strike that virtually shut down the industry. Of the twenty-five thousand workers who went on strike in western Pennsylvania, no more than a dozen were black. Although 85 percent of the black workers at the Illinois Steel Company in Chicago walked off at the start of the strike, most of them had a limited commitment to the strike and returned to work at the first opportunity. African Americans who worked in the Chicago mills lived on the city's South Side, a considerable distance from the steel factories. Consequently, few of them attended union meetings, and labor organizers failed to establish a presence in black neighborhoods or incorporate black workers into the life and culture of the union. Only in Cleveland, where the local lodges of the Amalgamated Association had organized black workers before the strike, did blacks join in the walkout in significant numbers. Elsewhere black support remained lukewarm at best.

While strike organizers failed to make a special effort to recruit black steelworkers, employers quickly realized their value in breaking the strike. The steel operators pursued a two-pronged approach. They recruited nonunion workers to work in the mills and waged a campaign of intimidation against those who went on strike. Steel operators relied on police forces, company guards, and deputized citizens loyal to the companies to pressure, harass, and break the resolve of those who went on strike. At the same time, employers assembled crews of nonunion workers, including an estimated thirty thousand black strikebreakers, to operate their mills. In western Pennsylvania, where employers relied heavily on black recruits from the South, white strikers clashed with the black newcomers in a series of bloody and deadly assaults. Employers escalated racial tensions by deputizing nonunion black workers and authorizing them to guard company property and intimidate strikers.

When black workers refused to participate in the strike, they acted in their own interests and not as pawns of the steel operators. From their perspective, crossing the picket line seemed the clearer path to steady employment in better positions at higher wages than joining a strike in solidarity with white workers who had always been openly hostile to them. Two types of black migrants joined the ranks of those who broke the strike. First were those whom the company recruited from the South at the height of the conflict. They were temporary workers who had traveled North without their families. Desperate for work of any kind, these men considered the immediate income from work in the mills as more significant than any elusive benefit that union membership might deliver. The second type of strikebreaker was one who had migrated during the war, had worked in the mills for the last few years, and had already brought their families to live with them. As regular millhands in the steel mills long before the strike, they had forged ties with their white coworkers and were at least somewhat receptive to the benefits of unionism. They also refused to walk off the job. Instead, they saw the strike as a rare opportunity to gain promotion to higher skilled, better-paying positions. Most black workers at the time were primarily concerned with making a living, regarding the union and the prevailing attitudes of white unionists as obstacles to their right to work and provide for their families.

Regardless of the reasons they had for crossing the picket lines, black strikebreakers alone did not cause the failure of the strike. Several other factors doomed the workers' cause. Native-born, skilled white workers, who had perhaps the most to gain from the strike, were among the first to give up and return to work and did so long before the operators began importing nonunion black laborers from the South and elsewhere. Strike organizers also did not receive much support from the country's other major unions. Employers effectively undermined public support by portraying the strike as a plot hatched by anarchists, revolutionaries, and radicals with ties to Soviet Russia. Given these conditions, union leaders had little choice but to call off the strike in early January 1920. Nevertheless, for years to come whites in the nation's steel industry blamed black scabs for the strike's failure.

The prospects for interracial unionism were far more promising in the Chicago meatpacking industry. In July 1917 labor activists in the Chicago stockyards created the Stockyards Labor Council (SLC), a coalition of craft unions that represented various trades in the meatpacking industry. The SLC launched an ambitious organizing drive to unionize the stockyards, and by the late fall of 1917, about 40 percent of Chicago's packinghouse workers had joined the SLC. Unionization paid off. When workers threatened to strike, the federal government intervened to preserve order in an industry considered essential to the war effort. In March 1918 a federal mediator subsequently issued a binding arbitration order that granted workers much of what the union had demanded, including an increase in the hourly wages of unskilled workers, an eight-hour work day at ten hours' pay, and compensation for overtime. It did not, however, require packers to recognize the union.

The SLC succeeded in part because organizers made genuine efforts to welcome black workers into the union. Unlike unionists in the steel industry, early on the SLC recognized that any effort to build industrial unionism required an active campaign to organize the twelve thousand African Americans who worked in the Chicago stockyards. Because most black workers remained skeptical of the union, labor leaders recognized that organizing blacks posed peculiar challenges that demanded special tactics. SLC organizers assigned black recruits to any one of the forty locals of the Amalgamated Meat Cutters and Butcher Workermen (AMC), which was one of the few unions affiliated with the SLC that did not bar black workers from membership. When black members complained of their minority status within these locals, the SLC reorganized the AMC locals on a neighborhood basis. It established Local 651, headquartered in the Black Belt, and Local 554 in a white immigrant neighborhood in close proximity to the packinghouses. By creating a community-based local, SLC leaders hoped to win over broad-based support for the union among blacks. In addition, the SLC expanded its credibility with black workers by hiring black organizers and appointing African Americans to leadership positions. White unionists supported black workers who filed grievances with management. The SLC sponsored interracial marches, picnics, and social affairs at which speakers declared their commitment to labor solidarity over racial division.

Yet black support remained uncertain. Even though some contemporaries claimed that the SLC enlisted as many as six thousand blacks during its membership drive, actual membership fluctuated. Many black workers admitted that they had joined with initial enthusiasm but had allowed their dues to lapse, revealing a recurring pattern of black interest in—but not a commitment to—the union. Because many African Americans remained skeptical of the union's sincerity, they often ridiculed the few dedicated black unionists, accusing them of acting as the flunkies of white unionists. Consequently, black unionists did not enjoy the same level of community support that their white counterparts did. Black churches, much of the black press, and the Chicago Urban League, because of their ties to employers, either outright opposed the unions or at best offered modest support and assistance. Residential segregation and weak community support for the union in the ghetto pulled blacks toward neighborhood race-conscious institutions even as class experience at work drew them into the union.

When the SLC mounted a new organizing drive in the summer of 1919, it put the SLC's commitment to interracialism to the test. SLC leaders hoped to make wartime employment gains permanent through a negotiated labor contract. To strengthen their hand, they launched a new campaign in June 1919 to organize 100 percent of the labor force in the stockyards. The campaign exposed troublesome racial divisions that gave the packers a powerful wedge with which to divide labor. White unionists accused ambivalent and nonunion blacks of reaping the rewards of the federal arbitration agreement without bearing the costs or sharing the risks of joining the union that delivered the agreement. Militant unionists on the shop floor pressured foremen to either fire nonunion workers or force them to join. If foremen refused, militants walked off the job. Employers replaced strikers with nonunion blacks. They also recruited black workers whom they paid to sabotage the organizing drive.

Racial tension exploded into riot on July 27. On that warm and muggy Sunday afternoon, a white man threw a rock that struck and killed a black teenager who swam across the invisible racial boundary line that segregated beaches along Lake Michigan. Over the next five days, a bloody race war engulfed the city's South Side, leaving twenty-three blacks and fifteen whites dead, more than five hundred injured, and more than one thousand, mostly African Americans, homeless after white gangs burned and looted their residences. Even though the conflict that sparked the riot happened several miles from the stockyards, the fighting quickly moved to the neighborhoods around the packinghouses. The city's official report on the riot blamed much of the violence on Irish street gangs who attacked blacks, including packinghouse workers, who crossed through their neighborhood to return to their homes. These gangs roamed the streets for the next several days, terrorizing black travelers on the city's streetcars and staging assaults into black neighborhoods. The riot was among twenty-five race riots that erupted across the country between April and October 1919.

The Chicago riot doomed the SLC's organizing drive. Throughout the riot, the SLC struggled to preserve order, staging interracial meetings and organizing relief efforts for riot victims. Immigrant workers largely restrained from participating in the violence. The racial calm that the SLC worked so hard to preserve among the packinghouse workers during the riot collapsed within a week. White unionists, without evidence, accused blacks of setting a fire that burned dozens of homes of Lithuanian packinghouse workers. The packers, who believed that the loyalty of black workers was critical to defeat the union, exploited the racial distrust opened by the riot. On August 8, they provided three thousand nonunion black workers with an armed escort to ensure that they could return to work safely. In protest, unionists, most of whom were white, staged a strike. The packers retaliated by firing six hundred of the strikers. The SLC's organizing campaign quickly unraveled, leaving most blacks alienated from the union. Mounting factionalism among the unions in the SLC coalition further weakened labor. Employers used the ensuing disarray among workers to slowly reassert their authority in the packing plants. When the AMC called a strike in late 1921 to contest wage cuts, its effort quickly collapsed. It no longer could command a reliable base of support among the workers, and it failed to reorganize black workers, most of whom preferred to accept the jobs offered by the packers rather than risk casting their fate with the untrustworthy AMC.

No matter how devastating the riot was to the SLC's organizing campaign, interracial unionism had little chance of enduring in the Chicago stockyards of the postwar years. Despite the genuine overtures that white organizers made toward black workers—and they went far beyond anything that white organizers in the postwar steel industry attempted—they ultimately failed to convince black migrants that their unions were interracial institutions capable of understanding and acting upon the specific conditions that confronted black workers. SLC leaders did not understand the circumstances of their migration to the city, their past experiences with exclusion from industrial employment and craft unions, or the obstacles they confronted in gaining promotions to higher-skilled and better-paying jobs. Although black workers showed an interest in unions and saw interracial labor organizing as one among many strategies for improving the conditions of their employment, most of them still considered the packinghouse unions as white men's institutions. They feared that committed membership to an institution that catered to the priorities of white workers would cost them access to the industrial employment that had attracted them to Chicago in the first place. Perhaps for these reasons, unions remained institutions external to the black migrant communities of Chicago. In the immigrant and white working-class neighborhoods, strikes and union activities became community events, and white ethnic unionists drew upon neighborhood institutions—churches, businesses, banks, newspapers, social clubs, fraternal lodges—for critical social and material support. In contrast, Local 651 never became part of the black community, and most residents there never identified its cause as their cause.

The labor defeats and racial violence of 1919 and the persistent underemployment of the 1920s did not necessarily generate apathy and political resignation among black migrants. Rather, the war and migration inspired a new style of black politics in the 1920s that was firmly rooted in the workplace struggles of the early years of the Great Migration. Many African Americans considered World War I a moment of great democratic promise. Because African Americans had sacrificed to make the world safe for democracy—President Woodrow Wilson's justification for American intervention in the war—many blacks believed that the time had come to make America safe for democracy. Inspired by the heroics of black troops in France and the anti-colonial struggles of Africans against western imperialists, they imagined the postwar period as a new "reconstruction" that could expand citizenship rights and economic opportunity for African Americans.

Membership in the NAACP surged during the war years. When the association launched an ambitious nation-wide membership drive in 1917, black workers responded by the thousands, organizing branches in the North as well as the South. Although local black elites spearheaded the organization of many new branches, the NAACP's executive secretary attributed the rapid growth of the association to the common people, whom he believed gave the organization its strength and salvation. The black labor activists who built many of these branches pursued an agenda that addressed the concerns of black workers. They flooded the national office with evidence documenting employment discrimination and brutal working conditions in southern agriculture, petitioned Congress to eliminate color bars in railroad employment, registered black, working-class voters and mobilized them in local elections, supported black workers on strike, and worked for the political education of the black working class. The NAACP's national leadership recognized that the participation of black workers opened new possibilities for political action. Inspired by the activism of black workers, some NAACP leaders even advocated the labor strike as the most potent weapon that black people had for demanding the abolition of Jim Crow.

Although black workers helped to transform the NAACP from a small, elite reform group into a national organization of more than ninety thousand members by 1920, the association could not capitalize on the surge of black labor activism that flowed into its growing network of branches. The national office lacked the resources, staff, and will to provide meaningful support to working-class branches. For example, in 1922 when the members of a branch near Tulsa, Oklahoma, appealed to the national office for help for seventy-five black workers who had been blacklisted for joining a strike, the association declined to intervene, claiming that it was not the kind of issue that it could handle. The NAACP never developed a clear labor agenda or strategy about how to respond to these kinds of appeals or how to mobilize black workers once they became members. More importantly, the national office lacked the ability to protect these branches and their members, particularly those in the South, when they became targets of political violence and legal intimidation, which forced many of them to disband or suspend operations within a few years of their organization.

The NAACP also had limited leverage with the AFL. The NAACP made periodic overtures to the labor federation. For example, in 1924 the association proposed to create a joint interracial labor commission to investigate the conditions of black workers, and in 1929 it offered to support the AFL's drive to organize southern labor. Both times the AFL declined to cooperate. Ambivalent about whether to consider the labor movement a friend or a foe, the NAACP concentrated its energies instead on defending blacks' right to work rather than on promoting the unionization of black workers. It also crafted an agenda—combating racial violence and discrimination in housing, education, and transportation, largely through the courts—that was relevant to the lives of black workers but that did not appeal to them directly as workers.

Marcus Garvey's Universal Negro Improvement Association (UNIA) had greater success in sustaining a mass following of working-class blacks in the 1920s. Born in Jamaica in 1887, Marcus Garvey founded the UNIA there in 1914 but moved its headquarters to Harlem in New York City shortly after he immigrated to the United States in 1916. The organization grew quickly. The branch in Harlem enlisted five thousand members by 1919, but more importantly, its reach was national and international. Some nine hundred local divisions of the UNIA operated in forty countries in the early 1920s. The organization's newspaper, *The Negro World*, circulated not only throughout the United States but in Central America, the West Indies, and Africa. Because the UNIA routinely asserted inflated claims that it had enlisted as many as 6 million dues-paying members, it is impossible to determine reliable estimates of the UNIA's membership. Regardless, the UNIA and its core principles attracted millions of followers and sympathizers, if not dues-paying members, around the globe, making it the largest black social movement of the early twentieth century.

Garvey was an avowed black nationalist who aspired to enlist the black masses behind race-conscious solutions—economic self-help, self-defense, racial pride, individual ambition, collective self-determination, the liberation of Africa from western imperialism—to solve the problems that confronted black people. The spectacle and pageantry of UNIA parades and meetings regularly drew crowds of several thousand in New York City who gathered to hear the flamboyant Garvey thunder about blacks fighting for their freedom, predict the coming dawn of a new Africa for Africans, and make self-confident declarations that the "New Negro Has No Fear." Unlike earlier apostles of black self-help such as Booker T. Washington, Garvey appealed directly to the black masses and did not seek to curry the favor of white philanthropists.

Despite the initial support and enthusiasm of its working-class base, the UNIA never became an organization capable of uniting African Americans or of winning economic and political rights for blacks. Garvey quickly became embroiled in conflicts with the black leaders of other civil rights organizations who opposed him. The Black Star Line, Garvey's ambitious all-black steamship company that had been supported by the exclusive sale of stock to African Americans, failed amidst financial mismanagement and internal corruption. The federal government conducted extensive investigations of the UNIA, and it finally arrested Garvey for mail fraud in 1922. He was subsequently convicted and eventually deported. But even as these problems with the UNIA caused its rapid decline after the mid-1920s, the organization itself had trouble sustaining the interest of its members. Local UNIA divisions had difficulty translating the racial enthusiasm of mass meetings into a tangible program for improving the material lives of working-class blacks. The growth of black enterprise, not the needs of wage workers, dominated Garvey's racial agenda. Consequently, he never endorsed the labor movement or encouraged his black followers to join trade unions or fight for universal suffrage. Working-class blacks may have remained attracted to the UNIA's core message, but the organization itself did little to encourage their active participation in the life of the organization. Nevertheless, central ideas of racial pride, self-determination, and self-defense resonated among black workers long after the UNIA's collapse.

If many black workers embraced Garvey's ideas, they did not necessarily share his indifference to labor activism. In their battle against employer discrimination, exclusionary unions, and racist white workers, African American workers often relied on their own organizations, which fused racial pride, self-defense, and labor activism. In 1919 sharecroppers in the Arkansas Delta formed the Progressive Farmers and Household Union to prevent landlords from hoarding the bounty of the wartime rise in cotton prices. Local authorities made fanciful charges that black unionists were plotting to massacre whites to justify deploying private armies of gunmen and vigilantes who broke the union in a reign of terror that killed twenty-five sharecroppers. Events in Arkansas underscored the imperative of self-defense. Black railroad workers, longshoremen, postal workers, and even teachers organized their own independent unions and initiated numerous strikes. Although most of these efforts failed, they nevertheless reveal a remarkable upsurge in independent black unionism that attracted thousands of workers in the immediate postwar years. The growth of working-class militancy and black protest in the period inspired black labor activists with hopes that they might succeed in organizing to improve their specific condition as black workers. As one black longshoreman put it, they had unionized not only to protect their rights as honest workingmen but also in defense of their race.

In the 1920s, the Brotherhood of Sleeping Car Porters (BSCP) emerged as the largest and most successful all-black union to combine racial solidarity and collective action. Porters worked as onboard servants to affluent white passengers on luxury railroad sleeping cars operated by the Pullman Sleeping Car Company. In the mid-1920s, more than twelve thousand black Pullman porters served 35 million white passengers annually, making Pullman the largest private employer of African Americans in the country. The Pullman Company built its success largely on the reputation for the excellent personal service that its porters provided. White travelers who paid for a ticket to a sleeping car expected porters to carry and stow their luggage, make their beds, clean their rooms, press their clothes, shine their shoes, cut their hair, serve them drinks, wake them before their stop, and perform any other services they requested. Pullman expected its porters to conduct themselves in an attentive and deferential manner and to carry out all of their tasks with a smile. Supervisors required porters to follow elaborate rules of etiquette that regulated everything from the proper way to fold sheets to the topics that they could discuss with passengers.

Porters worked long hours at low pay. Working an average of four hundred hours or 1,100 miles a month for modest wages, porters had to endure long periods away from their homes and families. Although they earned tips, which enabled some porters to make a decent living, they had to act in a solicitous manner to loosen the wallets of white passengers. Despite these working conditions, the job of porter compared favorably to the physical demands of sharecropping or factory work. In a labor market that restricted black occupational mobility, few black men could expect a job better than that of Pullman porter. Many porters were among the best educated black men in America, and because of their wide travel and urban living, they earned a reputation in the black community for sophistication and respectability. This tension between social prestige within their communities and social subservience at work defined the lives of many porters. But the Great Migration and the war had elevated the expectations of African Americans, many of whom no longer saw the servile status of Pullman porter as a worthy aspiration. A new generation of activists emerged who prepared not only to battle against long hours and low pay but also to fight for the abolition of a workplace culture that demanded their servility.

Figure 3.2. A white passenger asks a Pullman porter to deliver a telegram aboard the Great Northern Railway's Oriental Limited in 1929. Dubin I.17.19, Special Collections, Lake Forest College Library.

In the summer of 1925, a small group of porters gathered in New York City to form the BSCP. The Pullman Company's expert surveillance of its workers, which long frustrated past attempts to organize the porters, required that they enlist an organizer who could operate beyond the purview of company spies. They found their ideal candidate in Asa Philip Randolph, whom they appointed as the new union's president and chief organizer. Having never worked as a porter or for the Pullman Company, Randolph could operate free of company pressure. A native of Florida, Randolph had moved to Harlem in 1911, where he soon devoted himself to political activism. In 1917, he and Chandler Owen launched the *Messenger*, a radical monthly magazine dedicated to inspiring revolutionary economic and political action among black Americans. He especially urged African Americans, as workers, to abandon the Republican Party and vote for the Socialist Party because of its genuine commitment to the economic and political interests of the working class. As a proponent of trade unionism and collective bargaining, Randolph vowed to unionize the porters and win not only a full charter from the AFL but also secure a labor contract from the Pullman Company.

To succeed, Randolph and the BSCP had to win over not just the fiercely anti-union Pullman Company but they had to draw support from the broader black community skeptical of unions and often dependent upon the Pullman Company for charity. To do so, Randolph crafted a message linking the porters' struggle with the wider political and economic aspirations of all African Americans. Until porters asserted their manhood rights, Randolph declared, they would be unable to claim the economic rights of citizenship. Manhood contested the culture of servility at work and demanded recognition of the humanity of all blacks. Equating manhood with full citizenship rights, the unionized porters demanded freedom from white control and their rights as free laborers, including the right to negotiate the terms of their employment. To spread its message, the BSCP deployed a community-based strategy. It used the pages of the *Messenger* to circulate union propaganda and educate readers about the concept of manhood rights. Randolph challenged the community authority of black leaders who were more willing to curry favor with powerful whites than to make the sacrifices necessary to advance the cause of African Americans. It forged alliances with other organizations dedicated to challenging the racial status quo. In doing so, BSCP organizers created new protest networks of community activists who converted black ministers, editors, and politicians to the union cause and helped to convert the BSCP's union organizing drive into a social movement for the liberation not only of twelve thousand porters but also of all African Americans.

The BSCP campaign clarified that migration alone, without organization and social activism, could not complete the unfinished work of Reconstruction that so many thought was possible in 1917. The Great Migration transformed African Americans from an industrial labor reserve into a population integral to the workforce of America's major industries. Migrants broke racial barriers of exclusion in industrial employment, claimed the right to work, and won permanent places of employment in those industries. But even as they broke the barriers of entry, they discovered entrenched obstacles to promotion and opportunity within those industries. Their failure to advance beyond the low-skill, entry-level positions in the industrial labor market was not a legacy of their rural past, as so many contemporary social commentators assumed, but reflected the broader structural obstacles of the American labor market. The right to work alone did not confer the economic or political power necessary to expand opportunity in American industrial society. Although unions, especially in the aftermath of World War I, attracted significant black interest, most African Americans did not see them as institutions that represented their interests or as vehicles for overcoming their exclusions from full participation in American society.

The emergence of the BSCP signaled the emergence of a shift in the reputation of labor unions, labor activism, and the labor movement among African Americans. Randolph and BSCP activists offered a critical new model of social activism for claiming the economic rights of citizenship. Unlike the steel and meatpacking unions of the postwar years, the BSCP had the makings of a community institution built by and for black people. It self-consciously linked its struggle to the historic fight for the economic foundation of freedom that their ancestors had begun during Reconstruction. But these seeds of protest, planted in the 1920s, would not take root until the 1930s when African Americans confronted the economic crisis of the Great Depression.

CHAPTER FOUR

~

A New Deal for Black Workers

Beginning in 1929, the economies of the industrialized nations of the world collapsed, precipitating the Great Depression, which lasted throughout the 1930s. In the United States, the stock market lost 80 percent of its value between 1929 and 1932; nearly half of the nation's twenty-four thousand banks had failed by 1933; and as manufacturing output sank to about half of what it had been in 1929, millions of Americans lost their jobs, and the unemployment rate soared to more than 25 percent. By almost every standard of measure, African American workers suffered a disproportionate share of the Depression's misery. In the 1930s, more than 14 million African Americans remained in the rural South and earned their living as indebted sharecroppers or tenant farmers raising cash crops on land that they did not own, a condition now made infinitely worse by the free fall in the price of cash crops such as cotton. Although the Great Migration opened employment to African Americans in key industries such as meatpacking, steelmaking, and automobile manufacturing, most migrants had never gained job security or mobility into better-paying, higher-skilled jobs. As recent hires, most blacks lacked seniority and held a disproportionate share of the unskilled, common labor jobs, making them far more vulnerable to layoffs than white workers. These conditions contributed to the staggering rates of unemployment among urban blacks. In 1934, more than 40 percent of African American men of working age in Chicago were out of work; that rate was 48 percent in Pittsburgh and 60 percent in Detroit. For African Americans, the right to work, let alone equality of working conditions, appeared as elusive in 1933 as it had in 1915.

Nevertheless, many African Americans were not prepared to give up on the promise of the Great Migration. More than a million southern blacks had migrated to the urban North since the beginning of World War I in search of both economic opportunity and political freedom. Even if the urban North failed to live up to its reputation as a promised land, many working-class blacks had at least tasted the possibilities for a better life. When northern employers opened new opportunities for work to African Americans, they undermined the customs that had once restricted access to good-paying industrial jobs to white workers. The integration of African Americans into the industrial labor force elevated blacks' expectations for inclusion into the economic mainstream and emboldened their claims to full participation in American society as equal citizens. During the migration years many black workers experimented with new forms of political activism, joining civil rights groups, race-conscious organizations, and independent labor unions to pursue and advance their economic needs and civil rights. African Americans carried that new spirit of activism into the 1930s.

The presidential inauguration of Franklin Roosevelt in March 1933 kindled hope among many African Americans that the federal government might finally respond to their needs. Roosevelt signed into law dozens of pieces of legislation that created a host of new agencies, programs, and regulations—what was collectively called the "New Deal"—that significantly expanded the power and authority of the federal government to promote and protect the social welfare of working Americans, including the black masses. Despite the New Deal's undeniable advantages, it did nothing to promote the specific interests of black workers or to advance the citizenship rights of African Americans. In response to both the economic crisis of the Depression and the limitations of the New Deal, many black labor activists looked more and more to the path blazed by the BSCP in the 1920s. They combined black solidarity, labor activism, and mass action to claim not only their rights as citizens but also to demand the power to exercise them. Community activists challenged the reputation of black elites and organized hundreds of local movements to meet the direct needs of the struggling black masses. They rejuvenated the membership of the NAACP and worked to create a new civil rights agenda more attuned to the concerns of black workers. They helped to build a new labor federation—the Congress of Industrial Organizations—dedicated to protecting the rights of all industrial workers. On the eve of World War II, thousands of black activists mobilized a mass movement to demand that the federal government open employment in the nation's defense industries. The war inspired new forms of black labor militancy aimed at opening access to good jobs, improving working conditions, and fighting for equality within the labor movement. Throughout the 1930s and 1940s, thousands of black labor activists experimented with mobilizing the power of collective, mass action to advance the interests of African American workers and to give substantive meaning to the New Deal.

Unemployment took its toll on black working-class families and communities. Black banks and insurance companies collapsed, wiping out the little savings and economic security black families had accumulated. Extended unemployment forced black industrial workers to survive by hauling trash, collecting bottles, and selling scraps. Wages for black women in domestic service dropped to less than a dollar a day, and many now faced stiff competition from the expanding ranks of poor white women seeking domestic work. Joblessness begat homelessness. Landlords evicted unemployed families. Most shelters operated by private charities, such as the Salvation Army, refused to open their doors to blacks, forcing African Americans without homes to seek shelter in the many camps and shantytowns that they built on landfills, dumps, and abandoned lots.

Unemployed blacks had few places to turn for assistance. In the first years of the Great Depression, before the New Deal created the modern welfare state, private charities, and in some instances state and local governments, assumed the responsibility of providing relief to destitute Americans. The scale of the Depression overwhelmed the nation's charitable organizations, which had never been very generous to poor blacks, leaving them unable to meet the needs of the millions of Americans now desperate for emergency assistance. Sharp declines in tax receipts compromised the ability of state and local governments to provide public assistance. The economic collapse decimated the coffers of black self-help societies such as benevolent associations, fraternal orders, and churches, crippling their ability to respond to the social crises of poverty, joblessness, and homelessness in African American communities.

The Depression also challenged the community authority of black elites. The economic crisis exposed the limitations of the elite's faith in the goodwill of employers to provide the steady employment that they had hoped would underwrite the economic welfare of the black masses. Organizations that relied upon elite models of social welfare such as the National Urban League and Chicago's Wabash Avenue YMCA, dependent as they were upon the philanthropy of employers for their operating budget, had neither the resources nor the imagination to develop new programs capable of meeting the new conditions that confronted the black working class in the 1930s. The NAACP lost stature with black workers as well. Because many of its members could no longer afford to pay annual dues, the association lost thousands of members in the early years of the decade. Although officials in the NAACP's national office recognized that the association was failing to attract the interest of the black masses, the NAACP proved slow to adopt measures that might make it more relevant to black workers.

The failure of black elites to make substantive changes to their agenda and strategies inspired the rise of new networks of community organizers who were more attuned to the needs of black workers. Rather than rely on black elites to negotiate with whites on their behalf, some black working-class activists forged a new politics of protest that combined mobilization of the black masses, a spirit of racial consciousness, and confrontational tactics. In Gary, Indiana, for example, blacks in a number of community organizations worked together to block plans by city officials to forcibly relocate unemployed black migrants back to the South. Throughout the urban North, community activists launched "Don't Buy Where You Can't Work" campaigns in which black residents boycotted national chain stores that opened franchises in black neighborhoods but that refused to hire blacks. Success depended upon much more than a collective decision not to shop at offending stores but required daily picket lines outside stores and mass meetings to sustain interest, enthusiasm, and commitment. These kinds of campaigns inspired activists to form permanent organizations dedicated to the use of direct action tactics in a broader struggle for jobs.

Black women often spearheaded community organizing. In New York City, local activists Anna Hedgeman, Ella Baker, and Marvel Cooke conducted a series of investigations into the working conditions of the city's casual black domestic workers whose only hope of securing employment was through the many informal outdoor labor markets that had surfaced on the street corners of the Bronx since the onset of the Depression. Whatever the weather, black women—young or old and desperate for work—gathered and waited for white housewives who came in search of cheap labor. After giving the assembled women a careful and humiliating inspection, a housewife would barter for the services of one of the women, who would agree to perform the drudgery of household labor at a paltry wage that she had no guarantee of receiving from her temporary employer. Condemning the practice as reminiscent of antebellum slave markets, Baker and Cooke published an exposé that generated widespread publicity and eventually pressured city officials to intervene and regulate the day labor sites.

The presidential administration of Franklin Roosevelt (1933–1945) gave black activists new hope that the federal government might become an ally for the first time since Reconstruction. By distributing direct relief to the unemployed, putting people to work on massive public works projects, providing old-age pensions and unemployment insurance, setting a federal minimum wage, and protecting the rights of workers to unionize, the New Deal had a direct impact on the lives of millions of Americans, including the black masses. African Americans gained access to the White House when Roosevelt consulted his so-called black cabinet of prominent black scholars, economists, social reformers, and policy analysts. Although none of them held a formal cabinet position or formulated policy, they served as administrators in New Deal agencies and in executive departments of the federal government where they communicated the needs and interests of African Americans to the administration. African Americans responded with their votes. Whereas a majority of blacks had voted for the Republican Herbert Hoover in 1932, more than two-thirds abandoned the party of Lincoln to cast their votes for Roosevelt in 1936 and 1940. Blacks became part of the New Deal coalition of the Democratic Party and helped to transform it from a conservative party of small government, states' rights, and Jim Crow into a political party that embraced activist government on behalf of progressive reforms, including federal protection of labor rights and civil rights.

Although the New Deal had the capacity to improve the lives of African Americans, few programs targeted the specific conditions of black workers. To preserve the political support of the southern, conservative wing of the Democratic Party, Roosevelt never made civil rights an overt goal of the New Deal. Moreover, many New Deal programs, though federally funded, were locally administered and thus perpetuated local patterns of racial discrimination and economic subordination. Local administrators of the various federal work relief agencies seldom assigned African Americans to jobs that matched their skills and work experience. Most significantly, the Social Security Act of 1935, which established a system of old-age pensions and unemployment insurance for workers, excluded domestic servants, agricultural workers, and casual laborers from coverage, thus leaving most African American workers ineligible for benefits. Likewise, landmark New Deal labor legislation—the National Labor Relations Act (1935), which protected the rights of collective bargaining, and the Fair Labor Standard Act (1938), which established a federal minimum wage—exempted agricultural workers and domestic servants.

Whatever the limitations of the New Deal, African American activists organized to pressure New Deal agencies into meeting the needs of black workers. African Americans especially seized upon the New Deal's rhetoric of rights and democracy. The New Deal gave birth to the concept of social and economic citizenship, one that redefined the relationship between citizens and the federal government. President Roosevelt frequently claimed that American citizens possessed not only the right to be free from a government that infringed upon basic civil liberties such as freedom of speech and freedom of religion, but that they also had a right to live under a government that assumed the responsibility and the power to protect them from economic insecurity and poverty. As African Americans mobilized to broaden the reach of the New Deal, they staked their claim to these emergent social and economic rights of citizenship, insisting that they were not rights reserved for whites only.

One of the first places in which African Americans organized to challenge the inequities of the New Deal emerged in the rural South. In 1933, Congress enacted the Agricultural Adjustment Act (AAA), which established a federal crop reduction program designed to raise agricultural prices. Overproduction had created tremendous surpluses of agricultural goods that lowered their market value. Cotton prices, for example, had plummeted from a high of $0.40 a pound during World War I to $0.046 a pound in 1932. Because sharecroppers and tenant farmers were more dependent upon growing cash crops than farm owners, African Americans suffered a disproportionate share of the misery caused by the collapse of the cotton market. To reverse the decline in agricultural prices, the AAA paid farmers to deliberately take land out of cultivation. The government thus provided farmers with an incentive to grow less, creating a scarcity that would increase the market price of cash crops. By funneling millions of dollars of federal subsidies into the rural South, the AAA promised to provide critical relief to rural blacks dependent upon the land for their livelihood.

The legislation, however, favored the interests of large-scale landowners over those of tenants and sharecroppers. Although the AAA required planters to share their government subsidy payments with the farming families who worked their land, most planters defrauded tenants and sharecroppers of their rightful portion of the subsidies. Between 1933 and 1936, Delta planters in Arkansas and Mississippi received more than $4.6 million in federal subsidy payments, most of which never reached tenants and sharecroppers. Planters then used the federal payments to restructure the plantation economy. By investing the federal subsidies they received in tractors and then evicting whole families of croppers and tenants from their land, planters began to replace the decentralized, family-labor system of sharecropping with a consolidated, capital-intensive, and mechanized system of cotton production.

Sharecroppers and tenant farmers fought back by organizing the Southern Tenant Farmers' Union (STFU). Established in 1934 in Arkansas by an unlikely coalition of southern white socialists and black preachers, the STFU quickly grew into an interracial social movement of twenty-five thousand sharecroppers and tenant farmers across seven southern states. Nevertheless, if shared economic circumstances brought black and white croppers and tenants into an alliance, unionists drew upon a common cultural heritage of Christianity to strengthen those bonds. Both black and white organizers, many of them ministers, preached a gospel of unionism that applied the ethical teachings of Jesus Christ to expose the social injustices of a plantation economy that impoverished blacks and whites alike. Meetings often mimicked religious revivals in which organizers mixed biblical metaphors of deliverance and redemption with stirring denunciations of the arbitrary and unjust power of the planters.

If southern white radicals were the initial founders of the union, African Americans constituted the core of the STFU membership. Blacks in the Arkansas Delta proved particularly receptive to the STFU's message. For it was in this region that black sharecroppers had organized a rural cooperative in the wake of World War I before planters brutally suppressed it. Here blacks had organized, under great risk, branches of the NAACP and locals of Marcus Garvey's UNIA to contest planter control of the rural economy. Black organizers such as the Rev. E. B. "Britt" McKinney—a circuit-riding preacher, UNIA member, and communist sympathizer—fused religious zeal, racial consciousness, and a Marxist critique of the planter class in powerful appeals that spoke to blacks' historic and collective sense of injustice. Most importantly, the STFU emboldened impoverished rural blacks to demand their rights, as citizens, to receive the federal aid that they were entitled to under the law.

The STFU appealed to the men and women who bore the social costs of the collapse of cotton tenancy. On a practical level, the union used its organizational strength to challenge planter control of the AAA. Activists organized mass marches on AAA offices. Evicted tenants staged roadside demonstrations in which they refused to move until the federal government provided relief. Unionists testified before federal agencies on the need to reform farm programs so that they respected the rights of tenants and croppers. When planters reduced the wages that they paid to cotton pickers, the STFU organized a massive strike in the fall of 1935. Although planters threatened unionists with eviction, arrest for vagrancy, and violence, the strikers refused to return to the fields, forcing planters to relent and raise wages. STFU activism captured the attention of well-connected liberal allies. They published feature stories in nationally circulating magazines, exposing the poverty of sharecroppers, the greed of planters, the inequities of federal farm aid, and the brutal and repressive measures that planters used to suppress the STFU. The publicity pressured the Roosevelt administration to support minor revisions to federal farm legislation and to make rural poverty a target of the New Deal.

In the end, the STFU could not create a new deal in the rural South that provided land for the landless. In response to the STFU's agitation, the Roosevelt administration created the Resettlement Administration and the Farm Security Administration (FSA). Through these agencies, the government proposed to alleviate the problems of displaced sharecroppers and tenant farmers by offering them low-interest loans to purchase farms and to help them establish rural farming cooperatives. Despite the promise of this assistance, few sharecroppers ever received loans. The Depression displaced 192,000 African American families from the land in the South, but only 2,000 of them received FSA loans to purchase farms and only another 1,400 resettled onto FSA cooperatives. Unable to forestall the consolidation of landholdings and the advance of capital-intensive agriculture, croppers had little choice but to abandon the countryside and become wage laborers in the urban North and West. But even as they left, they carried with them a resolve and determination, forged through their struggle against the planter aristocracy, to demand their economic rights as citizens.

Black community activists in the urban North mounted their own campaigns against the limits of the New Deal. The Great Depression had weakened the BSCP, the organization that had emerged in the late 1920s as the leading voice of black workers. A sharp decline in the number of passengers traveling on railroads in the early 1930s forced Pullman to lay off porters. Membership in the BSCP declined from more than seven thousand to fewer than seven hundred by the early 1930s. Consequently, the BSCP had yet to establish itself as a labor union that could win the respect, attention, and ultimately the recognition of the AFL or the Pullman Company. Throughout the early 1930s, the AFL rejected the BSCP's application for a full charter. The porters, consequently, had little leverage with which to compel the company to the bargaining table. Rather than giving up, BSCP activists reached deeper into the community, mobilizing black Americans around a labor-oriented approach to citizenship, intensifying its efforts as a social movement.

The BSCP got a new lease on life when Congress passed the Amended Railway Act of 1934. Part of the New Deal, the new law guaranteed railroad workers, including those who worked on sleeping cars, the right to collective bargaining. When the company claimed that the BSCP had no legal authority to represent the porters, a federal mediation board intervened and authorized an election in 1935. Pullman porters overwhelmingly voted for the BSCP as their official representative. When Randolph tried to open talks, the company continued to stall. In 1936, the AFL finally awarded the BSCP full union status, marking the first time that the AFL gave an all-black union full recognition, which gave it additional resources and support. Finally, in 1937, twelve years to the day that the BSCP was founded, the union won a historic labor contract from the Pullman Company. Under the terms of the agreement, the first contract that an American company negotiated and signed with a union of black workers, porters won wage increases, a shorter work month, a reduction in the number of miles they were required to travel, and new grievance procedures that covered, among other things, racial discrimination by supervisory personnel.

Randolph and the BSCP won far more than a labor contract. The success of the BSCP transformed the reputation of labor unions, labor activism, and the labor movement among African Americans and established a critical new model of social activism for claiming the economic rights of citizenship. In the 1920s, many black leaders opposed the BSCP. They believed that black workers had more to gain through cooperation rather than confrontation with employers such as the Pullman Company. During the course of its organizing campaign, the BSCP eventually succeeded in converting many of these opponents into allies. Unionized porters demonstrated the tenacity, courage, and self-sacrifice to persevere for twelve years against one of the nation's staunchest anti-union employers. No longer, declared the editors of the *Chicago Defender*, one of the nation's leading premier black newspapers and one-time opponent of the BSCP, could white trade unionists exclude black workers from union membership on the grounds that blacks lacked the capacity to become reliable and dedicated unionists. By raising their own money and resources and organizing and waging their own fight for justice against the Pullman Company, BSCP unionists also won the respect, rather than just the pity, of sympathetic white allies. Finally, they inspired other African Americans to adopt the confrontational tactics of protest politics and organize and fight for their rights.

That new confrontational approach to black activism became increasingly visible. In February 1936 some eight thousand men and women representing more than five hundred organizations gathered in Chicago for the first annual meeting of the National Negro Congress (NNC). Making black rights to employment their principal demand and advocating collective action as their primary strategy, organizers envisioned the NNC as an alternative to the NAACP. Their selection of A. Philip Randolph as the NNC's first president reflected the confrontational, prolabor turn in African American protest politics. In his keynote address to the congress, Randolph captured the spirit of the new organization. He criticized the New Deal as an inadequate

Figure 4.1.   A. Philip Randolph delivered the presidential address at the Second National Negro Congress, which met in Philadelphia in October 1937. Photographs and Prints Division, Schomburg Center for Research in Black Culture, The New York Public Library, Astor, Lenox and Tilden Foundations.

remedy to the problems that confronted African Americans. He insisted that the fight for social and economic justice could not come through the courts alone but must be backed up by the tactics of mass politics, including demonstrations, rallies, parades, and propaganda campaigns. He urged them to organize around issues of "vital and immediate" concern to the lives of black workers.[1] Most significantly, Randolph advocated industrial unionism. Unlike craft unions, which too often excluded blacks, industrial unions embraced all workers, regardless of race, creed, or skill. Consequently, they had the capacity to combat the twin threats of racial hatred and class exploitation. The NNC endorsed Randolph's recommendation and passed a resolution to cooperate with the newly formed Committee on Industrial Organization (CIO), a dissident faction within the AFL, and help it to recruit black workers into industrial unions in the nation's mass-production industries.

Organized in 1935, the CIO advocated an aggressive campaign to build industrial unions. They argued that the AFL leadership failed to take advantage of the favorable political climate created by landmark New Deal labor legislation to expand the membership base of organized labor. AFL executives rejected appeals from industrial unionists that it extend its reach into the nation's mass-production industries. Determined to organize the unorganized, CIO activists went ahead and formed organizing committees that launched aggressive campaigns to unionize industrial workers. Denouncing industrial unionists as insubordinate, the AFL leadership expelled the new industrial unions that the CIO organized. In 1938, breakaway industrial unionists formally established their own rival labor federation, now officially named the Congress of Industrial Organizations.

Black labor activists saw the CIO as a promising ally. CIO activists targeted those industries that had all become major employers of African Americans since the Great Migration. Consequently, CIO unionists recognized from the start that the success of industrial unionism rested on their ability to recruit black workers. To do so, they depended upon an energetic group of young, white labor militants who embraced interracial organizing as a principled conviction rather than a pragmatic exercise. They adopted open membership policies, spoke an egalitarian language, appointed blacks to positions of leadership within their unions, and joined African Americans on the front lines of community protests against racial discrimination. Some CIO unions adhered to strict antidiscrimination policies, supported legislative racial reforms, and published editorials in the union press that took progressive positions on civil rights. The CIO also engaged in political action to elect and lobby prolabor legislators at both the state and federal level. Activists thus recruited African Americans not only as fellow unionists but also as key voters in a prolabor political coalition. Finally, the CIO pursued a dual strategy in which it tried to be both a social movement dedicated to the political mobilization of the working class and an effective bureaucracy capable of winning good contracts that guaranteed economic security for all workers.

Despite the CIO's reputation for racial liberalism, the new labor federation was far from free of the racial tensions that had long bedeviled the labor movement. Egalitarian rhetoric, no matter how earnest, could not erase the bitter legacy of distrust between black and white workers. Black steelworkers and packinghouse workers, in particular, labored under their lingering reputation in the eyes of white workers as the scabs who defeated the strikes of 1919. White organizers, no matter how committed they were to racial justice, seldom appreciated the hostile conditions that black workers had long endured. Many could not understand why many black workers, hardened by racism, harbored suspicions. As one black steelworker explained, white unionists needed black support, whether they liked it or not, to avoid a replay of 1919. So "they're sincere," he admitted, "if you can call that sincereness."[2] Nor did it help that white unionists often failed to live by the egalitarian principles that they preached in the union hall. According to one black worker, the same white unionist who denounced segregation and insisted upon the need for racial unity at CIO meetings refused to rent him a house that he owned.

Still, the CIO signaled a significant departure from the labor movement's long history of racial discrimination. Perhaps the main difference between early twentieth-century unions and the CIO was that the CIO organizing campaigns, for all of their limitations, opened up genuine spaces for African American participation. Black labor activists played a central role in transforming the CIO from a federation of white unions that counted African Americans among its members into an interracial labor movement that eventually combined the fight for industrial unionism with the struggle for civil rights. To overcome the challenges in building an interracial labor movement, CIO leaders recognized the need for new approaches to organizing black workers. When the CIO launched its campaigns to organize mass-production industries in 1936, activists were determined to win the support of the broader black community and to put experienced, well-trained black organizers into the field. To do so, CIO activists drew upon local black political networks associated with the NNC to gain access to the black community. NNC activists provided CIO organizers with unprecedented access to the black community. They introduced industrial unionists to community organizers, hosted labor forums at which unionists spoke to black workers, distributed thousands of union leaflets and other propaganda in the black community, provided bodies for picket lines, and connected CIO organizers with black activists committed to the new tactics of mass-action politics.

Most importantly, the reciprocal relationship between the NNC and the CIO provided the new industrial unions with black unionists trained in the arts of organizing. White organizers understood that black workers seldom responded with enthusiasm to their appeals to join the union. At best, white organizers enlisted black workers into the union, but they did not really organize them. Black organizers, on the other hand, convinced black workers to cast aside their suspicions of unions and were far more capable of not only signing up black members but also of enrolling them into the union as sustaining and active members. Hank Johnson, one of the founders of the NNC and a man with a reputation for powerful and eloquent oratory, mobilized thousands of black workers in the steel and meatpacking industries in Chicago and Northwest Indiana. The son of a radical West Texas unionist and an experienced labor militant in his own right, Johnson's assertive and fearless race consciousness attracted black workers like George Kimbley, a southern migrant and veteran of World War I who had settled in Gary, Indiana, to work in the steel mills. Johnson tapped men such as Kimbley to serve as a volunteer organizer for the CIO's Steel Workers Organizing Committee (SWOC). Through his involvement with the local branches of the NAACP, the UNIA, and the Chicago branch of the NNC, Kimbley developed extensive ties to black steelworkers and their families, many of whom shared a commitment to building working-class unity among African Americans. Volunteer organizers fanned out across the churches, saloons, and street corners of the black neighborhoods, conducting face-to-face meetings in a method Kimbley called chain recruiting. By targeting informal, community networks of work, leisure, and worship, organizers such as Kimbley expanded support for the union from just the workers to the broader black community.

As proven and effective organizers, blacks assumed leadership positions within the CIO unions. In various union lodges throughout the country, black workers won election, often by unanimous vote, to the principal offices such as president, vice president, and financial secretary. Many black unionists who aspired to leadership positions within their lodges preferred to serve as shop stewards or hold positions on the bargaining and grievance committees because it was in such positions that black unionists could do effective work. Blacks who served on the bargaining committee, for example, assumed the responsibility of ensuring that contract negotiations met the needs of black workers. Black unionists who served as chair of grievance committees used their position to call unauthorized strikes, to demand equal pay for equal work, challenge foremen who refused to promote black workers into better jobs, or protest managers who violated the terms of labor contracts.

Through this style of working-class activism, black unionists transformed CIO unions into organizations that not only recruited black workers but also that advanced their interests not just as workers but as African Americans. They exposed the limits of color-blind unionism and demanded the expansion of civil rights in the workplace—including the elimination of segregation within factories, discriminatory barriers to promotion, and racial wage differentials—as central to a meaningful industrial democracy. They saw their workplace grievances as inseparable from the broader struggle for civil rights beyond the factory gate. Black activists even won some white converts to their cause. Together they worked to build a more racially progressive social and political order in working-class communities across the country. They campaigned for new laws banning racial discrimination in housing, employment, and education, expanded the influence of African Americans in the Democratic Party, and challenged local segregation ordinances in the South to hold publicly integrated meetings. Recognizing the importance of integrated social spaces beyond the workplace, some black and white CIO activists organized union boycotts of local taverns, restaurants, and bowling alleys that denied service to black workers.

As black workers pressed their civil rights demands within industrial workplaces, they also transformed the composition and agenda of civil rights organizations, further blurring the distinction between labor and civil rights activism. Between the late 1930s and the end of World War II, black membership in the NAACP surged from 50,000 in 355 branches to nearly 450,000 in more than 1,000 branches. Many of these new members were among the half million black workers who joined unions affiliated with the CIO. As militant participants in the labor struggles of the nation's mass-production industries, these black workers emerged as the new vanguard of black activists who expanded the labor-oriented character of the NAACP's activism and helped to mobilize the broader black community around the interests of black workers. Baltimore's branch president worked with local black CIO unionists to organize longshoremen and steelworkers, insisting that the NAACP needed to recruit the masses rather than cater to the interests of black professionals. Such energy forced NAACP executives to concede that the association had to abandon its cautious conservatism and adopt the more aggressive and confrontational tactics that its membership base now expected.

The convergence of black workplace militancy and civil rights proved critical to the CIO's campaign to organize the nation's automobile industry.

Although African Americans constituted only 4 percent of the nation's automobile workers in 1940, their concentration in the fiercely anti-union Ford Motor Company made their recruitment vital to the United Automobile Worker's (UAW) campaign to organize the industry. Unlike other automobile manufacturers in Michigan, Henry Ford hired thousands of black migrants, most of whom worked at his company's massive River Rouge plant. Whereas companies such as General Motors Corporation (GM) and the Chrysler Corporation confined the few African Americans they did hire to either the most dangerous jobs or to their custodial staff, Ford employed some of its black workers on its assembly lines and even offered limited opportunities for occupational mobility into skilled, supervisory, and managerial positions. Black employment at Ford actually expanded during the 1930s. Whereas most Detroit-area employers laid off disproportionate numbers of black workers, Ford hired more than seven thousand African Americans to work at River Rouge at the same time that it cut the number of white workers there by more than fifteen thousand. By 1940 Ford employed more than half of all working-age black men, including nearly all black autoworkers, in the Detroit metropolitan area. Ford's reputation as a high-wage employer attracted many of these workers. New hires at Ford earned nearly twice as much as newly employed blacks in Detroit's other industries. Henry Ford cultivated close relationships with Detroit's black clergy and community leaders whom he relied upon to recruit dependable workers who would remain loyal to the company and hostile to unions. For Detroit's African Americans, a job at Ford opened a path toward economic security, upward social mobility, and even middle-class respectability. To the city's black elites, Ford confirmed their faith in the merits of cultivating the goodwill of enlightened industrial employers who would reward black workers for their loyalty. Despite the UAW's initial success in winning contracts at GM and Chrysler, the UAW's influence throughout the industry remained limited until it organized Ford's River Rouge plant and its more than fourteen thousand black workers.

By the late 1930s, signs had surfaced that Ford's command over its black workers was not absolute. Most black employees at Ford long understood that a River Rouge job was not without its costs. Despite Ford's promise to promote black workers into better-paying jobs, most African Americans at River Rouge had long been restricted to the most dangerous and labor-intensive work at the factory. Ford's black workers endured what many considered "man-killing" working conditions, not out of blind loyalty to Ford, but because they had no alternatives for earning comparable wages in the region's labor market. More than two-thirds of Ford's black workers were young, married men who needed the income from the dangerous work to meet the financial obligations of raising a family. By the late 1930s, UAW organizers hoped to tap growing resentment among black workers who were far less wedded to Ford than many had assumed.

As in the CIO's organizing drives in other industries, the UAW ultimately reached Ford's black workers through the persistent efforts of black community organizers. In 1938, the local NNC collaborated with the city's branch of the NAACP around a series of initiatives designed, as one area black newspaper explained, to serve the interests of the dispossessed masses rather than the local black elite. Those campaigns enhanced the reputation and appeal of the NAACP among black autoworkers, who started joining the NAACP by the thousands. At the same time, the NNC also cultivated ties with some of the UAW's black autoworkers. In 1940, a group of these black unionists at River Rouge formed a special committee to organize black autoworkers. On the job these seasoned community activists engaged their fellow workers in conversation, trying to persuade them to rethink their loyalty to Ford and support the UAW. They launched an expansive campaign outside the factory to spread the union's message into the black communities of the Detroit area. A ladies' auxiliary conducted home visits, distributed union literature, organized luncheons that solicited the support of community women's groups, and held pro-union rallies at the city's public schools. Organizers with the special committee spread the UAW message to African Americans through frequent radio broadcasts. Through these various channels, black unionists portrayed the campaign to organize Ford as a crucial battle for civil rights. They shared the vision of Randolph and BSCP organizers, insisting that the UAW offered blacks an unparalleled opportunity to claim freedom at work, assert the dignity of black labor, and reject the servility and humility demanded by employers such as Ford.

Despite the efforts of the special committee, many black workers remained reluctant to abandon their loyalty to Ford and cast their fate with the UAW. When the UAW intensified its organizing campaign by calling a strike in April 1941, many African American workers hesitated to support the union. Confident of their ability to mobilize their black employees against the UAW, Ford officials fed and housed several thousand black workers who refused to leave the factory and join the strike. For ten tense days, violent clashes between striking workers and Ford loyalists erupted along the picket lines outside the factory gates and spilled over into black neighborhoods. Ford's hope that it could rally the black community against the UAW backfired when community activists accused Ford officials of instigating racial confrontations. Black ministers supportive of the UAW came to River Rouge to persuade black workers to leave the plant; black youth in the local

Figure 4.2.   The Detroit NAACP Youth Council broadcasts a radio message from its sound car to striking workers marching outside of the Ford Motor Company's River Rouge factory in April 1941. Walter P. Reuther Library, Wayne State University.

NAACP distributed thousands of leaflets in support of the strike. And in a dramatic moment, the NAACP's executive secretary Walter White flew to Detroit in support of the strike. As he toured the picket line in a union sound truck, he thundered over the loudspeaker, urging black workers still in the plant to come out and support the union. The strike ended when government mediators ruled that Ford must hold an election, under the supervision of the National Labor Relations Board, to allow workers to vote on whether they wanted the UAW to represent them. Although a majority of Ford's black workers likely did not vote for the UAW in the May election, a significant number nevertheless did, ensuring that the UAW prevailed by a substantial margin over a rival AFL faction that Ford quietly supported. Shortly after the UAW victory, black workers joined the union in droves. The UAW's River Rouge Local 600 soon emerged as a center of civil rights unionism and the new institution of black political power in Detroit.

The NAACP's Walter White believed that the Ford strike represented what he called the new order in black Detroit. As he declared over the loudspeaker at River Rouge, no longer could black workers rely on the kindness and goodwill of any individual employer because what workers needed was justice. The grassroots activism across the country offered ample evidence of the effectiveness, indeed the necessity, of confrontational activism to pressure employers. White's support of the UAW and the black workers at Ford re-oriented the national agenda of the NAACP into a closer partnership with organized labor and committed the association to a program far more attuned to the needs of black workers. White further committed the NAACP to the new order of collective action when he collaborated with A. Philip Randolph later that spring to use the threat of a mass march of African Americans on the nation's capital to pressure President Roosevelt to demand that the federal government open employment opportunities to African Americans in the nation's defense industries and end discrimination in the armed services.

When the Second World War began in Europe in 1939, the Roosevelt administration began to invest huge sums of money into defense industries. The rapid conversion to a wartime economy initially seemed only to benefit white workers. As the military buildup shrank the rate of unemployment among white Americans, blacks found themselves excluded from full participation in the American industrial economy that was now emerging from the depths of the Great Depression. More than 50 percent of defense industries admitted that they refused to hire African Americans or observed a strict policy of only hiring blacks as janitors. The two major AFL unions in shipbuilding and aircraft production excluded blacks from membership and colluded with employers to prevent black employment.

Vowing to use the strategies and tactics that the BSCP had utilized in its struggle against the Pullman Company, Randolph planned to deploy the organized power of the black masses to pressure the federal government to intervene. Drawing upon the community networks that they had built in the 1920s and 1930s, BSCP organizers enlisted popular support for a march on Washington. They circulated leaflets, collected donations, sold buttons, staged demonstrations and rallies, and spread their message through the black press. They secured the enthusiastic support of national civil rights organizations, including the NAACP. By late spring 1941, Randolph's March on Washington Committee threatened to bring one hundred thousand African Americans to the nation's capital on July 1. Fearful of the consequences of a mass demonstration of dissent on the eve of world war, Roosevelt invited Randolph and White to the White House on June 18 hoping that he might persuade them to cancel the march. They refused to do so unless the president issued an executive order mandating the employment of blacks in defense industries. The president reluctantly relented. On June 25, he issued Executive Order No. 8802, which banned employment discrimination based on race, religion, or national origin by defense contractors and the government and established a Fair Employment Practice Committee (FEPC), an agency empowered to investigate complaints of discrimination and to redress valid grievances.

Randolph and White triumphantly proclaimed Executive Order No. 8802 as a Second Emancipation Proclamation. They had ample reason for optimism. Although the executive order did not desegregate the military, it did establish the FEPC, the first federal agency since Reconstruction committed to promoting and protecting the interests of black workers. By signing the executive order, the president admitted to racial discrimination in American workplaces, acknowledged that it caused blacks irreparable harms, and affirmed that the federal government had the responsibility and the authority to eradicate it. The federal ban on discrimination proved instrumental in opening doors of industrial employment to African American workers, especially to black women who would account for almost one-quarter of those blacks working in manufacturing by the end of the war. The promise of defense employment at good wages with guaranteed benefits lured millions of blacks from the rural South, spurring a second Great Migration far greater in magnitude than the first. The FEPC challenged the practices of the exclusionary craft unions of the AFL, thus opening to blacks the rights and benefits of full membership in the labor movement. Perhaps most importantly, Roosevelt's executive order declared in the universalist language of democracy and fairness that access to work and the opportunity to earn a living were basic civil rights that constituted the economic foundation of the rights of citizenship.

The political strategies and tactics that secured Executive Order 8802 were as important as the provisions that it guaranteed. Few people understood politics as power as clearly as Randolph. Only by making demands from a position of strength, Randolph long maintained, could black Americans expect to win their full recognition as citizens. That required blacks to forge a language of protest, organized into mass rallies and demonstrations, that would enable the voice of black Americans to penetrate the halls of power. Randolph thus saw the March on Washington not as a deferential petition to the federal government but as a demand backed by the power of the organized black masses of America. They did not seek promises of good intentions. They expected instead, Randolph explained to Roosevelt, concrete and definitive action. To many black activists, the lessons were clear. "We get more when we yell," concluded the editors of the black newspaper *Amsterdam News*, "than we do when we plead."[3]

The war opened black employment in shipbuilding, which emerged as the largest nonagricultural employer in the nation. Between 1940 and 1946, the federal government invested $35 billion in California to take advantage of the state's climate, abundant resources, and proximity to the Pacific theater of war. Federal spending sparked rapid industrial growth that transformed places such as the San Francisco Bay Area into the nation's premier center of shipbuilding. In 1939, only six thousand, mostly white men, worked in the shipyards of the Bay Area. Four years later, at the peak of wartime production, the Bay Area's twelve shipyards employed 240,000 men and women, accounting for more than 80 percent of all workers in heavy industry in the area. To meet wartime production schedules, shipbuilders shifted to new production methods that reorganized the work process, which opened employment to thousands of workers who had limited technical skills or experience. Rather than building the ships on site from the ground up, which depended upon the use of skilled labor, companies converted shipyards into assembly lines in which workers put together ships with parts prefabricated elsewhere. By shifting from a reliance on skilled labor that required years of training, employers now hired legions of unskilled workers, including African Americans and women.

By opening employment in shipyards and other wartime defense industries, the federal government during World War II went well beyond the New Deal in promoting the aspirations and protecting the rights of black workers. Access to industrial work, for one thing, enabled African Americans to abandon those low-wage occupations—agricultural work, domestic and personal service, and casual, common labor—that were not covered by Social Security, federal unemployment insurance, and minimum-wage legislation. As wage laborers in industry, black employees now had the rights to claim the protections of and collect benefits under the provisions of the welfare state. Most industrial defense jobs were covered by union-negotiated contracts. Unionized work not only guaranteed good wages but also established workplace rules that protected the health and safety of workers and instituted grievance procedures that prohibited foremen and supervisors from arbitrarily firing workers. To boost the morale of their workers who labored for long hours under the stress of intense wartime production schedules, major defense employers offered a range of recreational services and nonwage benefits. They operated subsidized cafeterias and shops, sponsored intramural sports leagues, and offered cheap entertainment at onsite theaters. To meet the needs of its many female employees, employers established child-care centers staffed by certified teachers, nurses, nutritionists, and child psychiatrists. Perhaps most significantly, defense industries offered their employees, regardless of race, a health insurance plan that provided thousands of workers their first access to professional medical care. For new black recruits to industrial labor, defense jobs provided a path to better work, greater educa-

Figure 4.3. Among the thousands of black women who secured work in defense industries during World War II was this woman who worked at a Douglas Aircraft Company plant in Los Angeles, California, in 1944. Farm Security Administration/Office of War Information Photograph Collection, Prints & Photographs Division, Library of Congress, LC-USW33-028625-C.

tional opportunity, and wages that enabled them to access urban worlds of entertainment, respectability, and homeownership.

By working for the nation's defense, blacks also grasped the symbolic importance of working to build what President Roosevelt called the "great arsenal of democracy."[4] In 1943, when the National War Labor Board abolished racial wage differentials, it did so by equating racial discrimination with Nazism. Not only did the nation need African Americans to win the war, claimed the board's commissioners, but a policy of equal pay for equal work committed the country to the ideals of democracy, freedom, and equality of opportunity that it claimed to defend. Such statements made it clear that American citizens, black as well as white, had rights to fair employment.

Despite its unmistakable importance in opening wartime industrial employment to African Americans, the FEPC lacked the power, resources, and administrative reach to eliminate discrimination in hiring and promotion.

Consequently, black workers entered industrial workplaces that were rife with racial inequalities. Many black migrants, for example, failed to secure employ-ment in defense industries commensurate with their work experience and expertise. Even if many entered the wartime shipyards with experience equal to or greater than that of their white coworkers, most black migrants had to settle for work as laborers on cleanup and maintenance crews or as unskilled welders and riggers. Despite the tangible gains of wartime employment, black women continued to labor at the bottom of the occupational ladder. Many firms disregarded FEPC pressure and persisted in their exclusion of black women from many manufacturing jobs, preferring to hire black women exclu-sively as janitors, bathroom matrons, elevator operators, or cafeteria workers.

Black migrants, whether male or female, experienced a world of caste and class within wartime shipyards. Wartime rhetoric of democracy, patriotism, and national unity of purpose did little to generate a spirit of racial tolerance among white workers. To the casual observer, the shipyards were a remark-able jumble of people from all walks of life—native-born, white Californians, southern white migrants, black migrants, men and women—working to-gether in support of the Allied war effort. Beneath the surface of cooperation, however, white workers expressed deep resentments toward blacks. Whites freely ridiculed black coworkers with racial epithets. They dismissed blacks as ignorant, lazy, lustful, and criminally inclined. They feared that blacks, once they entered the workplace, would threaten their job security and eventually take over their communities.

White workers at times acted on their fears. In scores of racially motivated hate strikes throughout the war years, white workers walked off the job to protest promotions of black workers into skilled or supervisory positions, the training of blacks in skilled trades, or the racial integration of facilities such as bathrooms and cafeterias at manufacturing plants. One of the twenty-five thousand white strikers who walked off the job at a Packard Motor Company aircraft plant in Detroit when the company upgraded three black men to the assembly line in 1943 captured the racist sentiments of many when he ex-claimed that he would rather see Germany and Japan win the war than work next to a black man. Although the FEPC settled many of these disputes, the simple threat of a racially motivated strike constrained many employers from advancing fair employment. Rather than provoke racial confrontations in their workplaces, employers refused to hire blacks, claiming that white work-ers would rather leave than work with African Americans. At times hate strikes exploded into race riots. In May 1943, the Alabama Dry Dock and Shipbuilding Company in Mobile suddenly complied with a six-month-old FEPC directive to promote black workers into skilled positions. The morning after it upgraded twelve of its seven thousand black employees to welding jobs, enraged white workers grabbed pipes, wrenches, and other tools and indiscriminately attacked their black coworkers for several hours until the U.S. Army arrived to restore order.

In many war industries, organized labor obstructed rather than facilitated the transition to fair employment. In the shipyards of the East Bay, white workers controlled black workers' access to employment through the power of their exclusionary unions. Early in the war, before the rapid expansion of employment, the International Brotherhood of Boilermakers (IBB), the major AFL union in shipbuilding, negotiated a closed-shop agreement with the shipyards of the East Bay that restricted employment to union members and gave the IBB control over hiring, promotion, and workplace rules. Pressure from the federal government and the sheer demand for wartime labor compelled the IBB to relent and permit black workers to work in the yards. White unionists, however, forced black workers to join subordinate, auxiliary unions that had no voice or vote in union affairs but were bound by its rules and regulations. IBB locals required black auxiliary members to pay full union dues but denied them full membership benefits. With consent of management, which valued meeting production schedules over enforcing workplace equality, exclusionary unions restricted black women from employment and barred black men from promotion. In doing so, they operated as potent weapons in the defense of the workplace privileges of white workers.

Confronted by hostile white workers, exclusionary unions, and reluctant employers, black workers fought back. Ironically, the segregated auxiliary unions often became the staging ground from which black workers launched their assault on workplace segregation and discrimination in hiring and promotion. Local A-36, the segregated auxiliary union of Boilermakers Local 513 in the East Bay, functioned as a transitional institution through which black newcomers acquired a union consciousness as well as a taste for collective, race-based, working-class activism. Local A-36 integrated thousands of black migrants into urban, industrial life and to the broader black community of the East Bay. Although Local A-36 had no formal authority to place black workers in shipyard jobs, under the spirited leadership of its president, it nevertheless managed to secure a significant number of jobs for black migrants in the yards as well as in other positions across in the region. Moreover, the auxiliary union provided a forum in which black workers discussed among themselves the conditions of their employment and in which they expressed the need for race-based solidarity to combat low wages and employment discrimination. Through this experience, black workers developed the skills to run an organization and communicate its mission to a broader audience.

Thousands of black shipyard workers along the Pacific coast organized local committees to challenge the authority of the IBB. These committees drew upon confrontational, direct-action tactics to challenge the auxiliary union system. In Richmond, black members of Shipyard Workers against Discrimination picketed and occupied the headquarters of Boilermakers Local 513 and sent a delegation to the IBB's national convention to protest the union's antiblack policies. In July 1943, they joined a national boycott of the auxiliaries by refusing to pay union dues. When white Boilermakers at the Marinship Company in San Francisco's North Bay demanded that management fire those who refused to pay their dues, thousands of black workers walked off the job in a spontaneous strike. Shipyard activists in San Francisco filed a complaint in federal court against the union, securing a temporary injunction that restrained the union from discharging blacks who refused to pay their dues and join the auxiliary union. Workers throughout the Bay Area joined in sympathy by refusing to pay their dues. These committees of black shipyard workers expanded their scope of activism beyond the workplace as well. They protested deplorable housing and living conditions, lobbied for improved child-care services, and conducted voter registration drives. In doing so, they mobilized the broader black community, including both working-class newcomers and the more politically cautious prewar black elite, around a civil rights agenda rooted in issues of direct concern to black laborers.

The war inspired black working-class civil rights militancy throughout the country. Detroit and its nearly one hundred thousand unionized black workers became a site of intense black working-class activism. Black unionists joined the local branch of the NAACP by the thousands, transforming it into one of the nation's largest branches. As workers flocked to the NAACP, the city's traditional black elites—lawyers, ministers, and teachers—remained active in the branch, but now they collaborated with unionists to develop confrontational strategies for a more urgent agenda. They worked together in 1942 and succeeded in defending the rights of black residents, desperate for adequate and affordable housing, to move into a federally funded public housing project. Energized by their victory in housing, they mobilized to pressure the city's many factories, which had now been converted to manufacturing munitions for the war effort, to open their doors to black employees. Sponsored by the Detroit NAACP's labor committee, a mass rally and march drew an interracial crowd of more than ten thousand people in April 1943. Those who gathered listened to community activists as well as UAW vice president Walter Reuther denounce racial discrimination in war plants and demand that defense employers be bound by the provisions of Executive Order No. 8802.

Militancy mattered. In the face of entrenched workplace discrimination at dozens, if not hundreds of plants and factories, black workers refused to remain passive and staged spontaneous walkouts to protest employers who refused to transfer or promote them to better, higher-paying jobs. In the fall of 1943, for example, black foundry workers at the Packard plant in Detroit staged a strike protesting the company's refusal to promote them. Management responded by upgrading two hundred workers, and to avoid more confrontations, they promoted another five hundred black foundry workers to production jobs that had previously been held by only whites. In Cleveland a local militant civil rights organization staged numerous demonstrations, organized boycotts, conducted investigations, launched letter-writing campaigns, and filed lawsuits to pressure many of the city's largest industrial employers to hire black workers, especially black women. By late 1943 grassroots activism, aided by severe labor shortages, opened industrial employment to some six thousand black women in Cleveland and compelled some of the city's largest employers to adopt, if not enforce, fair employment practices at their plants.

Black labor activism paid off in the courts as well. In a series of class action lawsuits that black workers filed against discriminatory unions, state supreme courts ordered unions to abolish the auxiliary union system. Citing the "fundamental right to work for a living" and the "constitutional right to earn a livelihood," the California Supreme Court ruled that a union could not deny black workers equal voice in their economic welfare.[5] The ruling, however, only applied to California. The Boilermakers disbanded the auxiliaries in the state, but the union continued its discriminatory system elsewhere in the nation. Without federal legislation prohibiting such practices, discriminatory unionism would persist into the postwar period.

The assertive independence of black unionists as well as the mounting racial tensions in wartime workplaces motivated the CIO leadership to defend black workers and to adopt a more aggressive stance on civil rights. In 1942, the CIO created a Committee to Abolish Racial Discrimination (CARD) to promote racial tolerance and cooperation among workers and to assist the federal government's fair employment mission. CARD produced and distributed a series of pamphlets to educate workers on the necessity of interracial collaboration. The committee hoped to neutralize white fears of working with African Americans by exposing racial discrimination as irrational. CARD literature urged unionists to treat their coworkers, regardless of race, with dignity and respect, encouraged interracial socializing, and reminded workers that union solidarity would create the economic prosperity that would defeat racial prejudice. To support blacks' access to industrial jobs, CARD developed model contracts that contained antidiscriminatory hiring clauses that some of its affiliated unions then adopted in collective bargaining negotiations. CARD also gave broad support to the FEPC and the black workers who filed grievances. By defending African Americans' right to work and arguing for their acceptance as full and equal coworkers, CARD helped to legitimize the integration of black workers into American industry and the labor movement.

Emerging wartime civil rights coalitions focused much of their energy on compelling the FEPC to fulfill its obligation to enforce fair employment practices. Recognizing that the FEPC had little support among employers and trade unions, NAACP executives warned its branches that it would take a concerted and coordinated effort to make the president's order effective. The association performed the critical work of gathering data about defense opportunities for black workers, processed complaints, and pressured the White House to appoint an African American to the FEPC. Thus, even if the FEPC obligated the federal government to challenge workplace discrimination, civil rights activists understood that it was up to black workers and their allies, not federal bureaucrats and investigators, to make the FEPC work. Aware of these realities, many black workers took matters into their own hands to force the committee to act. They wrote letters to investigators, filed complaints with the committee, and testified before FEPC hearings. In doing so, they offered compelling evidence of employers who denied them jobs or promotions, of racist unionists who forced them into second-class auxiliary unions, and of supervisors who ignored their complaints of unsafe and hostile working conditions.

But beyond providing a rich record of racial discrimination in the wartime workplace, African American appeals to the FEPC demanded fair employment as a right of citizenship. They drew upon wartime rhetoric to advance those claims. If blacks can fight and die for their country in defense of democracy, reasoned one typical editorial in the black press in 1943, then they have the right to enjoy the full fruits of their sacrifices, just as any other citizen. That logic informed the thinking of the black men and women who pleaded their case to the government. In numerous appeals, they claimed to ask no more than what every American citizen had a right to ask; they questioned a country that would draft a mother's son into the military but deny her the right to a job at home; and they exposed the injustice of denying work to citizens who, like everyone else, paid their taxes, bought war bonds, and donated to the community war chest. As one black complainant simply put it, she expected to be "treated as an American and not as a Negro."[6]

Local labor and civil rights activists forged a key partnership with the FEPC that enabled it, despite its many limitations, to make significant accomplishments toward fair employment. Throughout its operation, the FEPC handled more than twelve thousand complaints (nearly three-quarters of which involved blacks), reaching satisfactory settlements in nearly five thousand of them. It conducted thirty public hearings, involving 132 companies and thirty-eight unions. In places where labor markets were tightest the committee was particularly effective in opening wartime employment to African Americans. The committee advanced the cause of fair employment through crucial intervention that settled dozens of racially motivated hate strikes by white workers. It conducted a concerted educational campaign on employment discrimination that created an atmosphere more conducive to fair employment. As the president of one company explained, he decided to end discrimination at his factories because he accepted the central message of the committee that the country could not wage a war on fascism abroad while practicing racial discrimination at home. In areas with more plentiful labor supplies, entrenched Jim Crow practices, and deep local opposition to the committee, the FEPC proved ineffective, even powerless. Still, black workers regarded the committee as an essential defender of fairness and justice in the workplace. As one black worker in Cincinnati asserted toward the end of the war, the FEPC, despite its failures, broke the shackles of discrimination and freed blacks to demand the right to earn a living as equal citizens.

By the end of World War II, a new deal had in many ways emerged for black workers. Out of the struggles of the Depression and war years, black workers had become integrated into the urban life of the country, had secured a place in the nation's industrial labor force, and had become union conscious. Mobilized in new industrial unions and reinvigorated civil rights organizations, black workers had amassed the organizational strength that had forced union officials, employers, and government agencies to confront and redress civil rights in the workplace and beyond. Through organizations such as the STFU, the BSCP, the NCC, the industrial unions of the CIO, and the March on Washington Committee, black labor activists demanded economic justice, the right to earn a living, and fair employment. Black workers reoriented the agenda of the NAACP, transformed industrial unionism into civil rights unionism, formed scores of local committees against discrimination in wartime industries, filed grievances with the FEPC against discriminatory employers and exclusionary unions, and demanded that the government enforce its commitment to fair employment.

This activist spirit inspired African Americans to continue to push their demands for full participation in American life in the postwar years. They drew upon the strategies and tactics for social change that they had embraced since the early 1930s to build not only a mass social movement against Jim Crow in the South but also to expand their vision of a civil rights movement focused on fair employment, anchored in an alliance between the CIO and black community protest networks and committed to economic justice as the basis for racial equality.

CHAPTER FIVE

The Black Working-Class Movement for Civil Rights

On the eve of the 1963 March on Washington for Jobs and Freedom, the occasion at which Martin Luther King delivered his famous "I Have a Dream" speech, a national poll asked African Americans how discrimination had personally affected them. More respondents replied that they had suffered job and wage discrimination rather than discrimination in restaurants. The pollsters also found that six out of ten African Americans worked either in menial unskilled jobs, domestic or personal service, or were out of work. When pollsters asked blacks what jobs they would like to have for which they believe themselves qualified, eight out of ten aspired to jobs as skilled laborers, professionals, business executives, or white-collar workers. To the pollsters, these numbers clarified the obstacles that prevented most African Americans from enjoying the fruits of American postwar prosperity. Although 90 percent of African American homes owned a television set, television exposed the material comforts that whites freely enjoyed—suburban homes, modern appliances, new automobiles, and manicured lawns—but that remained elusive for most blacks. To attain a share of that prosperity, the pollsters argued, blacks needed better-paying jobs. To qualify for such jobs, blacks needed better education, which required that they live in neighborhoods that supported good public schools. But to live there, they needed the money to afford decent housing.

As the national poll revealed, African Americans regarded economic justice as the central demand, if not dream, of the civil rights movement.

While African Americans carried on a vigorous fight for school desegregation, access to public accommodations, and the right to vote during the civil
rights movement of the 1950s and 1960s, they never abandoned the struggle
for economic equality or dismissed unions as irrelevant to their quest for just,
fair, and full employment. Most African Americans adhered to a vision of
civil rights that combined access to good jobs, an end to employment discrimination, the desegregation of public space, and the right to vote. As Gloria Richardson, a community activist in Cambridge, Maryland, recognized in
1963, segregated lunch counters, schools, and buses were merely symbolic
of the deeper indignities that African Americans endured. Economic questions remained central, and African Americans regarded unions, despite
their flaws, as relevant institutions for waging the struggle for the economic
foundation of citizenship.

The results of the 1963 survey may appear surprising, for in the two decades
following World War II, black workers enjoyed greater access to employment
and earned higher wages than did their predecessors in the two decades that
followed World War I. Why, then, did the economic rights of citizenship
emerge as a central demand of the civil rights movement? To be sure, there
were significant signs of progress. The exodus out of the rural South accelerated in the postwar years, contributing to the dramatic declines in the
number of blacks employed in agriculture. At the same time, unprecedented
expansion in consumer spending and increased demand for the manufacture
of weapons and munitions during the Korean War (1950–1953) stimulated
economic growth that sustained high rates of nonfarm black employment.
With fewer African Americans working in agriculture, black workers made
impressive gains in other sectors of the economy, including manufacturing,
and retail and professional and semiprofessional jobs, especially in the public
sector. By 1960 nearly one in eight blacks—almost nine hundred thousand—
held jobs working for local, state, or federal government (see Table 5.1).
Black women also improved their occupational status in the postwar years.
Between 1950 and 1970 the number of black women employed in clerical
and sales positions and who worked in professional and technical jobs rose,
while those employed as private household workers fell dramatically. Even
more precipitous was the decline in the number of women working on farms;
by 1970, fewer than 1 percent of black women toiled in agriculture (see
Table 5.2). Employment in these new sectors paid higher wages and offered
more stable and secure employment, which enabled African Americans to
narrow the wage gap with white workers. Because thousands of blacks now
earned unionized wages, the average family income of African Americans in
the early 1950s was almost 60 percent of that of white families, up from less

**Table 5.1. Occupational Status of Nonwhite Persons,
1948–1962 (percentage distributions)**

Major Occupational Groups	1962	1955	1948
White-Collar Workers	16.7	12.0	9.0
Professional and technical workers	5.3	3.5	2.4
Managers, officials, and proprietors	2.6	2.3	2.3
Clerical workers	7.2	4.9	3.3
Sales workers	1.6	1.3	1.1
Blue-Collar Workers	39.5	41.8	39.7
Craftsmen and foremen	6.0	5.2	5.3
Operatives	19.9	20.9	20.1
Nonfarm laborers	13.0	15.8	14.3
Service Workers	32.8	31.6	30.3
Private household workers	14.7	14.8	15.6
Other service workers	18.1	16.8	14.7
Farm workers	11.0	14.5	21.0

Source: Matthew A. Kessler, "Economic Status of Nonwhite Workers, 1955–62," *Monthly Labor Review* (July 1963), 781.

**Table 5.2. Occupational Status of Nonwhite Women,
1950–1970 (percentage distribution)**

Occupational Category	1950	1960	1970
White-Collar Workers	12.0	18.6	32.8
Professional and technical workers	5.3	7.7	10.0
Managers, officials, and proprietors	1.3	1.1	1.4
Clerical and sales	5.4	9.8	21.4
Blue-Collar Workers	17.5	16.2	18.5
Craftsmen and foremen	0.7	0.7	0.8
Operatives	15.2	14.3	16.8
Nonfarm laborers	1.6	1.2	0.9
Service Workers	55.1	61.1	48.0
Private household workers	42.0	38.1	19.5
Other service workers	19.1	23.0	28.5
Farm Workers	9.4	4.1	0.5

Source: Alan L. Sorkin, "Education, Occupation, and Income of Nonwhite Women," *Journal of Negro Education* 41, no. 4 (Autumn 1972), 345.

Table 5.3. Income of Nonwhite Families, 1948–1961 (percentage distribution)

Annual Family Income	1961	1955	1948
Under $3,000	47.5	57.3	78.1
$3,000 to $4,999	24.4	28.3	16.3
$5,000 to $9,999	22.8	13.7	5.3
$10,000 and over	5.6	0.6	0.4

Source: Matthew A. Kessler, "Economic Status of Nonwhite Workers, 1955–62," *Monthly Labor Review* (July 1963), 787.

than 40 percent in 1939. Between 1948 and 1961, far fewer African American families earned incomes that placed them in the lowest income brackets; at the same time, the percentage of black families who earned more than $10,000 a year increased substantially.

Economic benefits translated into tangible social and political gains. In 1956 *Ebony* magazine exalted Gary, Indiana, as the city where African Americans came closest to realizing first-class citizenship. A robust unionized industrial labor force anchored the city's small but expanding black middle class. More than 20 percent of those who worked for the city government, including police officers and firefighters, were African American. The rate of homeownership among Gary's black residents far exceeded that of nearby Chicago. A new generation of blacks—the sons and daughters of the city's first black working-class migrants—had come of age in the urban North and were now determined to exercise their political rights. In 1956, black voters demonstrated their growing political influence by helping to elect three African Americans to the city council. African Americans also held seats on a variety of city boards, including those that governed zoning, public health, schools, and libraries. Such dramatic improvements in the economic and social conditions of African Americans confirmed the faith of many American liberals that postwar prosperity and the expansion of the affluent society would eradicate poverty, quicken the pace of racial integration, and dissolve racial inequality.

The living conditions of many black workers, however, did not confirm such boundless optimism. If one walked from one of Gary's all-white precincts to one of its all-black neighborhoods, insisted a former steelworker in 1956, he would take a "step off an economic cliff."[1] Family incomes were 30 to 40 percent lower in black neighborhoods. Although many black steelworkers had more than a decade of seniority they were denied promotions to higher-paying and higher-skilled jobs. Most blacks rented rather than owned their homes, had accumulated deep levels of consumer debt that restricted their access to credit, had endured one or two layoffs within the past year, and lived in perpetual fear of losing their jobs again. Although instability in the postwar steel industry threatened the economic security of all workers, most blacks had fewer economic resources to insulate themselves from the perils of hard times. Despite the city's professed commitment to racial integration, blacks lived in concentrated neighborhoods characterized by blight and decay, most black children attended racially segregated schools, and local businesses and other private employers refused to go beyond token integration of their workplaces. As one black resident explained, a tour of black Gary revealed more social disintegration than racial integration.

Black industrial workers in postwar Gary confronted new constraints to their employment opportunities that portended a bleak outlook for African Americans in manufacturing. Although African Americans constituted one-third of those who worked in the United States Steel Corporation's massive Gary Works, most of them toiled at jobs that were vulnerable to elimination through automation. As steel manufacturers introduced new technologies that mechanized the heavy, dirty, and dangerous manual jobs that had been overwhelmingly done by black workers, they terminated thousands of African Americans and hired in their place a much smaller number of higher-skilled white machine operators. These trends prevailed throughout the industry in the postwar decades. Years of seniority did little to protect black jobs. In numerous departments throughout the Bethlehem Steel Corporation in Johnstown, Pennsylvania, scores of blacks had labored since the first Great Migration in various hot and heavy jobs. By the mid-1950s, only a handful of blacks remained working in these departments, most of whom were well above the age of fifty. As one local NAACP activist and veteran steelworker of forty years explained, generations of African Americans that grew up in the shadow of the steel mills no longer had the opportunity to work where their fathers had.

Segregated systems of seniority compounded the problem of technological unemployment. Many industrial unions had won key provisions for seniority systems in contracts that established the terms and conditions under which employers could assign, promote, and lay off workers. Systems of seniority protected all workers, regardless of race, from foremen and supervisors who would otherwise exercise arbitrary authority in governing the workplace. Although seniority systems provided workers with job security, they were often racially segregated. Workers accumulated seniority within the department of the plant in which they worked. Employers hired blacks into departments in which the work was heavy, menial, and low paying and offered limited opportunities for advancement. White workers, on the other hand, were hired into production departments in which they would, over time, receive training that enabled them to move up to higher-paying, more skilled work. Steel operators, often with the consent of the union, only allowed black workers to transfer out of their departments if they sacrificed the years of seniority that they had accumulated. Thus, in many plants, black workers who had far more years of seniority than white workers worked at jobs with significantly lower pay. As long as seniority systems operated on a departmental, rather than a plant-wide basis, African Americans found themselves confined to the jobs that required the least skills, paid the lowest wages, and were most vulnerable to technological elimination.

Nor were these problems confined to the steel industry. Between 1956 and 1964, the nation's four biggest meatpacking companies restructured their operations to meet new competitive challenges posed by hundreds of new firms that cut into their market share. By gradually phasing out their older centralized plants in urban rail centers such as Chicago and replacing them with a decentralized network of modern, mechanized plants located closer to livestock feedlots in the rural Midwest and Great Plains, the packers substantially reduced their labor costs by eliminating thirty-eight thousand jobs. These changes were particularly devastating for the unionized packinghouse workers in Chicago, where African Americans constituted 40 percent of the industry's labor force at the end of World War II. By the mid-1960s, packs of wild dogs foraged among the weeds and rubbish of the crumbling packing houses that had once drawn thousands of black migrants out of the South with the promise of gainful employment. Mechanization, relocation, and the decentralization of industrial operations also restructured the automobile industry. Detroit's three major automobile manufacturers closed older inner-city plants and opened newer, more automated operations in the suburbs as well as in smaller towns in the Midwest and South, locations far removed from unions and black workers. The racial consequences of these economic decisions were particularly evident at the Ford Motor Company's River Rouge complex, the center of militant black labor unionism in the 1940s. By 1960, the number of workers at River Rouge had fallen from eighty-five thousand to thirty thousand. In the coalfields of Appalachia, mine operators began to introduce mechanical loaders and cutters that eliminated the jobs of thousands of black miners and replaced them with white workers who operated, maintained, and serviced the machines that now mined the coal. As in the steel industry, black miners with decades of seniority had no opportunity to acquire the training and skill to become operators. Black miners quickly disappeared once operators began to automate. The number of black miners in southern Appalachia dropped from more than forty-two thousand in 1930 to fewer than four thousand by 1970.

Rapid economic restructuring, plant closings in central cities, and the mechanization of manufacturing put thousands of African Americans out of industrial work in the 1950s. From a postwar low of 4.4 percent in 1953, the black unemployment rate climbed steadily throughout the decade, reaching more than 11 percent by 1960, a rate twice as high as that among whites. More devastating, African American men in their prime working years— ages twenty-five to forty-four—suffered an unemployment rate three times higher than white men in the same age category. As mechanization shrank the once-expanding labor market for unskilled, industrial workers, southern black migrants continued to arrive in industrial cities and contributed to a growing pool of casual, low-wage workers. The rapid expansion of mechanical cotton harvesters in the 1950s and 1960s displaced millions of southern farmers, black and white, many of whom headed north, intensifying the competition for jobs. As the *Detroit News* reported in 1959, too many black families had arrived in the Motor City within the last decade seeking jobs that no longer existed in the automobile plants.

The combination of persistent underemployment, job insecurity, continued black migration, industrial decline, and employment discrimination devastated black urban neighborhoods across the industrialized North. By the early 1960s, most urban African Americans lived in all-black communities that more closely resembled slums of decaying houses, poor schools, and boarded-up storefronts. When Martin Luther King toured northern cities in the summer of 1965, he found that black residents endured patterns of discrimination and segregation more rigid than in the Jim Crow South. To King, high rates of concentrated poverty, unemployment, and crime had converted northern cities from lands of promise into streets of disillusion. Economic conditions particularly confined the future prospects of many African American youths who, King feared, confronted bleak futures. Despite the prosperity of the postwar period, many urban blacks had yet to escape the Depression.

One way to protect the economic security of black workers, reasoned civil rights advocates, was to extend the federal government's wartime commitment to fair employment. Black labor activists supported a permanent FEPC with expanded powers that broadened the committee's reach to industries outside of defense and that strengthened its authority to investigate violations and enforce compliance. Hoping to channel the momentum of wartime labor activism into a national campaign, black activists helped organize the National Council for a Permanent FEPC in 1943, an interracial body that lobbied Congress, petitioned federal officials, and enlisted the help of prominent journalists to build public support for an FEPC bill. Their efforts ran into a stiff conservative counteroffensive in Congress. Southern Democrats raged against the FEPC as an outside agency that would revoke the fundamental right of employers to hire and fire whom they wished, compel employers to pay higher wages to black workers whom they regarded as unqualified, place white workers under the authority of black supervisors, and force white workers to accept social equality in the workplace. Northern industrialists and their Republican allies likewise opposed a permanent FEPC as an unwarranted federal intrusion in their business decisions. Congress failed to pass the bill in the fall of 1946. Proponents of the measure did not give up. Over the next twenty years, they introduced more than one hundred fair employment bills in Congress. None passed.

Advocates of fair employment legislation found lawmakers more receptive in the state legislatures and city halls of northern and western states. In the twenty years following the end of World War II, twenty-four states and dozens of municipalities enacted fair employment laws that protected nearly the entire nonwhite population outside the South from discrimination by employers, employment agencies, and unions. Passage of the laws revealed the growing importance of assertive and organized black voters who elected lawmakers committed to passing meaningful and substantive civil rights legislation. Although administrators reported that the new regulations opened the workplace to thousands of new workers, state and municipal fair employment laws lacked the power to effect fundamental, structural change. Most laws suffered two critical flaws. First, most state and local FEPCs lacked the authority to fine or penalize employers who continued to discriminate. Second, the law relied on workers to file complaints against employers who discriminated. Most workers lacked the resources, time, or expert advice to file effective claims. Rather than provoking strong enforcement and decisive intervention, complaints opened investigations that often dragged on for months without resolution. Fair employment laws at the state and local level remained an inadequate instrument for opening the workplace to African Americans; nevertheless, they signaled an important departure from the 1920s and 1930s, when black workers had no course for redress against employment discrimination.

As state legislatures and city halls across the North passed fair employment legislation that at least promoted nondiscrimination in the workplace, southern state legislatures enacted new laws that created a climate of anti-unionism that further blocked black workers' access to fair and just employment. In 1947 the conservative coalition in Congress passed the Taft-Hartley Act over President Harry Truman's veto. The new law contained a host of provisions that weakened the protections that workers had won under the New Deal. Taft-Hartley empowered states to pass so-called right-to-work laws that prohibited collective bargaining agreements requiring employees to join a union and pay union dues as conditions of their employment. Within a decade, every southern state but Louisiana had adopted some form of right-to-work legislation. Proponents claimed that the new laws protected workers from being coerced to join a union against their will. Unionists countered that such laws undermined union security because they enabled free riders to enjoy the benefits of collective-bargaining agreements without having to pay for or share in the burden of winning those contracts. The law thus encouraged divisions, especially racial ones, among workers that eroded union solidarity and made it nearly impossible for unions to sustain their membership. In 1947 North Carolina, for example, passed its right-to-work law in the midst of the CIO's spirited campaign to organize the southern lumber industry, including a successful effort to unionize the workers at the state's largest sawmill. The mill's mostly black unionists had difficulty encouraging whites to support the union, even after they won a contract from the company. Under the law, however, white workers were under no obligation to join, even though they now earned higher wages under the union-negotiated contract. Black unionists complained that whites freeloaded, refusing to pay dues to the union, which deprived it of the critical resources it needed to continue to represent its members. By weakening this upstart union of lumber workers, the law enabled the company to reassert its authority in the workplace and eventually suppress the union as an effective bargaining agent.

Anti-union legislation prevailed in the South partly because disfranchisement prohibited blacks from voting. Where blacks could exercise political leverage, such as in the industrialized states of the North, right-to-work initiatives failed. In 1958 when the National Right to Work Committee succeeded in placing before the voters of Ohio a proposed right-to-work amendment to the state constitution, the labor movement waged a campaign to defeat the measure that succeeded in large part because 85 percent of black voters opposed the initiative. For black labor activists the lessons were clear: blacks needed the ballot to enact public policies that promoted fair employment and to defeat those that discriminated against black workers; organized labor learned that it needed black voters to defeat anti-union legislation. Black voters would consistently vote with labor because they needed the same legislation that labor did. Indeed, some black civil rights leaders saw the labor movement and the black freedom movement as natural allies working together to become the architects of a new democracy that wiped away the

racial divisions among workers that had been imposed by those who benefitted from their disunity.

Forging a potent black-labor alliance was easier to imagine than to implement. Signs of trouble had surfaced shortly after the war when the CIO
launched Operation Dixie in 1946, its ambitious effort to organize industrial
workplaces in the South. Despite the extraordinary growth in union membership throughout the country since the late 1930s, the South remained a
bastion of anti-unionism. The CIO resolved to turn the tide and dispatched
250 organizers to the region, but conflicts over southern strategy divided the
federation. The CIO's top leadership wanted to focus first on the fragmented
textile industry. Stretching across the southern Piedmont from Virginia to
northern Alabama, the southern textile industry employed more than five
hundred thousand mostly white workers in hundreds of mills of varying sizes.
Organizers saw textiles as the gateway to the South. Success there would
enhance the reputation and prestige of unions among southern workers, enabling organizers to unionize scores of secondary industries such as furniture
making, food processing, and oil refining. Others within the CIO challenged
this strategy. Skeptical that concentrating resources on the notoriously
anti-union white textile workers would pay off, they argued that organizers
would have greater success focusing on workplaces—lumber, furniture, and
tobacco—that employed significant numbers of blacks, who were far more
likely to respond to the union's message. They urged the Southern Organizing Committee (SOC) to follow the path blazed by black unionists who had
already established strong interracial locals around an agenda that combined
civil rights and industrial unionism. CIO leaders, however, rejected such an
approach, fearing that too much agitation on race would narrow rather than
expand organized labor's appeal among the region's workers. They further
countered that despite their successes, interracial unions had only organized
a small segment of the working class and had not established a sufficient
enough precedent to serve as a model for a region-wide mobilization.

Regardless of the strategy that it deployed, the CIO ran into determined
employer opposition. Southern industrialists mobilized the communities in
which they operated plants, enlisting the help of churches, local officials,
civic groups, and chambers of commerce against union organizers. The local
press portrayed unionists as northern invaders who were more concerned
about converting southerners to their alien ideologies of political radicalism
and interracialism than in improving the lives of southern workers. Southern
elites exploited postwar communist hysteria to discredit unionists and their
agenda, slandering them as Soviet agents determined to do the Kremlin's
bidding within the United States. Employers fired workers suspected of

organizing intimidated employees into voting against union representation, and they deployed armed spies to infiltrate organizing meetings. In the end, the CIO's southern campaign produced disappointing results. The CIO had expended tremendous sums of money and diverted substantial resources for negligible gains in membership among textile workers. More fundamentally, the southern organizing drive failed to build a foundation of industrial union- ism that could serve as a political base for mobilizing against the region's repressive anti-union and segregationist political order.

Nor did the CIO's left-led unions, those that had been among the most aggressive in opening their membership to black workers, provide a promis- ing base for a viable black-labor coalition in the postwar years. Internal polit- ical conflicts within the CIO over communism, employer counteroffensives, and white worker resistance exposed the limits of working-class interracial- ism in these unions. Long-smoldering tensions within the CIO over com- munism erupted in 1949 and 1950 when the labor federation's mainstream leadership expelled eleven affiliated unions it accused of subservience to the Communist Party of the United States, and ultimately, to the Soviet Union. Caught in the firestorm were unions with large numbers of black members. In Memphis employers exploited disunity within the CIO to destroy its larg- est local of furniture workers. The Memphis Furniture Company, one of the city's staunchest opponents of the CIO, refused to bargain with the furniture workers. In January 1949, seven hundred black women went out on strike. Risking hunger and eviction from their homes, these desperately poor black women waged a militant strike, buoyed by initial support from the city's industrial union council. But after eight months the strike fizzled. Employers relied upon the police to intimidate strikers and escort strikebreakers across the picket lines; white workers remained loyal to the company and refused to join the strike; and the local union fell under an internal CIO investigation for alleged communist activity. Under such pressure, the furniture workers' union collapsed. Unionized black sugar workers in Louisiana also struggled to win the support of their white coworkers. In 1942 the CIO had organized the state's sugar refineries, establishing biracial unions that won economic gains for black and white workers but which sustained discriminatory employment and promotion practices. Shortly after the sugar locals affiliated with the racially progressive United Packinghouse Workers of America (UPWA) in 1947, black sugar workers moved to implement the UPWA's antidiscrimi- nation action program. Alarmed by the challenges to job discrimination and segregated workplace facilities, white workers in twelve sugar locals seized upon the language of anticommunism to organize a revolt against the UPWA. Their effort to disaffiliate twelve sugar locals from the UPWA and join with AFL unions willing to reverse the civil rights program ultimately failed, but not before it brought the sugar locals to the brink of collapse. Although white workers eventually accepted desegregation of the workplace, they neither promoted the union's progressive racial policies nor participated in future union affairs.

Although anticommunism provided opponents of interracial unionism with a powerful language to discredit the black leadership and civil rights orientation of these unions, it alone does not account for their collapse. Anticommunism exposed more fundamental weaknesses—the failure to win white allies, the inability to forestall mechanization, and the vulnerability to employer power—that isolated activists. Other southern unions with robust black membership—including those that organized iron ore miners, tobacco factory workers, and lumber workers—succumbed to similar pressures.

Despite these defeats, black workers remained fervent, even stalwart unionists throughout the postwar years. In the 1950s, when reports of internal corruption and scandals tarnished the reputation of organized labor among Americans, black workers continued to see unions as vital institutions. Despite the limits of CIO support for black workers and the open hostility of many white unionists, blacks were more likely than whites to join and remain consistent supporters of unions. The country's major civil rights organizations continued to take pro-union positions, black voters overwhelmingly supported political candidates that labor unions endorsed, and blacks exercised more influence within the labor movement than ever before. An estimated 1.5 million African Americans belonged to unions in 1955 compared to around sixty thousand in the late 1920s. Even unions that did little to combat racial discrimination attracted black workers because union-negotiated wage increases and benefits enabled them to attain the material prosperity that had long eluded them. As one black union veteran explained, black workers in the 1930s wore secondhand clothes and drove beat-up old jalopies, but by the 1950s, unionized blacks could afford suits and ties and drive Cadillacs.

In addition to their commitment to fighting for the fair wages of unionized pay scales, black unionists sustained the connections between labor and civil rights activism. An infusion of younger, militant black workers who joined the industrial labor force after the war resented continued discrimination within workplaces as well its persistence within unions. Many of these workers were veterans of World War II and the Korean War who were more racially conscious and anxious for racial change than the older generation of workers. They had risked their lives in defense of the country and believed that they were entitled to a better deal. Instead of crumbs, they expected a slice of the pie. Impatient with incremental change, some black workers took advantage of union contracts and grievance procedures to demand jobs from which they had been excluded. They also threatened to walk out when the companies vacillated in desegregating their plant facilities. Others filed lawsuits to challenge barriers to job promotions. Black unionists pressured union locals to adopt antidiscriminatory policies and establish fair employment committees within their unions. At times, dissident black unionists formed independent caucuses to pressure the labor movement to support the interests of black workers.

But black unionists did not confine their civil rights activism to the workplace. They also launched movements for economic justice and racial equality in their communities. Black unionists in the South devoted energy and resources to educate, register, and mobilize black working-class voters. Black unionists cultivated working relationships with local branches of the NAACP and the National Urban League and joined the struggle to desegregate schools and other public facilities, end housing discrimination, and expose and challenge police brutality. Whether in New Orleans or New York, black unionists kept alive a working-class vision of civil rights that remained centered upon the fundamental question of economic inequality and continued to use their unions as a base for organized civil rights activism.

In the mid-1950s, when mass movements against segregation in the South emerged, they drew much of their support from the participation of experienced black unionists. In the wake of *Brown v. Board of Education*, the Supreme Court's 1954 landmark decision ruled that racially segregated public schools were unconstitutional, black activists across the South mobilized to force states and municipalities to enforce desegregation. Over the next decade, southern blacks marched to integrate public schools, launched boycotts against segregated public transportation, staged sit-ins to demand the integration of lunch counters, organized freedom rides to integrate interstate buses, and engaged in other mass demonstrations to demand equal access to theaters, parks, swimming pools, beaches, libraries, hospitals, and department stores. Black trade unionists and working-class blacks filled the ranks of civil rights organizations and acted as the shock troops of the movement's most celebrated struggles. As one black veteran unionist explained, labor activism had taught him valuable lessons about fighting racial discrimination, which prepared him to join the civil rights movement in the 1950s.

The Montgomery bus boycott—the first sustained, mass demonstration against segregation in the wake of *Brown*—illustrates the working-class character of the civil rights movement. Although there had been signs of racial moderation in the city's government, Alabama's capital remained a city firmly in the grasp of militant segregationists. Excluded from jobs with the city and state government, African Americans had few employment opportunities outside of domestic service or unskilled day labor. To get to work, most black workers relied on the city's buses, where they frequently became embroiled in testy confrontations with overbearing white bus drivers who used their police power to enforce segregation. After waiting at bus stops in segregated lines, black passengers encountered white drivers who commanded them to enter buses through the rear, dictated where they could sit, and often forced them to stand while seats reserved for whites remained empty.

These indignities inspired an activist spirit among Montgomery's blacks. Few embodied that spirit more than Jo Ann Robinson and Edgar D. Nixon. Robinson, an English professor at Alabama State College, served as president of the Women's Political Council (WPC), a group of more than three hundred female educators, nurses, social workers, and other semiprofessionals who were determined to use what she called women power to combat the humiliations of Jim Crow. Nixon boasted an impressive resume of labor and civil rights activism. A Pullman porter by trade, Nixon had organized a successful challenge to the city's policy of excluding blacks from federal public works projects in the 1930s. He also served as president of the Alabama division of the BSCP, had been an active leader in the local and state NAACP, founded the Montgomery Voter's League, and headed the all-black Progressive Democrats that challenged the state's all-white Democratic Party. As a devoted disciple of A. Philip Randolph, Nixon believed that the tactics of mass working-class action could be used against the city's system of segregated transit. Robinson's group likewise advocated a boycott, and the local NAACP branch hoped to mount a legal challenge. What they needed was a catalyst.

On the evening of December 1, 1955, activists got their test case. City police arrested Rosa Parks, a tailor's assistant, for refusing to give up her seat for a white passenger as she was riding home from work. Parks was no stranger to confrontation. She was among the first black women to register to vote in Montgomery, served as an adviser to the local NAACP's youth council, and had become involved in dozens of local protests. Parks's devotion to civil rights activism grew in part from her own personal work history. Trained as a stenographer but denied employment in her trade, Parks settled for work as a low-wage seamstress, but she used her skills to work as the secretary of the local branch of the NAACP, which her husband had founded in the 1940s. Parks sharpened her activist spirit in the summer of 1955 when she attended a workshop for community organizers at the Highlander Folk School in Tennessee. In 1932, Myles Horton founded Highlander as an interracial training center for union activists, civil rights campaigners, religious dissenters, and community organizers. Horton's own experiences working under the oppressive conditions of the South's farms, mines, and mills combined with his later theological training convinced him of the need to establish a sort of school of life in which ordinary working people could meet to develop their own strategies for social change. Some of the mid-twentieth century's most famous social activists, including Martin Luther King, Pete Seeger, Fannie Lou Hammer, and Woody Guthrie, all attended Highlander. By educating activists through workshops in which participants exchanged tales of their experiences and shared ideas about how to solve their problems, Highlander workshops prepared grassroots organizers for the fight for social change. Parks returned from Highlander with a renewed sense of purpose and a commitment to putting what she had learned into action.

When news of her arrest broke, black activists swung into action. Robinson and the WPC mimeographed and distributed thousands of leaflets announcing a boycott. Nixon and a group of black clergy organized the Montgomery Improvement Association (MIA) to coordinate the boycott. He recruited Martin Luther King, a young Baptist minister who recently moved to Montgomery from Atlanta, to serve as MIA's president. Addressing a mass meeting of black supporters of the boycott at a local Baptist church, King connected the black struggle against segregation to the battle the labor movement had fought against capitalism. He urged his audience to follow the labor movement's model and organize to demand their rights. For the next thirteen months, fifty thousand blacks, most of whom were among the working class, endured death threats, violence, unwarranted arrests, and what one journalist called economic warfare to sustain the boycott of the city's buses. Determined to force supporters of the boycott into submission, white employers fired their maids and house servants, landlords raised rents and evicted tenants, the city cut off utilities to black residents who had fallen behind in their payments, a grand jury indicted more than one hundred organizers of the boycott, and vigilantes hurled a bomb at King's home. The manner in which Montgomery's whites fought back convinced King to frame the conflict as a struggle for political and economic power. Throughout 1956, King insisted that defeating segregation and discrimination required more than rearranging where blacks and whites sat on buses; it required the transformation of an economic system that had produced gross inequalities.

African Americans in Montgomery were not without resources of their own. After enduring several evictions by white landlords, MIA located its headquarters in the building owned by Montgomery's predominantly black bricklayers' union. Blacks organized an extensive carpool system, run out of a black-owned parking lot on cars fueled with gasoline purchased from black-owned filling stations; black business owners provided critical relief funds; and residents walked to work, regardless of the weather. Their endurance in the face of white intransigence soon brought national and international attention to the boycott and with it extensive outside support. As the city's black workers found alternative ways to travel, lawyers pressed their case through the federal courts until the Supreme Court ruled in December 1956 that the bus segregation laws were unconstitutional. The boycott demonstrated black workers' capacity to make common sacrifice, stick together, and defeat massive resistance with mass action.

Many labor unions provided financial support for the Montgomery boycott, revealing the broader commitment that both the CIO and the AFL made to the emergent civil rights movement of the 1950s. The CIO continued to cultivate its alliance with black workers and with national civil rights organizations that dated back to the early war years and encouraged its affiliated unions to promote racial justice within their unions and their workplaces. The CIO's most visible leaders endorsed the civil rights platform of the Democratic Party, including calls for the creation of a permanent FEPC, and denounced racism as a national disgrace that compromised the country's international standing as a defender of freedom in the Cold War. The CIO's reputation for racial liberalism forced the AFL to moderate its policies toward blacks. The AFL enlisted seventeen black organizers and adopted a new policy calling for equal employment opportunities for black workers and the full participation of African Americans within the AFL and its affiliated unions. After the two labor federations merged in 1955, the AFL-CIO and many of its affiliated unions lobbied for civil rights legislation pending before Congress, gave critical funding to civil rights organizations, funded civil rights litigation, freedom rides, and voter registration campaigns, provided bail money for jailed civil rights protesters, and mobilized its membership in support of the civil rights movement. Perhaps no other non–civil rights organization gave more support for civil rights reform than organized labor.

If the AFL-CIO leadership understood the political benefits of an alliance with the civil rights movement, few southern white unionists shared the same conviction. AFL-CIO operatives tried, often in vain, to convince southern white unionists of the economic benefits of labor's support for civil rights. In explaining why they did not vote for a racially progressive Democrat with strong ties to organized labor who ran for the U.S. Senate in 1950, white workers in North Carolina admitted that they would rather work for lower wages than allow their children to attend public schools with African

Americans. Labor activists who canvassed the South on behalf of the AFL-CIO found such sentiment to be widespread. They despaired that white workers expressed greater loyalty to the White Citizens Councils—groups that organized to defy desegregation—than to their own unions. AFL-CIO president George Meany emphasized the dangers that Citizens Councils posed to organized labor and tried to expose them as groups headed by anti-union employers who exploited fears of racial integration to disguise their anti-labor agenda. Such arguments persuaded few southern white unionists. Throughout the civil rights years, southern white unionists joined the Ku Klux Klan, raised funds to support a host of segregationist causes, threatened to disaffiliate from their parent unions, and even created a short-lived Southern Federation of Labor as a segregationist alternative to the AFL-CIO.

The depth of this hostility often paralyzed national union leadership. Because of state right-to-work laws, membership in southern unions was voluntary, and national union leaders feared that if they expressed overly aggressive support for *Brown* or pushed uncompromising positions on civil rights, white unionists would flee. As one Mississippi unionist warned Meany, if southern unions expelled all of those who supported segregation, as UAW president Walter Reuther seemed to have suggested, there would be no one left to fight for labor's cause in the South. Given these circumstances, unions such as the UAW often acted as modest rather than militant defenders of shop floor civil rights. For one thing, institutional structures that protected the independence of affiliated locals limited the leverage that national leadership had over their Jim Crow southern locals. When the UAW insisted that its locals in Atlanta abolish racially separate seniority systems, which confined black workers to lower-paying, lower-skilled nonproduction jobs, local officials simply refused on the grounds that white workers would not tolerate integration of the shop floor. Other efforts to pressure southern locals were equally ineffective. Nor did the UAW exercise any leverage over its skilled tradesmen, who retained control over the rights of entry to their craft. UAW staffers feared that skilled tradesmen, who never had been enthusiastic supporters of an industrial union that they believed favored unskilled workers, would abandon the union if pressured to open their trade to African Americans. Consequently, the skilled crafts in the UAW remained more segregated than the infamous AFL building trades.

The CIO's Civil Rights Committee (CRC) acted with similar restraint and avoided tense workplace confrontations that might disrupt the independence of affiliated unions. The CRC exerted limited authority and had only the power of moral suasion and expulsion to compel compliance, neither of which it seemed very willing to use. CRC officials refrained from publicizing discriminatory practices of affiliated unions for fear that doing so would tarnish the public image of the labor movement in general. When committee members recommended revoking the charters of unions that discriminated, the committee often rejected the suggestion as counterproductive. Little wonder that many African Americans dismissed the CRC as a fruitless waste of resources that devoted more energy to promoting labor's public image than to confronting internal problems of racism.

Thus despite the many hopeful signs of a potentially robust black-labor coalition, many black workers doubted labor's commitment to eradicating racism in its midst. Too often, it seemed, white unionists proved quick to expel communists and political radicals but tolerated racists. Inspired by the achievements of civil rights activists in the South, black unionists launched their own assault on the patterns of racial inequality within the labor movement. Rather than rely on the goodwill and promises of national union leaders to promote change, black workers turned to civil rights organizations to pressure unions to comply with their own antidiscrimination resolutions. As black workers increasingly appealed to the NAACP to attack segregation and discrimination within the labor movement, the civil rights organization struggled to develop a consistent strategy that would both advance the interests of black workers but that did not jeopardize its fragile but critical alliance with organized labor. Much of that work fell to Herbert Hill, the director of the NAACP's labor department from 1951 to 1977. Originally hired to serve as the association's liaison to the labor movement, Hill expressed confidence that African Americans could use unions as a base from which to fight and eliminate racial discrimination in industrial employment. Hopeful in his ability to help the AFL-CIO realize its pledge to eliminate racism within trade unions, Hill advocated mediation over litigation and strove to build working relationships with union officials to secure job opportunities and promotions for black workers.

But by the end of the 1950s, Hill came to the conclusion that negotiation and persuasion had produced only a "piecemeal and inadequate" response.[2] He issued scathing indictments of the AFL-CIO's failure to eliminate racial discrimination in its affiliated unions. What little progress had been made, Hill contended, came only through the relentless efforts of black activists and civil rights agencies and not through the initiative of federation officials. Hill produced a mountain of evidence that revealed that the problems were neither isolated nor incidental but part of a systemic pattern of antiblack employment practices. Throughout the country and all employment sectors, unions tolerated affiliates that barred blacks, maintained segregated locals, sustained racially separate seniority systems, and excluded blacks from apprenticeship training programs under union control, which were essential if blacks were ever to escape the low-paying, unskilled jobs that had become most vulnerable to elimination through automation. Hill accused labor leaders of moral corruption for their failure and unwillingness to recognize the disturbing disparity between their own public pronouncements and the living conditions of black workers.

By the late 1950s, uneasy tensions strained the alliance between African Americans and the labor movement. Although the white leaders of the AFL-CIO and the country's major unions remained firmly committed to racial equality, they were uncomfortable with black militancy. The white working-class rank and file demonstrated a capacity to make common cause with black workers on economic issues so long as they did not have to forfeit racial privileges in the workplace. Black workers continued to embrace unions as vital institutions for building a fair and just social and economic order but had grown increasingly frustrated with the gradual pace of racial reform within the labor movement. Across the country, as black activists accused unions, especially those with racially progressive reputations, of perpetuating entrenched patterns of racial discrimination, they exposed these fragile fault lines. For many black unionists, white unionists' defense of long-standing racial privileges combined with labor leadership's inability and unwillingness to respond to intensifying demands for racial change convinced them to regard the NAACP as a more committed defender of their interests than their own unions.

Those tensions exploded into open conflict at the AFL-CIO's 1959 convention. Randolph, the nation's foremost black trade unionist, who was one of two African Americans on the labor federation's executive council, introduced a series of resolutions to commit the AFL-CIO to decisive action against affiliated unions that continued to discriminate. The most heated conflict erupted over Randolph's proposal to liquidate and eliminate all segregated locals among AFL-CIO affiliates. AFL-CIO president George Meany demurred, arguing that the federation had to respect the democratic rights of its local unions. Many black workers, after all, preferred the segregated locals in which they had long held positions of leadership. Neither he nor Randolph had the right to interfere with black unionists who wished to maintain the union that they had belonged to for many years. Randolph rejected such thinking. No matter what benefits they may offer black workers, segregated locals deprived African Americans of influence within their union and of access to equal employment. Meany, in a tense moment that he later regretted, defended the rights of black workers to maintain segregated locals, demanding of Randolph "who in the hell appointed you as guardian of the Negro members in America?"[3] Black unionists rallied to Randolph's support. One angry black unionist defended Randolph, explaining that no one had appointed Randolph to speak on behalf of America's black workers but that he had earned that right by devoting fifty years of his life to their cause.

Disillusioned by the unwillingness of the AFL-CIO to push for antidiscrimination within its own ranks with the urgency that they believed it deserved, Randolph and his allies launched the Negro American Labor Council (NALC) in May 1960. They envisioned two broad purposes: to advocate for the rights of black workers in general and to champion the interests of black unionists within organized labor. They did not create the NALC as a separatist organization—a black federation of labor—but as one dedicated to pressuring the federation's leadership from within. At the NALC founding convention, Randolph insisted that although the NALC rejected the doctrines of racial separation and black nationalism, African Americans alone must assume the burden of completing the unfinished work of emancipation. The failure of white liberals and labor leaders to comprehend the depth and scope of racial discrimination, to recognize their complicity in its perpetuation, and to grasp the civil rights revolution in their midst made it clear why black unionists could not rely upon white union leaders to promote and protect the interests of black workers. Instead blacks had to take control in order to maintain an independent agenda.

NALC activists hoped to harness the energy and momentum of the southern civil rights movement in its fight against discrimination in the labor movement and employment. Shortly after its organization, the NALC claimed more than ten thousand members organized into chapters in twenty-three cities. Operating from that base, black trade unionists coordinated with local civil rights and community organizations on a range of issues—housing discrimination, police brutality, collective bargaining rights for black municipal workers, and campaigning for racially progressive political candidates—that gave the NALC an influence far beyond its membership numbers. Most importantly, NALC activists remained dedicated to the principal that unions were vital to ending blacks' status as second-class citizens. Black unionists maintained that they stood a far greater chance of success by placing maximum pressure on the labor movement from within than by seceding from the movement altogether. They resolved to shake the house of labor to its foundations, to cleanse it of discrimination, and to secure for blacks positions of authority within organized labor. As Randolph declared in 1960, black workers were in rebellion.

One did not have to look far for evidence of open rebellion. Black workers, in alliance with black civil rights organizations such as the NAACP, intensified their demonstrations against unions that discriminated. In several cities across the North, black workers challenged racism in the building-trades unions with the same direct-action tactics that civil rights groups were using in the South. Protesters disrupted construction projects, picketed city halls, occupied public spaces, and clashed with police and white unionists. Some of the most intense protests unfolded in Philadelphia during the spring of 1963. Black labor activists in city's branches of the NAACP and Congress of Racial Equality (CORE) waged a vigorous campaign to force unions and contractors to employ blacks on public construction projects. The movement's leading advocate was Cecil B. Moore, a brash criminal defense attorney who as president of the local branch of the NAACP vowed a militant agenda that addressed the needs of Philadelphia's poor and working-class neighborhoods. Described by a supporter as "an arrogant foul-mouth radical" with a passion for racial justice, Moore insisted that African Americans demanded full racial integration and were prepared to hurt their friends and cross swords with their allies, if necessary.[4] A two-month insurgency against the city produced results. After demonstrators clashed with police outside a school construction site on which work had been suspended because of the

Figure 5.1. Picketers protesting employment discrimination in the Philadelphia building trades block a delivery truck at a school construction site in a predominantly black neighborhood, May 1963. Special Collections Research Center, Temple University Libraries, Philadelphia, PA.

protests, the city's Building and Construction Trades Council agreed to the immediate hiring of black plumbers, steamfitters, and apprentice electricians. As the council's president admitted, they accepted the NAACP's terms rather than see the protest escalate into a deadly confrontation.

Throughout the spring and summer of 1963 hundreds of local movements in other parts of the country pushed an aggressive civil rights agenda centered on the economic needs of black workers. When activists with CORE launched a community organizing project in rural Louisiana to expand voter registration among blacks, desegregate public facilities, and train residents in the arts of nonviolent protest, they discovered that most blacks did not see the desegregation of restaurants as nearly as vital as fair employment, wage discrimination, and access to good jobs. Activists in the working-class community of Cambridge, Maryland, organized a local movement that explicitly connected the demand for civil rights with the aspiration for economic justice. Gloria Richardson, the movement's strident leader, declared that black residents were most in need of resources—low-rent public housing, job training, and employment. Desegregated schools meant little to families who could not afford to buy schoolbooks for their children. In Mississippi, activists initiated a Freedom Vote, a mock political campaign designed to demonstrate what black Mississippians would vote for were they free to register and exercise their political rights. They staged a mock political convention in which delegates voted for a platform that demanded the basic economic foundations of citizenship: low-interest loans for small farmers, government aid to farming cooperatives, public works for the unemployed, fair employment practices in hiring, and an expansion of federal minimum wage protections to agricultural workers and domestic servants.

At the same time, black trade unionists planned a march on Washington to dramatize the economic crisis that confronted the nation's black population. Veteran civil rights strategist Bayard Rustin suggested to Randolph that they organize a two-day mass-action protest to demand full employment to reverse the structural inequalities of the national economy. To advocates of full employment, the federal government had an obligation to provide all adult Americans with the right to an equal opportunity for paid employment at a just rate of compensation. Randolph endorsed the concept but suggested that such a march should link the economic agenda of the NALC with the aspirations of the southern movement for civil rights. Over the next several months organizers enlisted the support of the nation's other major civil rights organizations—NAACP, the National Urban League, Southern Christian Leadership Conference (SCLC), CORE, and the Student Nonviolent Coordinating Committee (SNCC)—in helping black workers march on the nation's capital. Although some activists such as John L. Lewis of SNCC favored mass demonstrations of civil disobedience that would paralyze the nation's capital, organizers settled upon a peaceful, one-day march followed by a program of speeches that emphasized the dual agenda of civil rights and economic justice. As Randolph explained, he preferred mobilizing people by the thousands under the umbrella of a broad coalition rather than encouraging the militant protest of a few thousand. Moreover, President John F. Kennedy proposed a civil rights bill in June that civil rights activists welcomed but criticized for falling far short of their expectations. As planning for the march proceeded, organizers shifted their focus to using the demonstration to pressure Congress not only into passing but also in expanding the provisions of the bill.

In early July organizers circulated their official call for a March on Washington for Jobs and Freedom to convene on August 28, 1963. Insisting upon the inseparability of economic and civil rights, the marchers demanded public policies that not only protected civil rights but also that promoted economic justice. These included the passage of robust and effective federal civil rights legislation, the immediate desegregation of public schools, and the abolition of police brutality against civil rights workers and peaceful demonstrators. They also demanded a massive federal public works program to achieve full employment, federal fair employment practice legislation, and an expansion of the Fair Labor Standards Act that not only raised the federal minimum wage but also granted protections to domestic servants and agricultural workers. As Randolph testified before Congress that summer, all civil rights were built upon the right to earn a decent living.

The March on Washington Committee drew upon the community protest networks that had first emerged during the Great Depression and World War II to recruit 250,000 people to the nation's capital. Responding to the call to march on Washington, community groups—churches, settlement houses, youth centers, and neighborhood associations—raised thousands of dollars to provide food, lodging, and transportation for marchgoers. They chartered trains and buses, organized convoys of automobiles, and coordinated with state police patrols to facilitate travel. Despite the AFL-CIO's unwillingness to endorse or participate in the march, seventeen national unions and a number of state and municipal labor councils supported it and provided the experience, skill, money, and leadership at the local level that proved indispensable in mobilizing thousands to Washington. The UAW printed two thousands signs for marchgoers to carry, rented out two hundred area hotel rooms, coordinated the transportation of five thousand marchers, and helped to underwrite the cost of the sound system at the Lincoln Memorial. The United Packinghouse Workers and National Urban League subsidized the trips of 250 unemployed black Chicagoans. One Chicago black school teacher and community activist raised $30,000 to send another one thousand unemployed workers to the march. Busloads of domestic workers from New York City, white coalminers from Kentucky, and black farmers from the South joined the Freedom Train to the National Mall. Although reporters counted fewer unemployed and working poor among the marchers than organizers had initially hoped to recruit, Whitney Young of the National Urban League counted plenty of the "most victimized" blacks in America among the crowds who effectively dramatized the connections between economic deprivation and Jim Crow public policy.

Those who gathered on the National Mall constituted what Randolph called "the advance guard of a massive moral revolution for jobs and freedom."[5] They carried picket signs that announced in bold letters the core demands of the march: "decent housing, *now*," "jobs for all at decent pay," "equal rights, *now*," "an FEPC law, *now*," "first class citizenship," "full employment," and "Civil rights plus full employment equals freedom." In his opening remarks, Randolph endorsed the civil rights bill making its way through Congress, but he warned that the racial integration of public accommodations would mean little to the masses who could not afford to use them. Others echoed that theme connecting economic discrimination and racial subordination. The NAACP's Roy Wilkins demanded effective fair employment legislation to empower African Americans to claim the dignity and self-respect of those who had equal access to jobs. CORE's James Farmer, whose speech was read because he was imprisoned in Louisiana for civil rights activism, pledged direct action until every black American had work that matched their skills, enough food to feed their families, and schools that expanded the minds of their children. John Lewis of SNCC asked what good the current civil rights bill would do for a maid earning $5 a week working for a family whose income exceeded $100,000. Martin Luther King gave the final speech of the day. Instead of focusing on the specific demands of the rally, King used his time to express the transcendent purpose of the struggle and to articulate the transformation—the dream—that sustained the movement forward. With the Lincoln Memorial at his back and gazing at the Jefferson Memorial in the distance, King reiterated how the full promise of American citizenship had eluded African Americans. One hundred years after Lincoln issued the Emancipation Proclamation, the black masses remained exiles in their own country, trapped in islands of poverty surrounded by vast seas of prosperity. King vowed that African Americans would continue the struggle until they fulfilled the dream of an America that lived up to its creed of justice, equality, and freedom for all.

Figure 5.2. Civil rights demonstrators on the National Mall, Washington, D.C., carry signs that announce the core demands of the March on Washington for Jobs and Freedom, August 28, 1963. Walter P. Reuther Library, Wayne State University.

Over the next few years, civil rights activists accomplished much of their agenda. In 1964 Congress passed the Civil Rights Act, a sweeping assault on the legal foundation of Jim Crow. The law prohibited discrimination in all public places such as hotels and restaurants, theaters and stadiums, restrooms and drinking fountains, terminals and ticket counters, and any other accommodation engaged in interstate commerce. Under the law, state and local governments could no longer deny people access to public facilities—parks, playgrounds, swimming pools, libraries—on the basis of race (as well as on the grounds of religion and national origin). Any agency that received federal funding could no longer discriminate. The law also empowered the federal government to file lawsuits to enforce the desegregation of public schools. Crucially, Title VII of the law prohibited employment discrimination and thus required companies to integrate factory facilities, unions to merge segregated locals, and both to eliminate racially segregated systems of seniority and all other forms of employment discrimination. A year later, in August 1965, Congress passed the Voting Rights Act, which banned the elaborate practices that southern states used to deny the ballot to African Americans. By restoring the right to vote to black southerners, the act completed the legal demise of Jim Crow.

Despite these undeniable political and legislative achievements, March on Washington organizers knew that without full and fair employment, African Americans would remain second-class citizens and lack the ability to participate in the full promise of American life. In the wake of landmark civil rights legislation, black activists warned that the success of winning racial equality before the law would do little to generate an economic transformation capable of alleviating the problems that confronted millions of black Americans. Yet the menace of unemployment continued to threaten black neighborhoods. Unless the United States invested massive sums in schools, job training, social welfare, and public works, declared civil rights leaders, African Americans would lack the resources to improve their living conditions. The recent civil rights legislation, Randolph pointed out, failed to provide affordable housing, quality education, access to good jobs, or a guaranteed income. Even if the Civil Rights Act of 1964 promised to end employment discrimination, Herbert Hill noted that the act would not enforce itself and required the activism of workers to compel the government to intervene. In assessing the challenges that confronted civil rights activists, King reminded Americans that the Civil Rights Act and the Voting Rights Act had cost the country little. It required no expenses or taxes to permit blacks to sit at lunch counters or cast ballots in elections. The real costs, he asserted, lay ahead. Expanding payrolls would be far harder and costlier than expanding voter rolls.

Still, labor and civil rights activists had achieved much since the end of World War II. They won scores of state and municipal fair employment laws, challenged racial discrimination within the labor movement, and most importantly, dismantled the segregationist political order of the South. Now that the law no longer sanctioned racial discrimination and exclusion in employment, African Americans anticipated a new era of fair employment that promised unprecedented opportunities to move into the economic mainstream of American society. The victories of the civil rights movement would provide African American workers with access to good-paying union jobs, occupational mobility, decent housing in safe neighborhoods, and good schools, making possible the emergence of a blue-collar black middle class. Most black workers, however, understood that change under the new laws would neither be immediate nor automatic. They knew that they could not remain content with what they had accomplished. Having mobilized thousands of blacks in hundreds of local movements in the 1950s and 1960s, many black labor activists now prepared to forge new forms of activism to fulfill the promise of the new legislation and break open the remaining barriers to the American workplace.

~

CHAPTER SIX

Opening the American Workplace

Late in the afternoon of February 1, 1968, Echol Cole and Robert Walker—two African American sanitation workers in Memphis, Tennessee—took shelter from a cold, driving rainstorm inside their crew's aging garbage truck. They rode out the downpour as the truck headed for the dump, when suddenly something—perhaps an electrical shortage—accidentally activated the truck's garbage compressor. The driver pulled the truck over, hopped out, and tripped the safety switch, but to no avail. The compactor's hydraulic ram had already crushed the two men to their deaths. The accident left the widows of the two men practically penniless. Neither Cole nor Walker had been able to afford the expensive insurance policy that the city offered its employees, nor did they qualify, as unclassified, hourly employees, for coverage under the state's workmen's compensation program. The city had no obligation to pay the widows anything more than one month's severance pay. More than a week after the accident, while the bodies of the deceased workers remained in a funeral home and the widows struggled to collect the money to cover burial expenses, the city offered each family a modest settlement of $500, which was insufficient to cover the $900 funeral costs. Without the means to pay for her husband's burial, Earline Walker, the pregnant widow of Robert Walker, had no choice but to transport her husband's body to Mississippi and bury him in a pauper's grave near the Delta community where they had once lived as sharecroppers.

Infuriated by the city's response to the deaths of their fellow workers and fed up with deplorable working conditions, nearly 1,3000 sanitation workers refused, without notice, to report for work on February 12, the birthday of Abraham Lincoln. They demanded a pay raise, union recognition, a written contract, increased wages, guaranteed benefits, and improved working conditions. The mayor and city council refused to heed the strikers' demands, claiming that they were in violation of a state law that prohibited public employees from striking. The city's intransigence sparked outrage throughout black Memphis. Under the leadership of Rev. James Lawson, a veteran strategist of the civil rights movement, a group of more than 150 ministers and community activists rallied the black community behind the strikers.

The workers and their supporters soon united behind the slogan "I Am a Man." With that simple phrase, striking sanitation workers asserted their dignity and demanded to be treated as men—as full and equal citizens—and not like children. By asserting their manhood rights, the strikers echoed the themes of the Brotherhood of Sleeping Car Porters (BSCP) organizing campaign of the 1920s and 1930s. Thirty years after the BSCP won its historic labor contract from the Pullman Company, sanitation workers in Memphis still labored in a paternalistic environment that demanded black subservience and deference to the white elites who governed the city. Ultimately, the slogan connected the demand for dignified labor with the rights of citizenship and linked the cause of the sanitation workers to the aspirations of all African Americans to achieve the full realization of equality in the wake of the civil rights movement.

The labor–civil rights coalition that emerged in Memphis impressed both national civil rights strategists and labor leaders. They hoped that the strike could serve as a model for the kind of mass mobilization needed to lead the civil rights movement into what Martin Luther King called its second phase, the realization of equality through the elimination of poverty, illiteracy, and slums. Speaking before a mass audience in Memphis in support of the strike in March, King echoed a key metaphor from his speech at the March on Washington in 1963. The sanitation workers reminded the nation that most African Americans continued to perish "on a lonely island of poverty in the midst of a vast ocean of material prosperity." Though they lived in a rich nation, the working poor earned "starvation wages" to perform vital labor that the country neither valued nor recognized. Union rights were thus an essential civil rights demand. By highlighting "the economic issue," the strike, declared King, took the movement "beyond purely civil rights" and converted it into a struggle "for genuine equality, which means economic equality."[1]

Figure 6.1.   The success of the 1968 sanitation workers' strike in Memphis depended upon the wider support of the black community. Black women especially helped to sustain the economic boycott of downtown Memphis in support of the sanitation workers throughout the strike. Special Collections, University of Memphis Libraries.

Indeed, black workers across the country in the late 1960s and 1970s adopted what black labor organizer William Lucy called the Memphis spirit. Black activists built labor–civil rights coalitions in which black unionists drew their strength from community support networks. A new confidence and pride borne of the civil rights movement created an upsurge in black unionism. Black workers joined existing unions in large numbers or established new unions that drew thousands of low-wage, unorganized workers—trash collectors, hospital workers, municipal transit drivers, teachers, social service employees, and workers in the retail and service trades—into the labor movement. More than forty-five AFL-CIO unions counted substantial numbers of black members. The number of black workers in the Laborers' International Union and the International Longshoremen's Association, for example, exceeded 40 percent. Several other unions such as the American Federation of State, County and Municipal Employees (AFSCME) and the Steelworkers had black memberships of more than 20 percent. According to some estimates, nearly one-third of black workers belonged to a union in 1970, and close to 20 percent of the country's 14 million union members were African American. Black unionism was part of a broader working-class rebellion of the late 1960s and 1970s. During these years, American workers walked off the job in more than 1,400 spontaneous and unauthorized strikes per year. In 1970 alone, more than 3 million workers, one out of every six union members, participated in more than 5,700 strikes. This new mood of rebellion gave civil rights activists hope that a new stage of the civil rights movement had dawned, one that understood that political and social justice could not emerge without economic justice.

Although many of the jobs that African Americans initially secured in the public sector paid poorly and required few skills, public employment nevertheless offered unprecedented benefits and advantages over casual labor and personal service. Public employees generally enjoyed greater job security, earned higher wages, and collected more generous benefits than African Americans who worked in the private sector. For many African Americans, regular, full-time work for the government was a source of pride and respectability. Will Robinson, whom the city of Chicago hired as one of its first black bus drivers in 1945, recalled how he and his coworkers showed off the prestige of their job by wearing their drivers' uniforms rather than suits to Sunday church service. Public-sector employment also had broader social and community significance. States and municipalities emerged as critical employers of black workers at the time that deindustrialization and automation accelerated the decline of manufacturing jobs. For many African American families, especially in the urban North, access to unionized public-sector work provided the economic security that had long eluded their parents and grandparents. Work within government agencies that provided social services such as departments of housing, social welfare, and public health particularly attracted black women. Black social service employees used the authority of their positions within local welfare bureaucracies to ensure that local government responded to the needs of black urban communities.

Unionization vastly improved working conditions for African Americans in the public sector. Before the 1960s, few public employees belonged to unions, and many states and cities had laws that prohibited such workers from joining unions or going on strike. In 1962 President John F. Kennedy issued Executive Order No. 10988, which granted federal employees the right to engage in collective bargaining, which encouraged federal workers to unionize. Kennedy's order also created an atmosphere conducive to union organizing among public-sector workers at the state and municipal level. Under mounting pressure from newly organized and increasingly politicized teachers, nurses, transit drivers, and sanitation workers, thirty-seven states passed laws granting public workers the right to organize unions and negotiate collective bargaining agreements. Public-employee unionism became the fastest growing sector of the labor movement in the late 1960s and 1970s. Between 1955 and 1973 membership in public employee unions exploded from four hundred thousand to more than 4 million, paralleling the growth of private-sector unionism in the 1930s during the New Deal.

Blacks, particularly sanitation workers, were central to this upsurge in public-sector unionism. Their militant activism won both broader union recognition and the right to strike for public employees. For nine weeks the striking sanitation workers in Memphis and thousands of their supporters defied court injunctions, mass arrests, police intimidation, curfews, martial law, and the use of strikebreakers. On March 28, 1968, King and his staff from the Southern Christian Leadership Conference came to Memphis to stage a mass, nonviolent march in support of the strike. When the march degenerated into a violent melee under the pressure of police intimidation, organizers disbanded the march, but King vowed to return to Memphis to hold a second march in early April. On the night of April 3, in the midst of a powerful thunderstorm and weakened by illness and a sore throat, King addressed the sanitation workers and their supporters who gathered at a local church. He urged his audience to maintain their unity, warned that the powerful maintained their rule by keeping the oppressed fighting among themselves, and insisted that they keep their focus on the injustice of poverty. He concluded with a rousing declaration that God had taken him to the mountaintop and showed him the promised land. "I may not get there with you," he cried, but "we as a people will get to the promised land."[2] The next evening, while King stood on the balcony of the Lorraine Motel, a sniper's bullet killed him. King's assassination put mounting pressure on municipal administrators to settle the strike. Finally, on April 16 the city settled with the strikers, meeting most of the union's demands, including wage increases, grievance procedures, guarantees of fair treatment, and most importantly, union recognition.

In the wake of Memphis, municipal employers around the country feared that hard line tactics against insurgent black strikers ran the risk of transforming labor disputes into racial conflicts that invited political risk and bad publicity. Lyn Andrews, the city manager in St. Petersburg, Florida, learned that lesson a few months after the Memphis strike settled. When the city's mostly black garbage workers called an illegal strike in May, Andrews refused their demand for a pay raise and instead threatened to fire the strikers and hire replacement workers. Inspired by the success of sanitation workers in Memphis, more than fifty workers defied Andrews and remained on strike. Andrews quickly terminated them, ordered replacement workers to collect city trash under the protection of police escorts, and declared victory, boasting that there was no one to negotiate with because all strikers had been fired. Andrews's stance backfired. More than 150 other black sanitation workers walked off the job in sympathy, transforming the dispute into a struggle over the right to strike rather than a fight over wages. The strike galvanized the black community. Black churches and civil rights organizations collaborated and launched a series of marches and rallies around city hall that brought national attention to the conflict. With racial tensions mounting, Andrews resolved to prevent the city from becoming the epicenter of a civil rights conflict and settled the strike and rehired the strikers.

Over the next several years, strikes by sanitation workers in other cities followed a similar pattern. Although municipal employers had the legal authority to terminate strikers, they increasingly refrained from using it. Labor management experts recommended that city officials opt for a middle ground and negotiate with striking public employees. Many even advocated that states and municipalities repeal laws that banned strikes by public-sector workers. Even when city officials still fancied that they had the absolute power to crush labor militancy, mounting public pressure forced them to change course. In 1972, when Atlanta's white mayor Sam Massell threatened to terminate 1,400 striking black sanitation workers, civic groups, churches, and civil rights activists mobilized to convince him to come to terms with the strikers. Maynard Jackson, the African American vice mayor, came to the strikers' defense and urged the mayor to negotiate. Fearful of bad publicity that would damage his political career, Massell relented, rehired the strikers, and agreed to a 4.3 percent pay raise. By 1975, then, the labor militancy of black sanitation workers had forced most city administrators to negotiate with rather than punish striking public employees, effectively eliminating legal bans on public-sector strikes.

Successful strikes by sanitation workers underscored the critical importance of labor activism in fulfilling the promise of the civil rights movement. Throughout the 1970s and the 1980s, public-sector unions that had a significant African American membership operated as some of the most important black political organizations in urban America. They mobilized black voters and helped to elect African Americans to a range of city-wide political offices, pressured city halls to influence public policy to deliver social services and resources to meet the needs of black residents, and shifted the balance of political power in cities by significantly weakening the influence of their political opponents in city government. Unionized African American sanitation workers also paved the way for other public employees, black and white, to unionize and to secure collective-bargaining agreements that guaranteed better wages and fair working conditions. In many cities they helped to organize firefighters, policemen, city court clerks, auto inspectors, and workers in city zoos, public hospitals, boards of education, housing authorities, and departments of parks and recreation. Perhaps the strikes of sanitation workers made their biggest difference by opening workplaces and job opportunities to African Americans that had always been closed. Before 1968, recalled Taylor Rogers, one of the veterans of the Memphis sanitation workers' strike and who subsequently became president of their union, local banks only employed African Americans as janitors. But in the wake of the strike, they all hired tellers. Many of the schools began to hire black teachers and black principals, and city hall became one of the major employers of African Americans in Memphis. As James Robinson, another sanitation striker explained, the strike made a big difference not just to the sanitation workers, but to all black workers who now worked in places that they never had before.

As black labor activism succeeded in winning higher wages, better working conditions, and good benefits for African American government workers, public employment emerged as one of the best jobs available to working-class blacks in the last third of the twentieth century. The public sector—including jobs in police and fire departments, post offices, public hospitals, government agencies, urban transit systems, public school districts, and departments such as public works and parks and recreation—employed more than 18 percent of all black men. It remains the second biggest employer of black women, more than 23 percent of whom work at government jobs. African Americans in the public sector earned 25 percent more than black workers in the private sector, experienced greater occupational mobility and career paths working for the government, and earned more money relative to whites than they did in the private sector. Even if some of these jobs paid poorly and had limited prestige, such as laundry workers in veterans' hospitals, ground maintenance crew members, security guards at government buildings, and food service employees at government installations, they enabled many African Americans to ascend into the middle class. These jobs were stable and offered health insurance, paid vacations, sick leave, and pensions. Unionism had conferred dignity and respect to a whole range of occupations that lacked status and had offered little hope for social mobility. As one black union leader recognized at the conclusion of a successful strike in the late 1960s, "From now on, we won't be just garbage men. We're city employees."[3]

But even as black labor activists won improved working conditions within the public sector, unionists confronted limits to what they could achieve. Beginning in the late 1970s, new economic and political circumstances began to check the power and influence of public-sector unions. Because of economic stagnation and high inflation at the end of the decade, many local governments confronted fiscal crises that they managed through budget cuts, wage freezes, and a new confrontational approach with public-sector unions. At the same time, an emergent anti-tax movement galvanized city residents who had grown tired of strikes by bus drivers, school teachers, and trash collectors. City administrators across the country reached the conclusion that they could no longer meet the demands of their public employee unions. These conditions first surfaced in Atlanta in 1977 when the city's sanitation workers went on strike to demand a modest pay raise to keep pace with 7 percent inflation. Maynard Jackson, the city's first black mayor and a man who had supported striking sanitation workers when he was vice mayor in 1972, resolved to fight rather than negotiate with the union. Jackson fired striking unionists and hired replacement workers, forcing the union to call off the strike and admit defeat. By speaking the language of fiscal responsibility and expressing sympathy for taxpayers, Jackson made the union's demands seem excessive, selfish, and irresponsible and consequently won much black public support for his tactics. Other municipalities soon adopted the Atlanta model. Throughout the country, budget woes converted black elected officials, who had once been allies of black labor activists, into hard-bargaining employers. Public-sector unions survived, but their ability to strike had been weakened. Consequently, labor conflicts increasingly evolved into budget disputes as they did in Atlanta in 1977 rather than expanding into community struggles over social and racial justice as they had in Memphis in 1968.

Black labor militancy also emerged within older industries such as steel, transportation, and automobiles to challenge the slow pace of racial change both on the shop floor and within industrial unions. In the late 1960s, inspired by the language and aspirations of the civil rights movement, and growing out of the long-standing black pursuit for genuine and equitable power within the labor movement, a new breed of black unionists emerged who made their demands more explicit. When they concluded that their unions had become complacent and failed to take decisive action against employment discrimination, Jim Crow unionism, and deteriorating working conditions, black insurgents formed independent caucuses, study groups, and ad hoc committees within their unions. They used their race-based organizations to challenge unresponsive white union leaders, expand their voice and power within their plants and unions, and fight for the changes they demanded. In New Orleans and Baltimore, black dock workers, for example, refused to unload cargo imported from the African nation of Rhodesia in protest of that country's racially oppressive apartheid government. In Pittsburgh black bus drivers went on strike to protest the suspension of a fellow driver who wore a button in support of Angela Davis, a black radical political activist on trial in California. In Atlanta black workers across the city staged a general strike against employment discrimination and intolerable working conditions in factories, hospitals, and chain grocery stores. In all of these cases from the late 1960s and early 1970s, black workers acted with a growing sense of militancy, drew upon widespread community support, and demonstrated their ability to tie up key sectors of the American economy.

The most radical black caucus movement emerged in the automobile plants of Detroit. In the spring and summer of 1968, black workers at the Chrysler Corporation's Dodge Main plant—many of whom had joined the newly organized Dodge Revolutionary Union Movement (DRUM)—walked out in a series of spontaneous and unauthorized strikes that crippled production. DRUM's insurgency alarmed city administrators, corporate executives, and UAW officials, all of whom explained the walkout as a sudden outburst orchestrated by a handful of militant radicals. On the contrary, DRUM voiced deep resentments that had long been growing among black workers at Dodge Main. During the 1960s, automakers expanded employment. Chrysler alone, the largest employer of African Americans among the major automobile manufacturers, practically doubled its payroll to more than 130,000 workers, about one-quarter of whom were black. Many of the new recruits to the industry were black men under the age of the thirty who worked heavy, dirty, monotonous, and dangerous production jobs. Chrysler made the work even tougher when it introduced a series of innovations to increase production from forty-nine to sixty-eight cars an hour. The speed up of production quickened the pace of work on the assembly line, but workers received neither extra pay for the increased work nor did managers place more workers on the line to ease the stress of the job. White foremen and supervisors routinely barked orders at black workers and spoke to them with racial slurs and derogatory insults; black workers who could not keep the pace lost their jobs; and others quit under pressure, creating a high degree of labor turnover. Many of these young black workers equated the demeanor of white foremen to the manner in which Detroit's white police force patrolled black inner-city neighborhoods. In 1967 a series of violent riots erupted in Detroit's ghettos, sparked in part by outrage at police brutality. After the riots, a group of black labor activists began to publish *The Inner City Voice*, a radical newspaper that they circulated in black neighborhoods.

Under the terms of union contracts, these recently hired black workers had to join the UAW, which they found unresponsive to their grievances. Black workers complained that union officials concentrated on negotiating wages and benefits but ignored the deteriorating conditions under which production workers labored and dismissed black workers' grievances about the culture of racial hostility on the shop floor. Black workers exerted little influence in shaping union policy because union officials allowed retired white union workers to vote in UAW elections. Black workers also expressed impatience with the union's bureaucratic procedures for calling a strike, which they complained moved too slowly and forced workers to endure intolerable conditions.

Black workers were thus poised to take matters into their own hands. In early May 1968, while most of the local UAW leadership was away at the UAW annual convention in Atlantic City, black workers joined a wildcat strike over speedups on the production line. The UAW intervened, settled the grievances, and enabled the workers to return to their jobs. Even though white women had initiated the first walkout and white and black workers participated in the wildcat work stoppages, Chrysler managers blamed black workers, especially some of the militant radicals, for the disruption. They promptly fired seven and suspended a dozen other black workers. The UAW refused to defend the terminated strikers. In response, DRUM mobilized to demand that Dodge reinstate the workers. Over the next several weeks, DRUM activists organized rallies and demonstrations, and on July 8, they called for a walkout in which 70 percent of Dodge Main's black workers went on strike. For five days, local black college students and other community supporters joined workers on the picket lines. The strike pressured Local 3 of the UAW to negotiate for the reinstatement of five of the seven black workers that Dodge had fired. Dodge also agreed not to fire anyone for the July walkout.

DRUM's success inspired black workers to organize similar groups at other plants in the Detroit area. Revolutionary union movements emerged in Ford Motor Company and General Motors plants as well as other area companies such as Blue Cross and Blue Shield, United Parcel Service, Henry Ford Hospital, and the *Detroit News*. Calling themselves the vanguard of the new social revolution, black activists soon established the League of Revolutionary Black Workers to coordinate their efforts and connect their workplace struggles to the broader problems that confronted their communities outside the plant. To do so, the league hoped to transform the UAW from a complacent bureaucracy into an aggressive advocate for the needs of its production workers and a political force for progressive reform. Accordingly, it urged UAW to fire its long-time president, Walter Reuther, elect instead a black president, and hire an executive board and paid staff that would be 50 percent black. League activists insisted that the UAW must resist speedups on the production line, agitate for a five-hour work day and a four-day work week, and demand the doubling of wages of all production workers. Beyond the shop floor, the league called for such things as a general strike against the Vietnam War and advocated that the federal government divert tax revenues from defense spending and use them instead to meet the social needs of the nation's working poor.

Even though the black reform caucuses challenged racism on the shop floor and within the union bureaucracy, they attempted a wider appeal to all workers to unite against what they identified as the inhumane working conditions in the industry. Many of the black caucuses distributed mimeographed shop papers that they distributed to workers. *The Stinger*, a paper edited by black workers at the Mack Avenue Chrysler plant in Detroit, made a key distinction between the "whitey" who worked on the shop floor and the "whitey" who either represented company interests or served as a union bureaucrat. As the black editor explained, although black workers had organized to fight racial discrimination, their movement attracted the interest of many white workers because it challenged the automation and speedups that threatened all workers. Moreover, the UAW's failure to protect production workers from the quickening pace of the assembly line left all shop-floor workers vulnerable. As one black activist explained, many white production workers who had initially been reluctant to join cause with "raving black militants" came to understand that they shared many of the same grievances with the company and the union.[4]

Black caucuses never became a national force capable of transforming the UAW bureaucracy or of enabling the rank and file to take control of the union. For one thing, labor turnover among young black workers made it difficult for the league to sustain their organization and its militant focus. The movement's self-described revolutionary leaders often spent more time trying to convert black workers into disciples of radical, abstract political theories, which failed to inspire young men who were more concerned about the practical, everyday problems that they confronted on the shop floor. Many black nationalist members championed a racial exclusivity that compromised their ability to appeal to and connect with white workers who shared many of their shop-floor grievances. Revolutionary union leaders often alienated other potential allies when they criticized older black UAW unionists, dismissing them in crass, abusive, and derogatory terms. Union officials responded to the league by addressing some of the insurgency's basic demands. They appointed more African Americans to the UAW staff, supported the election of blacks to leadership positions within union locals, and implemented a series of other reforms that partially restored many black workers' confidence with the UAW. Still, the union's response ultimately did more to create token change and left a series of problems unresolved, including blacks' continued exclusion from most skilled jobs and ongoing racial tensions on the shop floor and within the union hall.

African American workers also pursued legal action—which emerged as another important form of black labor activism in the years following the civil rights movement—to compel the federal government to enforce new equal employment rights guaranteed under the Civil Rights Act of 1964. Title VII of the act prohibited employers, unions, and employment agencies from discriminating on the basis of race, color, religion, sex, or national origin. It defined categories of unlawful employment practices and created a new federal agency—the Equal Employment Opportunity Commission (EEOC)—to address complaints and monitor compliance. Much like President Franklin D. Roosevelt's Executive Order No. 8802, Title VII committed the power and authority of the federal government to the elimination of racial discrimination in the workplace and to the protection of the employment rights of African Americans. Despite the promise of federal equal employment law, nothing about it—warned the NAACP—suggested that it was self-enforcing. Congress limited the enforcement powers of the EEOC, only authorizing it to achieve voluntary compliance through negotiation and persuasion. If the commission failed to mediate a resolution within sixty days, complainants could then file civil suit against alleged violators. The law thus placed the burden of proving employment discrimination onto workers who had to file complaints and ultimately seek remedies through the courts. Furthermore, because Congress provided the commission with a limited budget and a skeletal staff, the EEOC soon confronted a backlog of cases that took months if not years to resolve. By itself, the law brought no immediate end to workplace discrimination.

Black workers understood this. Sharing the NAACP's conviction that the federal government would only intervene on their behalf if they came forward to file grievances, more than fifteen thousand black workers filed complaints within the first eighteen months of the law, far exceeding the number that the architects of the legislation anticipated. By the mid-1970s, the EEOC received more than fifty-five thousand complaints a year. In Memphis, for example, the local NAACP forwarded more than four hundred complaints to the EEOC between July 1965 (when the law went into effect) and May 1967. Black workers complained that city employers, often in collusion with unions, routinely refused to hire or promote them out of menial service positions and maintained a hostile workplace culture of racial deference and servility. Even though they had a range of skills, decades of seniority, and had often trained the white workers who now supervised them, black workers testified that employers rejected their applications for promotion or transfer to higher-paying production jobs. Their affidavits exposed supervisors who bossed black workers with abusive language, who refused to address them with titles of respect, who routinely referred to adult male workers as boys, and who disciplined African Americans for failing to conduct themselves in a manner "consistent with 'Negro behavior.'"[5] One black woman who had secured a promotion to a nurse's position complained that her employer fired her for refusing to wear the green uniform required of black maids. By utilizing the grievance procedures authorized under Title VII, black workers created a public forum in which they articulated their definition of racial justice at work and insisted upon dignity and respect as essential to equal employment.

Despite its limitations, federal equal employment law eventually made a profound difference for African Americans. By resorting to the law, black workers, with the crucial assistance of civil rights attorneys, EEOC commissioners, and sympathetic judges, converted Title VII into a weapon that opened broad sectors of the American economy to black workers. Their actions generated a series of court decisions, consent decrees, and federal initiatives that became the basis for a national policy of affirmative action. By the early 1970s, federal administrators had come to regard fair employment as more than an abstract concept but as an enforceable mandate for achieving substantive results. The federal government applied the law not just to ensure the prohibition of discrimination in future hiring but to redress the long-term effects of past discrimination.

The phrase *affirmative action* first surfaced in an executive order that President John F. Kennedy issued in 1961. Under the provisions of the order, firms under contract with the federal government must take "affirmative action" to achieve equal opportunity in hiring and employment. Four years later President Lyndon Johnson, in his commencement address at Howard University, declared that freedom and equal opportunity were essential but not enough to overcome the consequences "of ancient brutality, past injustice, and present prejudice." Committed to a vision of seeking equality as more than "a right and a theory but as a fact and as a result," Johnson issued an executive order that called for affirmative action to achieve fair employment by prohibiting government contractors from discriminating in employment, promotion, job transfers, recruitment, training, and wage rates.[6] The Nixon administration created the Philadelphia Plan, which established a formula for achieving hiring targets and goals in construction under government contracts. The administration extended the principles of the Philadelphia Plan to all government contracts that exceeded $50,000. By the early 1970s, the federal government had quadrupled the size of the staff at the EEOC, which now hired legions of African Americans who built the commission into an effective agency for combating racial discrimination and enforcing affirmative action.

The courts also weighed in. In 1967 a federal court ruled in *Ethridge v. Rhodes* that firms must demonstrate that they had integrated their workforce before they could bid on public contracts. In its 1971 landmark decision in *Griggs v. Duke Power Co.*, the Supreme Court ruled that plaintiffs only had to demonstrate a discriminatory effect of past hiring practices, not a discriminatory intent. *Griggs* also upheld the constitutionality of minority hiring targets, promotion goals, and timetables, all key remedies in emerging affirmative action policy. In 1974, the nation's major steel companies, under the pressure of more than four hundred cases pending before the EEOC, signed a consent decree with the federal government. Under the agreement, the industry agreed to a series of targets, goals, and timetables for advancing African American and female workers into skilled positions and established a fund of more than $30 million to compensate the fifty-five thousand workers eligible for back pay under the agreement. By the mid-1970s, state and local governments and many private industries, often to avoid the expense and burden of litigation, voluntarily adopted affirmative action plans based on federal regulations.

The battle to integrate the cotton textile and paper manufacturing industries in the South reveals the critical role that black workers played in compelling federal officials to implement and enforce equal employment law. Before 1965, the southern cotton textile industry—the region's largest employer—excluded African Americans from production jobs, a practice that had long been the custom of mill operators and enforced by state law in places such as South Carolina. More than eight hundred thousand people worked in the southern textile industry, which dominated the economy of the Piedmont region, accounting for nearly 45 percent of all manufacturing jobs in the Carolinas. The work required little skill or experience, paid low wages, was nonunion, and subjected people to dangers and health risks such as brown lung disease. Nevertheless, jobs in textile mills offered white men and women with limited education far more than most work available to African Americans. White textile workers in North Carolina in 1967, for example, earned more than twice as much as the state's nonwhite workers. By contrast, the southern paper industry hired many more African Americans than cotton textiles did, but these manufacturers confined blacks to jobs in the wood yard and to other heavy, outdoor manual work. Unlike in textiles, most workers in the paper industry belonged to a union, which colluded with employers to restrict African American job prospects. The unions that represented paper mill workers relegated blacks to segregated locals with limited influence in union policy and negotiated collective bargaining agreements that protected the wages and status of white workers through racially segregated lines of promotion and a discriminatory seniority system that prevented blacks from ever advancing to skilled and supervisory positions. Employers consistently denied that they discriminated and objected to efforts to compel them to comply with Title VII. As one paper mill executive remarked, blacks simply lacked the educational opportunity and experience to be considered good prospects for skilled work.

Given the pervasive unwillingness of employers to comply with Title VII, black workers seized upon the law's provision that granted them the right to sue for fair treatment. Between 1965 and the mid-1970s, the NAACP assembled a team of attorneys and investigators and filed thousands of class-action lawsuits on behalf of black workers in a coordinated effort to abolish what they called labor apartheid in the South. They interviewed thousands of defendants and collected a wealth of evidence from men and women who attended community meetings and turned over compelling evidence, some of it decades old, documenting how they had been denied opportunities in favor of whites. In a series of landmark cases that affected both the textile and the paper industries, federal judges ruled that firms and unions were guilty of sustaining systematic patterns of racial discrimination in hiring and promoting. The courts ordered companies to cease discriminatory hiring practices, abolish segregated systems of seniority and promotion, and hire more African Americans. Black litigants thus exerted the pressure that accelerated the integration of these workplaces. By 1980, African Americans constituted 25 percent of all production workers in the southern textile industry. Black women made particularly impressive gains. In South Carolina alone, the number of black women who worked in the textile industry increased from 240 in 1960 to more than 8,000 by 1970. Change came slower to the paper industry. Whereas blacks sued for access to entry-level production work in cotton textiles, they battled for promotion to higher-paying jobs in the paper mills. Still, by the late 1980s, African Americans constituted 25 percent of all workers in the industry, up from 15 percent in the mid-1960s. Once the industry adopted a new system of seniority, blacks began to advance to positions as millwrights, mechanics, and even supervisors.

Many white workers did not quietly accept these dramatic changes, and their resistance made implementation of these court orders slower and more difficult than overall employment numbers suggest. When companies integrated factory facilities, white workers responded by refusing to use company bathrooms, cafeterias, and water fountains. At one paper mill, white workers rented a building across the street in which they constructed their own shower and locker facilities. When African Americans gained access to production jobs in the textile industry, many white workers responded by refusing to train the black new hires. In both industries, disgruntled white workers created a culture of intimidation in which they persecuted black workers who aspired to advance within the company. After A. C. Sherrill became the first African American promoted to a production job at the J. P. Stevens and Company textile plant in Stanley, North Carolina, he quickly earned a reputation as one of the best workers on his shift. When he asked for a promotion to supervisor, however, white workers responded with rage. His immediate superior discouraged him, telling him that the plant would not tolerate blacks in a position of authority. Other whites harassed him by stuffing trash in his car, verbally abusing him, and telling him that if he ever became a supervisor that they would all walk out. One even threatened him with a knife. But Title VII had changed the balance of power at work. Sherrill had the ability to challenge the company, and he subsequently became the lead plaintiff in a successful class-action lawsuit against J. P. Stevens for denying promotions to black workers.

As Sherrill's experience underscores, litigation remained vital to blacks in their struggle against entrenched workplace cultures of racial intimidation.

Although African Americans in the South gained access to service sector jobs in hotels and restaurants from which they had long been excluded, they continued to encounter formidable barriers that confined them to menial work well into the 1980s. In 1988, a white couple who managed a Captain D's seafood restaurant in Marianna, Florida, was fired for refusing to "lighten up" their store, company code for reducing the number of black employees on staff. When Tommy Warren, a local attorney, investigated their case, he discovered that their story was no isolated incident but compelling evidence of a systematic culture of racism at Shoney's Inc., the parent company that operated Captain D's, Shoney's, and Big Boy restaurants. Wall Street analysts had long regarded Shoney's as one of the nation's best managed restaurant companies and showered high praise on its rags-to-riches CEO, Ray Danner. Warren teamed up with civil rights attorney Barry Goldstein, and soon they uncovered mounting evidence of Danner's employment strategy: blacks were bad for business. To Danner, blacks lacked the qualifications to manage a restaurant, run a kitchen, or work in positions that made them visible to the dining public, especially in predominantly white neighborhoods. When blacks applied for work, white managers color-coded their applications by blackening the letter "O" in the word Shoney's to sabotage their chances for employment. The company retaliated against low-level white managers who refused to implement their racist policies. Even though the company based its promotions on length of service and job performance, black workers testified that whites with inferior performance records and shorter terms of service received promotions. Others charged the company of hiring inexperienced whites as supervisors over blacks with extensive experience and seniority with the restaurant. The company routinely restricted the number of blacks who could work on any given shift. Black workers endured a working environment that subjected them to relentless verbal, racist abuse. Sharon Johnson told of one harrowing tale on New Year's Eve in 1984. Shortly after midnight, the store's white manager received word that area supervisors were on their way to make a surprise inspection of the premises. In a panic because she had four black waitresses on duty that night and fearful that she would lose her job, the manager pleaded with Johnson and another black waitress to hide and lock themselves in the women's restroom until the supervisors left. Johnson, who had trained most of the white waitress staff at the restaurant, had had enough. In February, she filed a complaint with the EEOC.

It took five years of meticulous and careful class-action litigation to abolish the so-called Danner way at Shoney's. Warren filed suit in 1989, seeking more than one-half billion dollars in back pay and damages as well as an extensive and aggressive affirmative action plan. In 1993, the plaintiffs and

Shoney's finally agreed to a compromise settlement of $132.5 million—the largest ever in a racial discrimination suit—for nearly twenty-one thousand complainants. Under the terms of a consent decree, Shoney's agreed to a plan to hire and promote African Americans. Within a few years of the settlement, Shoney's had made considerable progress toward compliance. In 1995, 12 percent of Shoney's managers were black, up from 1.8 percent in 1988. The number of black assistant managers increased from 5 percent to 21 percent; the number of black dining room supervisors rose from 3 percent to 13 percent; and servers from 7.6 percent to more than 18 percent. Blacks experienced similar changes at the corporation's other restaurants, including Captain D's, where the number of black managers increased to 22.4 percent in 1995, up from less than 10 percent in 1988. By 1996, Shoney's had two black vice presidents, an African American woman on the board of directors, thirteen black-owned franchises, and conducted $17 million in annual business with minority-owned companies. Legal action produced dramatic changes in company culture. Warren praised the turnaround at Shoney's, from a company that systematically thwarted black opportunity to one that gained a reputation among African Americans as an employer where one could get ahead.

By breaking open the doors to the American workplace in the decades after 1965, black labor activists—whether striking sanitation workers, militant unionists, or crusading litigants—helped to elevate the economic status of African Americans throughout the country. Between 1947 and 1973, black family incomes doubled and the poverty rate among them declined by one-third. For the first time in American history, a majority of black workers escaped the ranks of the working poor and stepped into the American economic mainstream. Despite the many drawbacks and limitations of minimum-wage production jobs in a textile mill, such work enabled thousands of black women to escape the drudgery of working as maids and housekeepers in the private homes of whites. After going to work in the mills, many black women bought their first houses, purchased automobiles, and sent their children to college. Integration of the workplace made it possible for many African American industrial workers to have the kind of residential mobility that enabled them to search for better jobs and to purchase homes in safe and stable neighborhoods that gave their children access to a public education in decent schools.

Unprecedented economic opportunity opened a path to the middle class. Whereas before the civil rights movement, the small black middle class was largely confined to the owners of small-scale businesses that catered to a black clientele and a small number of black professionals—lawyers, physicians, teachers—who lived and worked in a segregated world. In the two decades after 1970, especially as access to higher education expanded in part because colleges applied affirmative action policies in admissions, the number of black workers in the professions surged. In 2000, 10 percent of African American men and 15 percent of black women earned college degrees, a remarkable change from 1940 when fewer than 1 percent of black men and 2 percent of black women earned degrees. Many of these went on to earn advanced degrees in business administration, law, and medicine. Partly out of fear of litigation, employers in both the public and private sector reformed their hiring practices not only to employ black professionals but to actively recruit a diverse workforce. At the same time, the expansion of the number of federal contracts to black-owned businesses underwrote the expansion of thousands of black businesses. By the end of the twentieth century, 58 percent of African American households earned an annual income that placed them in the middle class or higher, up from just 38 percent in 1970. The suburbanization of the black population expanded with the growth in black incomes. By 2000, 35 percent of all African Americans lived in suburbs, up from just 13 percent in 1960. Some middle-class African Americans integrated into white middle-class neighborhoods, whereas others built their own affluent enclaves such as Woodmore, in Prince George's County, Maryland, near Washington, D.C., and Baldwin Hills near Los Angeles. Many of these African Americans not only now earned middle-class incomes, they also began to acquire the assets—job security, higher education, home ownership, health insurance, inheritable wealth—that would enable to them to preserve their middle-class status.

As important as these changes were in the material lives of African Americans, the expansion of economic opportunity enabled black workers to claim dignity and respect that the American economy had long denied them. As the sanitation workers of Memphis recognized in 1968, the formal legal equality and desegregation of public space that the civil rights legislation of the 1960s guaranteed was insufficient to eliminate the economic subordination that remained the cornerstone of the racial order of much of American society. In the years after the civil rights movement, black working-class activists overcame insurmountable obstacles and made painful sacrifices that finally broke down the culture of exclusion that had dominated American workplaces and denied generations of black workers their full standing as citizens. The black workers who came of age after the civil rights movement now entered workplaces that had become openly committed to promoting equal opportunity employment. Access to good jobs provided a new generation with the economic security that was essential for their full participation in American life, enabling them to build strong families and communities and plan for futures that promised possibilities rather than dead ends and limits. Corine Cannon, who in 1962 became the first African American to work at Cannon Mills in Kannapolis, North Carolina, understood this essential connection between the right to work and citizenship. The opening of textile jobs enabled black women to finally become "full-fledged citizens," she recalled. "And that comes from their work. You can't even pretend to be free without money."[7]

Yet black labor activism, for all of its accomplishments, had its limits. Thirty years after Title VII went into effect, clear signs had emerged that the employment gains that blacks had made in the wake of the civil rights movement had stalled. Two statistics stand out. First, the racial wage gap, which had narrowed significantly between 1960 and 1975, no longer improved. School desegregation, federal funding on impoverished public school districts, the expansion of public-sector employment, unionization, and equal opportunity law had all combined to reduce wage inequality between blacks and whites. In 1976 African Americans earned annually 73 percent of what white workers did, up from 57 percent in 1960. Yet at the end of the 1990s, that figure remained unchanged. Even African Americans who attained high-status jobs in well-paying professions earned only about two-thirds the salaries of white professionals. Second, the unemployment gap between blacks and whites proved even more enduring than the racial wage gap. Since the 1940s, with only a few brief periods of exception, the rate of unemployment among African Americans has remained twice as high as the rate among white Americans. The legal elimination of job discrimination had thus neither eliminated poverty, unemployment, nor the concentration of African Americans in low-paying, low-status sectors of the economy.

The persistence of racial economic inequality confounded social science researchers and policy analysts. Some experts argued that continuing racial inequality in educational achievement explains the racial employment gap. Although African Americans have far greater access to education in the twenty-first century than they did at the beginning of the civil rights movement, blacks still lag behind whites in the attainment of high school diplomas and college degrees. Because of their lower levels of education, African Americans find themselves confined to low-wage service sector employment and lacking in the skills to escape the lower rungs of the labor market. Other researchers documented connections between expanding rates of immigration, especially after 1980, and depressed wages and lowered employment rates among African Americans, especially low-skilled men. Still others cited the effects of high rates of incarceration among American blacks. In 2009, nearly 40 percent of the 7.2 million Americans detained in the criminal justice system were African American. When inmates left prison and reentered the labor force, they faced tremendous obstacles finding work as many employers refused to hire job applicants with criminal records.

Deeper structural trends in the American economy and the labor market—ones that threatened the economic security of all working Americans—also limited the economic gains that blacks were able to make. Since 1970, when more than one-quarter of all jobs in the United States were in the manufacturing sector, industrial employment has been in steady decline. By 2008, no more than 10.1 percent of American workers held manufacturing jobs, and African American job losses in manufacturing were sharper than that of whites, especially after the early 1990s (see Table 6.1). Over the same period, the real wages and economic opportunity for low-skilled workers, regardless of race, declined dramatically. These so-called race neutral factors, however, contributed significantly to the perpetuation of racial economic inequality. In the late 1960s and 1970s, African Americans gained access to better-paying, higher-skilled employment in manufacturing just as American industries began to go into decline. Thus, even as the southern textile industry opened to African Americans for the first time in the 1970s, the industry as a whole lost more than a half million jobs the following decade, curtailing their ability to break into an industry that had long excluded them. Deindustrialization hit the steel industry particularly hard. In the wake of the 1974 court-ordered consent decree, African Americans finally gained access to promotions to supervisory positions as well as to jobs in departments that had long been dominated by white workers. Yet within a decade, the industry began to hemorrhage jobs. Steel companies that had once employed large numbers of workers entered bankruptcy and eventually closed their factory gates, throwing their remaining employees out of work as well as depriving thousands of retired steelworkers of their health benefits and pension payments. African American steelworkers suffered a disproportionate burden of these layoffs because they worked in those departments that had historically depended upon unskilled black labor. Steel mills replaced open hearth furnaces with more efficient furnaces and adopted processes such as continuous casting that eliminated a whole series of labor-intensive middle steps in steelmaking that reduced energy costs and the need for unskilled black workers. Plant closings devastated black communities that had relied on the steel industry. Shrinking tax revenues tightened municipal budgets, forcing city governments to cut or suspend public services and reduce the number of public employees on their payrolls even as they faced increasing demand to provide social services to families reeling from job loss.

Table 6.1. Percentage of Workers Employed in Manufacturing, by Race, 1979–2007

Year	Black	White	Overall
1979	23.9	23.5	23.8
1985	20.2	20.1	20.4
1990	18.4	18.4	18.6
1995	16.2	16.8	16.9
2000	13.6	15.0	15.1
2005	10.7	11.8	11.9
2007	9.8	11.7	11.6

Source: John Schmitt and Ben Zipperer, "The Decline in African American Representation in Unions and Manufacturing, 1979–2007," Issue Brief, Center for Economic and Policy Research (February 2008), 8.

In April 1985, Richard Hatcher, the black mayor of Gary, Indiana, and other city officials addressed a crowd of dignitaries gathered to celebrate the steel city's newest business: a Wendy's fast-food restaurant. With unemployment over 20 percent, one-fifth of its households living below the poverty line, and the steel industry declaring that it had no plans to expand employment in the mills, Gary welcomed any new business willing to open in the city. Hatcher heralded the coming of Wendy's and the eighty jobs it brought as the first sign of a new economic recovery. Among the first employees of the restaurant were former steelworkers, who, having lost their union jobs in the mills, eagerly accepted the $3.35 hourly wage offered by the hamburger chain. Of course the city would rather have the $15 to $20 hourly jobs that the steel mills once provided, admitted Hatcher, but the city needed to recruit jobs that put people to work before it could be selective.

As the arrival of Wendy's in Gary suggests, African Americans confronted not only a crisis of unemployment at the end of the twentieth century but also a crisis of bad jobs. At the same time that the economy deindustrialized, it generated a proliferation of low-wage, service sector jobs, such as those at Wendy's, that employed a disproportionate number of African Americans. In the 1990s, almost one-fifth of the net job growth in the economy emerged in occupations that ranked in the bottom 10 percent in wages paid. Three-fourths of the workers who took these jobs were either African American or Latino. By contrast, white workers in the 1990s took three-fourths of the new jobs that ranked in the top 20 percent in wages paid, thus contributing to a stark racial polarization of job growth in the decade. Not only were they the lowest-paying jobs in the economy, they provided little, if any, economic security. Those who worked in these occupations did not receive health insurance, retirement plans, or other nonwage benefits. Such work was often temporary or part time with unpredictable and unstable hours. These jobs offered limited opportunities for promotion. Because most of these jobs were in nonunion workplaces, employees lacked protection from arbitrary and abusive supervisors and had to endure unsafe working conditions. In 2000, more than one-quarter of all African Americans worked in occupations that had these characteristics, including nursing home aides, home healthcare workers, cooks, office custodians, hotel maids, cashiers, and secretaries. Not only did these jobs pay poorly, they commanded little dignity and respect. Even though a job as a secretary, for example, relieved black women from the drudgery of domestic service, it offered few rewards, little hope for occupational mobility, and little respect from their supervisors.

The decline of good-paying jobs in manufacturing and the rapid expansion of low-wage employment sparked a sharp decline in the power of unions in the last twenty years of the twentieth century. Although the number of workers who belonged to unions and worked under union contracts fell among all workers, the rate of unionization declined more rapidly among African Americans than it did for the labor force as a whole. In 1983, nearly one-third of all black workers either belonged to a union or worked under a union contract; by 2007 only 15.7 percent of black workers did so.

The decline in black union membership accelerated in the first years of the twenty-first century, dropping by 14.4 percent from 2.5 million union members in 2000 to 2.1 million in 2004. White union membership declined over the same time, but only by 5.4 percent. Consequently, the loss of unionized jobs, and the bargaining power that came with union membership, contributed to the decline in black earning power (just as it did for many white workers). In 2005, for example, the median weekly wage for African Americans declined by 5 percent, whereas it only declined by 1 percent for white workers.

Aggressive anti-unionism by employers, not just industrial decline, contributed to falling unionization rates. In the 1980s and 1990s, foreign automobile manufacturers such as Nissan, Toyota, and Hyundai opened

Table 6.2.   Percentage of Workers in Unions, by Race, 1983–2007

Year	Black	White	Overall
1983	31.7	22.2	23.3
1990	24.2	17.7	18.3
1995	22.2	16.1	16.7
2000	18.9	14.7	14.9
2005	16.5	13.9	13.8
2007	15.7	13.5	13.3

Source: John Schmitt and Ben Zipperer, "The Decline in African American Representation in Unions and Manufacturing, 1979–2007," Issue Brief, Center for Economic and Policy Research (February 2008), 5.

nonunion plants in the South that succeeded in defeating the UAW's vigorous campaigns to organize those factories. Although nonunion workers in the southern automobile industry regarded the pay and benefits packages that they received as welcome alternatives to the overabundant minimum-wage jobs in the region, they labored under the fear that the companies will relocate in search of cheaper labor elsewhere, leaving workers at the mercy of the power of their employer. Other factors contributed to the decline in unionism among blacks. When the U.S. Postal Service automated a number of its processes, such as letter sorting, it reduced its labor force, including thousands of members of the National Association of Letter Carriers and the American Postal Workers Union, both of which had significant numbers of black members. A number of other businesses replaced their unionized black employees with nonunion white workers by relocating from central cities to the suburbs. The Communication Workers of America lost thousands of its black members when customer service call centers moved out of New York City and reopened in regions inaccessible to urban blacks.

Because of the rapid decline of industrial jobs, the growth of low-wage service-sector employment, and the waning influence of unions in the private sector, public employment offered the best jobs available to working-class blacks at the end of the twentieth century. Still, public-sector employment, despite its undeniable advantages, remained contingent upon government budgets. Under pressure from taxpayers to operate government more efficiently, many public administrators at all levels of government began to privatize a whole range of public-sector work. In the 1990s throughout the country, private contractors started collecting trash, cleaning government offices, operating cafeterias, providing security guards, collecting tolls, and paving roads and sidewalks. In doing so, they converted unionized public-sector jobs that carried good benefits into bad jobs with low pay, little security, and limited benefits. Then in the fall of 2008, the catastrophic collapse of the banking and housing sectors precipitated the Great Recession. State and local governments soon faced steep budget shortfalls as tax revenues fell dramatically in the wake of sharp declines in real estate prices, the foreclosures of houses, and a stagnating real estate market. Governments responded by cutting their payrolls. Since the beginning of the recession, state and local governments cut more than 750,000 jobs. Not only did governments reduce their payrolls, but some states such as Wisconsin and Indiana passed new laws that curtailed or eliminated the collective-bargaining rights of public employees, arguing that such measures were necessary to close budget deficits. Even as the private sector slowly recovered from the Great Recession, adding 1.6 million jobs in 2011, state and local governments continued to eliminate jobs in a relentless quest to balance their budgets. Cuts in public-sector spending have a disproportionate impact on black urban communities, for they reduce black employment as well as reduce the social services on which many African Americans depend. Tight government budgets threatened to do to public-sector employment what deindustrialization had done to employment in manufacturing.

The Great Recession that began in 2008 exposed the fragility of the economic gains that blacks had made since the civil rights movement. Rising unemployment and growing foreclosures have created a mounting economic crisis among African Americans. Black unemployment soared after the recession began, to 16.8 percent (up from less than 9 percent in 2007). In the summer of 2012, the unemployment rate among blacks remained high, at 14.4 percent, compared to 7.4 percent among white workers. African American median household income declined sharply in the first decade of the twenty-first century, wiping out the gains in median black income of the 1990s. The percentage of African American households that earned middle-class incomes shrank while the percentage of those living in poverty increased sharply, especially after 2007 (see Table 6.3). Black homeowners and black neighborhoods were far more likely than whites to suffer the impact of the nation-wide foreclosure crisis, which wiped out the savings and retirement accounts of many black families as they struggled to hang on to homes with declining values. Between 2009 and 2012, an estimated 11 percent of all black homeowners lost or were at imminent risk of losing their homes to foreclosure (compared to 7 percent of non-Hispanic whites). The recession thus widened the tremendous wealth gap that had already existed between blacks and whites. The median wealth—the net value of a household's assets against its debts—of African American households declined by 53 percent between 2005 and 2009, from just over $12,000 to less than $6,000. The net wealth of white households also declined, but only by 16 percent, from nearly

Table 6.3. African American Income Brackets, 1970–2010 (percentage)

Year	Upper Class	Upper Middle Class	Middle Class	Working Class	Poverty
1970	0.2	2.2	35.8	33.0	28.9
1980	0.1	3.3	34.6	31.4	30.6
1990	0.5	5.9	37.1	27.3	29.1
2000	1.7	9.3	46.9	27.7	14.5
2010	1.2	8.4	37.2	27.2	25.6

Source: Akiim DeShay, "African American Income," BlackDemographics.com/income (accessed August 10, 2012).

$135,000 to just over $113,000. Most black household wealth was tied up in the declining value of their homes; white families, by contrast, owned other assets, such as retirement funds, pension accounts, and stocks. Foreclosures depreciated the values of adjacent properties, creating far-reaching and long-term indirect costs that threatened not only the financial security of individual families but also the wealth and stability of black neighborhoods and communities.

Forty years after King came to Memphis in support of 1,300 striking sanitation workers and denounced a nation that paid its working poor starvation wages, a new generation of black working poor appeared to be in the making. The decline of manufacturing and the weakening of the labor movement stalled the emergence of King's vision of a robust and sustained second phase of the civil rights movement dedicated to the realization of full equality. Far too many African Americans remained trapped, as King often remarked, on lonely islands of poverty surrounded by vast oceans of material prosperity. In 2008, when the nation elected Barack Obama as the first black president, African Americans remained "almost entirely a working people" who still needed the same resources that all working people did: decent wages, fair employment, affordable housing, secure retirement, health insurance, and quality education. King's dream of genuine, racial equality built upon economic justice remained as elusive as it did during his lifetime.

Despite the persistence of high rates of unemployment among African Americans, the proliferation of bad jobs, and seemingly entrenched income inequality, we should not lose sight of the fact that black workers today encounter a workplace far more open and inclusive than they did forty years ago. That they do so reminds us that people in the past had the vision, courage, and, at times, the ability to change the circumstances that structured their lives. Ex-slaves mobilized to expand the meaning of emancipation, black trade unionists worked across the color line in the Appalachian coalfields and waterfronts of New Orleans, black migrants seized new opportunities for work in the industrial North, community activists built new protest networks in the 1930s, black industrial unionists helped to build the CIO in the 1930s and 1940s, organizers created a March on Washington to pressure the federal government into opening employment to blacks in the defense industry, civil rights activists in the 1950s and 1960s helped to overthrow Jim Crow and challenged the practices of racial exclusion in the labor movement, urban sanitation workers staged numerous strikes in the 1960s and 1970s that improved the working conditions and labor rights of public workers, and waves of black workers filed Title VII complaints. In all of these cases and many others like them, black workers played key, at times even decisive, roles in building the kinds of coalitions and implementing the confrontational strategies that transformed the fortunes of millions of African Americans at work and in their unions. Just as dismal conditions in the past did not entirely dampen the spirit of dissent among black workers, a new generation of black working-class activists will build upon these memories in developing new strategies capable of confronting today's seemingly intractable problems. Having built, against great odds, a more inclusive workplace in the last one hundred years, they will carry on the struggle to defend and expand the rights of work that fulfill the promise of equality.

Notes

Chapter 1

1. W. E. B. Du Bois, *Black Reconstruction in America, 1860–1880* (New York: Harcourt, Brace, 1935), 55–83.

2. Frederick Douglass, quoted in James McPherson, *Battle Cry of Freedom: The Civil War Era* (New York: Oxford University Press, 1988), 354.

3. William T. Sherman, *Memoirs of General W. T. Sherman*, vol. 2 (New York: Charles L. Webster and Co., 1891), 180–81.

4. James A. Garfield, "Oration Delivered at Ravenna, Ohio," in Burke A. Hinsdale, ed., *The Works of James Abram Garfield*, vol. 1 (Boston: J. R. Osgood and Company, 1882–1883), 86.

5. Lieutenant W. B. Stickney to Capt. Thos. W. Conway, July 2, 1865, in Steven Hahn et al., *Freedom: A Documentary History of Emancipation, 1861–1867*, ser. 3, vol. 1, *Land and Labor: 1865* (Chapel Hill: University of North Carolina Press, 2008), 235.

6. Whitelaw Reid, *After the War: A Southern Tour* (New York: Moore, Wilstach, and Baldwin, 1866), 59.

7. William E. Strong to Major-General O. O. Howard, January 1, 1866, "Reports of the Assistant Commissioners," Sen. Exec. Doc. 27, 39th Congress, 1st Sess., p. 83.

8. Captain T. M. K. Smith, quoted in James Smallwood, "When the Klan Rode: White Terror in Reconstruction Texas," *Journal of the West* 25 (October 1986), 7.

9. "Reports of the Assistant Commissioners of Freedmen, and a Synopsis of Laws Respecting Persons of Color in the Late Slave States," Sen. Exec. Doc. 6, 39th Congress, 2d. Sess., pp. 223–24.

10. Frederick Douglass, "What the Black Man Wants," in *Equality of All Men before the Law* (Boston: Press of George C. Rand & Avery, 1865), 37.

Chapter 2

1. Theodore Rosengarten, *All God's Dangers: The Life of Nate Shaw* (New York: Vintage Books, 1974), 499.

2. Richard Wright, *Black Boy* (New York: HarperPerennial, 1991), 188.

Chapter 3

1. "Checking Migration," *Chicago Defender*, August 9, 1919.

Chapter 4

1. "'Forward!' Exhortation of A. Philip Randolph to Congress," *Chicago Defender*, February 22, 1936.

2. Quoted in Horace R. Cayton and George S. Mitchell, *Black Workers and the New Unions* (Chapel Hill: University of North Carolina Press, 1939), 220.

3. Quoted in Thomas J. Sugrue, *Sweet Land of Liberty: The Forgotten Struggle for Civil Rights in the North* (New York: Random House, 2008), 57.

4. Radio Address Delivered by President Roosevelt from Washington, December 29, 1940, in U.S. Department of State, Publication 1983, *Peace and War: United States Foreign Policy, 1931–1941* (Washington, DC: U.S. Government Printing Office, 1943), 598–607.

5. Quoted in Risa L. Goluboff, *The Lost Promise of Civil Rights* (Cambridge, MA: Harvard University Press, 2007), 209.

6. Quoted in Eileen Boris, "'The Right to Work Is the Right to Live': Fair Employment and the Quest for Social Citizenship," in *Two Cultures of Rights: The Quest for Inclusion and Participation in Modern America and Germany*, edited by Manfred Berg (New York: Cambridge University Press, 2002), 140.

Chapter 5

1. Warner Bloomberg Jr., "They'll Go Democratic Anyway: The Negro in Gary, Indiana," *The New Republic*, October 15, 1956, 13–15.

2. Herbert Hill, "Racism within Organized Labor: A Report of Five Years of the AFL-CIO, 1955–1960," *Journal of Negro Education* 30, no. 2 (Spring 1961): 109.

3. George Meany, quoted in F. Ray Marshall, "Unions and the Negro Community," *Industrial and Labor Relations Review* 17, no. 2 (January 1964): 190.

4. James R. Moses, quoted in Thomas Sugrue, *Sweet Land of Liberty: The Forgotten Struggle for Civil Rights in the North* (New York: Random House, 2008), 293.

5. *New York Times*, August 29, 1963.

Chapter 6

1. Martin Luther King Jr., "All Labor Has Dignity," AFSCME mass meeting, Bishop Charles Mason Temple, Church of God in Christ, Memphis, March 18, 1968, in *"All Labor Has Dignity"* edited by Michael K. Honey (Boston: Beacon Press, 2011), 172, 174, 175.

2. Martin Luther King Jr., "To the Mountaintop," AFSCME sanitation strike mass meeting, Bishop Charles Mason Temple, Church of God in Christ, Memphis, April 3, 1968, in *"All Labor Has Dignity,"* edited by Michael K. Honey (Boston: Beacon Press, 2011), 195.

3. Quoted in Joseph McCartin, "'Fire the Hell Out of Them': Sanitation Workers' Struggles and the Normalization of the Striker Replacement Strategy in the 1970s," *Labor: Studies in Working-Class History of the Americas* 2, no. 3 (2005): 70.

4. Charles Denby, "Black Caucuses in the Unions," *New Politics* 7, no. 3 (Summer 1968): 15.

5. Maxine Smith, Executive Secretary of the Memphis NAACP, quoted in Laurie B. Green, "Race, Gender, and Labor in 1960s Memphis: 'I Am a Man' and the Meaning of Freedom," *Journal of Urban History* 30, no. 3 (March 2004): 477.

6. Lyndon B. Johnson, "Commencement Address at Howard University: 'To Fulfill These Rights,'" June 4, 1965, *Public Papers of the Presidents of the United States: Lyndon B. Johnson, 1965,* vol. 2 (Washington, DC: Government Printing Office, 1966), 636.

7. Oral History of Corine Lytle Cannon, in Victoria Byerly, *Hard Times Cotton Mill Girls: Personal Histories of Womanhood and Poverty in the South* (Ithaca, NY: Cornell University Press, 1986), 160.

~

Documents

This Is Not the Condition of Really Freemen

In the autumn of 1865, when the black settlers of the Sherman Reserve learned that they were about to lose their land claims under President Andrew Johnson's proclamation of amnesty, settlers on Edisto Island, South Carolina, appointed a committee to draft appeals to General Oliver Otis Howard, the Commissioner of the Freedmen's Bureau, and to the president. In moving language, their letters convey the deep sense of betrayal among former slaves, their suspicions of the ill intent of their former masters, and their conviction that the ideals of free labor were insufficient to secure the economic conditions necessary for freedom.

Freedmen of Edisto Island to General O. O. Howard, October 1865
General

It Is with painfull Hearts that we the Committe address you, we Have thuroughly considerd the order which you wished us to Sighn, we wish we could do so but cannot feel our rights Safe If we do so,

General we want Homesteads; we were promised Homesteads by the government; If It does not carry out the promises Its agents made to us, If the government Haveing concluded to befriend Its late enemies and to neglect to observe the principles of common faith between Its self and us Its allies In the war you said was over, now takes away from them all right to the soil they stand upon save such as they can get by again working for <u>your</u> late and <u>thier all time enemies</u>.—If the government does so we are left In a more unpleasant condition than our former.

We are at the mercy of those who are combined to prevent us from getting land enough to lay our Fathers bones upon. We Have property In Horses, cattle, carriages, & articles of furniture, but we are landless and Homeless, from the Homes we Have lived In In the past we can only do one of three things   Step Into the public <u>road or the sea</u> or remain on them working as In former time and subject to their will as then. We can not resist It In any way without being driven out Homeless upon the road.

You will see this Is not the condition of really freemen

You ask us to forgive the land owners of our Island, <u>You</u> only lost your right arm. In war and might forgive them. The man who tied me to a tree & gave me 39 lashes & who stripped and flogged my mother & sister & who will not let me stay In His empty Hut except I will do His planting & be Satisfied with His price & who combines with others to keep away land from me well knowing I would not Have any thing to do with Him If I Had land of my own.—that man, I cannot well forgive. Does It look as if He Has forgiven me, seeing How He tries to keep me In a Condition of Helplessness

General, we cannot remain Here In such condition and If the government permits them to come back we ask It to Help us to reach land where we shall not be slaves nor compelled to work for those who would treat us as such

we Have not been treacherous, we Have not for selfish motives allied to us those who suffered like us from a common enemy & then Haveing gained our purpose left our allies In thier Hands There is no rights secured to us there Is no law likely to be made which our Hands can reach. The state will make laws that we shall not be able to Hold land even If we pay for It Land-less, Homeless, Voteless, we can only pray to god & Hope for *His Help*, <u>your Influence & assistance</u> With consideration of esteem

Your Obt Servts

In behalf of the people

Committee

Henry Bram
Ishmael Moultrie
yates Sampson

Henry Bram et al. to Major General O. O. Howard, n.d., B-53, 1865, Letters Received, series 15, Washington Headquarters, Bureau of Refugees, Freedmen, and Abandoned Lands, Record Group 105, National Archives.

Freedmen of Edisto Island to President Andrew Johnson, October 28, 1865

To the President of these United States. We the freedmen Of Edisto Island South Carolina have learned From you through Major General O O Howard commissioner of the Freedmans Bureau. with deep sorrow and Painful hearts of the possibility of goverment restoring These lands to the former owners. We are well aware Of the many perplexing and trying questions that burden Your mind and do therefore pray to god (the preserver of all and who has through our Late and beloved President (Lincoln) proclamation and the war made Us A free people) that he may guide you in making Your decisions and give you that wisdom that Cometh from above to settle these great and Important Questions for the best interests of the country and the Colored race: Here is where secession was born and Nurtured Here is were we have toiled nearly all Our lives as slaves and were treated like dumb Driven cattle, This is our home, we have made These lands what they are we were the only true and Loyal people that were found in posession of these Lands we have been always ready to strike for Liberty and humanity yea to fight if needs be To preserve this glorious union. Shall not we who Are freedman and have been always true to this Union have the same rights as are enjoyed by Others? Have we broken any Law of these United States? Have we forfieted our rights of property In Land?—If not then! are not our rights as A free people and good citizens of these United States To be considered before the rights of those who were Found in rebellion against this good and just Government (and now being conquered) come (as they Seem) with penitent hearts and beg forgiveness For past offences and also ask if thier lands Cannot be restored to them are these rebellious Spirits to be reinstated in thier <u>possessions</u> And we who have been abused and oppressed For many long years not to be allowed the Privilige of purchasing land But be subject To the will of these large Land owners? God fobid, Land monopoly is injurious to the advancement of the course of freedom, and if Government Does not make some provision by which we as Freedmen can obtain A Homestead, we have Not bettered our condition.

We have been encouraged by Government to take Up these lands in small tracts, receiving Certificates of the same we have thus far Taken Sixteen thousand (16000) acres of Land here on This Island. We are ready to pay for this land When Government calls for it and now after What has been done will the good and just government take from us all this right and make us Subject to the will of those who have cheated and Oppressed us for many years God Forbid!

We the freedmen of this Island and of the State of South Carolina—Do therefore petition to you as the President of these United States, that some provisions be made by which Every colored man can purchase land and Hold it as his own. We wish to have A home if It be but A few acres without some provision is Made our future is sad to look upon. yess our Situation is dangerous we therefore look to you In this trying hour as A true friend of the poor and

Neglected race for protection and Equal Rights with the privilege of purchasing A Homestead—A Homestead right here in the Heart of South Carolina.

We pray that God will direct your heart in Making such provision for us as freedmen which Will tend to united these states together stronger Than ever before—May God bless you in the Administration of your duties as the President Of these United States is the humble prayer Of us all.—

In behalf of the Freedmen

Committee

Henry Bram
Ishmael Moultrie
yates Sampson

Henry Bram et al. to the President of the United States, October 28, 1865, P-27, 1865, Letters Received, series 15, Washington Headquarters, Bureau of Refugees, Freedmen, and Abandoned Lands, Record Group 105, National Archives.

The Rural Household Economy

In 1898 the U.S. Congress created the U.S. Industrial Commission and granted it the authority to investigate conditions in American manufacturing, agriculture, and business. On March 23, 1900, Peter Edmondson, a black farm owner from Tennessee, testified before a subcommittee chaired by South Dakota senator James H. Kyle. Edmondson, a former slave, began renting farm land on shares in 1884. Throughout the interview, he describes his faith in his ability to get ahead through hard work, his ambition to own land, and his reliance on the household economy, especially the labor of his wife and dependent children.

Testimony of Mr. Peter Edmondson, 1900

Q. So you think by the same kind of economy practiced in the past that you can get ahead?—A. Yes; that is what I am trying to do. I worked 3 years, and I made 20 bales of cotton a year.

Q. (By Mr. RATCHFORD.) What part of that was your own?—A. Half of that was my own.

Q. (By Senator KYLE.) So you had 10 bales to sell this last year?—A. Yes.

Q. That would amount to how much a bale?—A. All the way from $36 to $38.

Q. Nearly $400?—A. Yes.

Q. During this time were you able to raise some garden truck and keep a pig or two?—A. Yes, sir. I bought two male pigs for $5, and I just weighed them, and they weigh 213 pounds one and 210 the other.

Q. So you were able to save part of this sum of money each year?—A. Yes.

Q. Well, with ordinary good luck, so to speak, in the course of 3 or 4 years you will be able to buy a piece of land?—A. Yes.

Q. That is your ambition?—A. That is my ambition; yes. I have got a good family, and I work them hard.

Q. (By Mr. Ratchford.) How large is your family?—A. I have 8 boys.

Q. All working?—A. I have 3 of age; the balance of them are working.

Q. Your wife work in the field?—A. Yes.

Q. Got any daughters?—A. They are not with me.

Q. Did you work them in the field when you had them?—A. Yes; I worked them in the field to the full extent.

Q. (By Senator Kyle.) That is good education for them?—A. Yes. Yon will never find any in the workhouse or penitentiary when you work them in the field.

Q. You also sent them to school?—A. Yes.

Q. What about the school facilities?—A. Well, they are pretty good, you might say. I sent them over to Mount Zion, over there; they have a good teacher over there.

Q. Average about 3 months in the year, do they?—A. Yes; the time is pretty well out now, and they must come in.

Q. You think the ambition you possess in regard to yourself and family is a characteristic of your race?—A. Yes.

Q. You think they generally work to get ahead?—A. Well, the majority do, and then there is a part that do not, that just want to come out even, and then start again, but that is not my ambition. I do not like that.

Q. Do you think that the opportunities for a colored man are better in the country than in the town?—A. I would take my own in the country before I would in town; yes. I believe a man can make a better living in the country. If he is a man of my standing, wants to farm and wants to work for a living, I believe the country is his place.

Q. Sometimes in town there is a little more cash return?—A. Yes.

Q. More amusements, etc., for the time being, but in the end they do not save as much?—A. No, sir. The dollar comes this week and goes Saturday night.

Q. (By Mr. RATCHFORD.) What part of your success do you owe to your large family? How much in other words, would yon have been able to accumulate as much as you have accumulated if you had but yourself and wife and a couple of children to support?—A. No, sir.

Q. Has every colored farmer the same number of children—the same opportunities that you have?—A. They have the same opportunities that I have—the wife and himself, yes, but do not have the children.

Q. The children are a material help to the family?—A. Yes.

Q. That is to say, they are worth more than it costs to support them and clothe them?—A. Yes.

Q. (By Mr. SMYTH.) It is a good investment to have a large family?—A. If a man has children he has peace at home and peace in the field.

Q. Peace with mankind?—A. Yes.

Source: Testimony of Mr. Peter Edmondson, House Documents, 57 Cong., 1 Sess., No. 179: *Report of the Industrial Commission on Agriculture and Agricultural Labor,* Vol. 10 of the Commission's Report (Serial 4340, Washington, 1901), 501–2.

The Georgia Race Strike

In May 1909, white, unionized railroad firemen went on strike, accusing the Georgia Railroad Company of replacing its white workers with lower-paid black firemen. Thus began the infamous Georgia Race Strike, one of hundreds of such efforts by white workers to force employers to exclude blacks from industrial employment. When the railroad refused to meet the strikers' demands, white residents along the railroad came to the aid of the unionists by mobbing trains operated by black firemen. The black newspaper the Atlanta Independent *captured the national outrage that the Georgia Railroad Strike created among African Americans. While affirming the rights of unions to organize and protect the interests of workers, the editors denounced the white railroad firemen who acted not as unionists in defense of their rights as workers but as a mob determined to oppress the rights of black workers. Episodes such as the race strike on the Georgia Railroad left many African American workers reluctant to consider labor unions as trustworthy allies in their pursuit of economic and industrial equality.*

"The Georgia Railroad Strike and Its Menaces," 1909

The INDEPENDENT believes in the right of Union Labor to organize for mutual protection and helpfulness. The INDEPENDENT believes in the divine law of selfdefense, and if it is necessary to organize and form a cooperative union in order to protect life, secure the rights of labor, or to secure an equitable distribution of its efforts, we stand ready to assist in every way reasonable to affect these just ends. Labor has the God-given right to organize for the purpose of securing just and fair returns for honest service, and for protection against greed and avarice and corporate wealth. But such organization and maintenance must be effected with due regard to the rights of other men and property. Labor in its zeal to protect its inalienable rights must not forget that other people have vested rights equally entitled to respect and consideration. The right of organized labor to petition employer for an equitable adjustment of economic differences, or reasonable grievance can not be denied, but the right to force its opinion and contentions by lawlessness and violence does not lie within the personal right of any individual.

Organized labor in protecting its rights and economic equities must not deny its employer the inalienable right to protect life, limb and property. It is axiomatic that, "Where public injury begins, personal liberty ends." The cause of labor is not promoted by violence. "He that would ask equity must come into court with clean hands." Labor has the personal right to quit work and use reasonable means and persuasion to keep other men from filling their places until their contentions can be heard and adjusted, but it has no right to endanger the peace of the community, confiscate property and throttle commerce to enforce its personal rights. It has no right to use violence to keep other men from filling positions it has voluntarily vacated. When organized labor disregards the rights of other men equally entitled to work, destroys property, and menaces the public good by tying up the mails, paralyzing freight and transportation, it is no longer an economic factor, deserving the protection of the law, but it is a mob that ought to be suppressed by the law. The official of the law who has official knowledge of such disorder and neglects so far as lies in his power to suppress and afford both labor and capital every reasonable protection guaranteed in the law is unfit for the position he dishonors and ought to be impeached.

The Georgia railroad strike, boiled down to its last analysis, is not a manly struggle for industrial efficiency or economic independence. It is nothing less than a cowardly subterfuge and inuendo clothed in the livery of Union Labor for the purpose of oppressing black working men because they are black. It is simply an effort on the part of a certain class of white men who are afraid to stand on their merits against black men and who hope by coercion and violence, to force their employers to choke off helpful competition so they can force their service upon public carriers, with or without merit.

A trust that oppresses labor, confiscates property, and intimidates other men in the exercise of their just rights to work, is none the less a trust, vicious and wicked, because it is operated in the garb of Union Labor. It is just as wicked and hurtful to society for working men without capital to enter into a conspiracy in restraint of trade and commerce, create social disorder and shut off competition in the trade as it is for corporate wealth to enter into a pool to stifle labor and arbitrarily lower or raise the prices of the necessaries of life for the purpose of shutting out competition. . . .

We [African Americas] are daily fitting ourselves in the fields, on the farms, in the shops, in the factories and on the railroads to perform satisfactory and trustworthy service. We are daily preparing ourselves to fit helpfully in the economic life of the South and we are going to hold our own in spite of bias, labor unions and church meetings to the contrary. We are entitled to a chance to make an honest living for ourselves and families and we shall manfully struggle to maintain our rights with due regards to the rights of other men.

Source: "The Georgia Railroad Strike and Its Menaces," *Atlanta Independent,* May 29, 1909.

Black Coal Miners and the Anti-Unionism of the Black Elite

The African American coal miner, Richard L. Davis, worked as a tireless organizer for the United Mine Workers of America (UMWA) in the 1890s. In this article, which appeared in the Labor Advocate, *a working-class newspaper published in Birmingham, Alabama, Davis argues that only employers—what he calls the monied classes—benefit from racial conflict. He denounces a black newspaper, the* Southern Sentinel, *and a black minister whom the coal operators paid to preach against unionism to members of his congregation.*

Richard L. Davis, Administers a Scathing Rebuke to the Colored Ministers and *Southern Sentinel,* 1897

Since coming into the state of Alabama I have not communicated with your valuable paper as I should, yet I assure you that it is not because I do not fully appreciate it. I know of no agent that can do more for the upbuilding of labor's cause better than a good live exponent such as the LABOR ADVOCATE is.

Again, I am sure that if our people would read more they would find themselves in a better condition than they now find themselves, and instead of being in the present unorganized state, they would be in a state of thorough discipline brought about by organized effort.

I have noticed since coming into the state that men, instead of being free men, act more like slaves, and the reasons are plain. One of these reasons is because of the differences between the white and the colored miner. I do not know positively from what source these differences eminate [*sic*], but it strikes me very forcibly that it is the work of the monied classes, who bring about these differences so that they may be enabled to prey upon their ignorance.

Is it not strange that men will allow themselves to thus be made tools of? Do they not know that the monied classes do not care for the color of the I skin so long as the work is performed and at the lowest possible cost?

It is to be hoped that the coal miners whose lot it seems is hardest will learn that a man is a man be he as white as the driven snow or as black as the vidian night.

We find also that those who should do all in their power to elevate the poor laboring man, at least, many of them are engaged trying to make his condition worse. I will cite the *Southern Sentinel* in one instance. In another I will cite a minister of the gospel whom I met only a few days ago, who had been away gathering up new men to go to the already too muchly crowded mines of Walker county and I dare say that on Sunday in the pulpit that self same individual espoused the cause of the lowly Saviour. Oh! consistency thou art a jewel. I sometimes think that the religion of a few years ago is almost a thing of the past and men will stoop to anything if the almighty dollar is there.

This should not be, but it is, and when a preacher resorts to such a low thing as to try to starve his flock for the paltry few dollars that he can get from some soulless corporation it is about time for such to be relegated to the rear. His congregation should allow him to go down into the bowels of the earth and dig out his living like the rest of the common herd.

Source: R. L. Davis, "Administers a Scathing Rebuke to the Colored Ministers and *Southern Sentinel*," *Labor Advocate* (Birmingham, AL), December 25, 1897.

The Great Migration

In 1917 James Weldon Johnson joined the staff of the National Association for the Advancement of Colored People (NAACP). Serving as the association's first black field secretary, Johnson oversaw the NAACP's aggressive nationwide campaign to expand its membership base, especially in the South. The following article from the black newspaper the Baltimore Afro-American *summarizes Johnson's visit to Baltimore, Maryland, in which he made a speech before the local branch of the NAACP. Johnson described what he saw as the political and economic potential of the migration of southern blacks to the urban North, claiming that it opened the greatest opportunity since the end of the Civil War for African Americans to claim the economic rights of citizenship.*

James Weldon Johnson, "A Man's Chance in the North," 1917

That the migration of colored labor to the North on account of the scarcity of white labor due to the European war may be turned into the advantage of securing to the Negroes of this country every right guaranteed other classes of American citizens was asserted by James W. Johnson, organizer for the National Association for the Advancement ct Colored People and contributing editor of the New York Age, in an address at Trinity A M E Church Tuesday evening.

Mr. Johnson was invited here by Bishop John Hurst, a vice president of the association, and despite the fact that the prelate only had two days in which to work up interest more than 400 people heard the organizer speak.

Mr. Johnson detailed a recent visit South, where he interviewed twentysix editors of daily newspapers, one governor and the mayor of a thriving city. He said that he had heart-to-heart talks with the editors and others over the exodus of Negroes Northward, and that they had agreed with him in the view that if the South would retain the larger element of its dependable class of labor that the Negro must have better schools, a larger share of funds spent for municipal betterment, better living conditions in the rural sections and less police persecution, as well as a fair show in the courts.

"Today the South," he went on to say, "is fully alive to the question of Negro migration Northward. Never before has the pocket book of the South been so touched as by this immigration. The Negro now has his greatest opportunity since 1865, and there is a double blessing in the movement Northward. Heretofore the Negro in the North has enjoyed a modicum of civil rights with little or no industrial opportunities. In the South he has, enjoyed no rights, but plenty of industrial opportunities. He now has a chance to live in the North upon a solid economic basis with all rights and privileges.

"I was told by an official of a great railroad that his company could get 1,000,000 colored men. These men scattered through the North, employed at lucrative wages, would have good schools for their children and could cast a ballot that would be counted. In the ballot they would have an instrument in their hands with which they could demand their rights. It is history that a race of people gets nothing that it cannot demand, and our people must prepare to wrest their rights. We now ask the Republicans on our knees to grant us a few rights, and we may wear our knees out in asking the Democrats. If there was from 800,000 to 1,000,000 colored voters from New York to California their power would be such that they would have not to beg for their rights, but they could demand them and the whites will listen, believe me. The Negro all over the country would be benefitted by such a situation.

"If the Negro becomes master of the industrial situation, just as the Irish became financially and politicall powerful through their master and the Italians and Greeks were beginning to do prior to the European war, the Negro problem will be solved. The Northern Negro not only has the key to the situation in the North, but can shape the destiny of his race in the South. . . . A Negro in Massachusetts is not free as long as one in Mississippi is oppressed."

He then declared that Southern Negro leaders must tell the white South what they must do for the race if the Northern migration would be stemmed, and asserted that the Southern white man now has his ears and heart open and is disposed to grant any reasonable demands. The European war, he said, has paved the way for this situation, and means financial and political strength for the race if the matter is handled correctly.

Northern colored people, he declared, cannot hold aloof from their Southern brothers coming North, and to do so would result eventually in a curtailment of the privileges enjoyed by those living North of Mason and Dixon's line. Baltimore could not escape this responsibility of caring for new comers, he said.

He said that the Negro had shown his genious for co-operation and organization along many lines, but that practically nothing had been done in the way of organizing to secure manhood rights. The National Association for the Advancement of Colored People, he asserted, was the one body doing this work, and he bespoke for it larger and more sincere support. . . .

Bishop Hurst declared that he wanted for his son every right and privilege that a white man had for his and that he was willing to contend for the same. The race must be properly organized to demand every right and privilege, he said.

Source: Baltimore Afro-American, January 20, 1917.

A Black Labor Organizer in the Chicago Stockyards

In early July 1919 the Stockyards Labor Council organized a massive, interracial parade and rally on Chicago's South Side as part of its campaign to organize 100 percent of the packinghouse labor force. Black labor organizer John Riley, who wrote a regular column in the black newspaper The Chicago Whip, *offered the following account of the parade. City authorities claimed that the march would incite racial conflict and forced unionists to change their original plans. Riley captures the enthusiasm and optimism of the crowd of native whites, European immigrants, and African Americans who united around a program of shared economic interest.*

John Riley, "Big Parade by Stockyards Workers Features Big Drive for Members," 1919

More than two weeks ago members of the Executive Board of the Stockyard's Labor Council and the Organization Committee planned to have a monster parade and organization demonstration on the South Side for the purpose of showing the numerical strength of the organization which was to terminate into a great mass meeting for the benefit of the workers who have not as yet joined the union.

Someone with more authority and influence than common sense, apparently got in a hard knock by painting a horrible picture of some terrible unseen evil that would be the direct cause of a race riot in case the parade was staged as it had been planned, and most naturally some fell for this capitalistic bunco game. . . .

[Union leaders] were compelled to change the plans to conform with the wishes of those who claimed that they desired to avoid disaster or probably the permit would have been revoked and yet the history of the labor movement has proven beyond all reasonable doubt that when people get together and understand each other, there is no chance for misunderstanding that will cause what these people claim they expected to be the result of this parade on the South Side. Those who are in power will eventually, through some legal procedure or technicality, deny the working men and women the right to even breathe in their presence if such were possible. We would not be surprised if some . . . some fanatic will come forward with a formula or some advanced scientific thought for the benefit of these people that would like to see all workers born minus a brain with a strong physique and nothing else to conform with what is generally considered Intelligence in the average workers. The only thing he needs are a strong back and a weak mind. Some would give him the strong back and deny him the right to have a mind altogether and compel him to produce everything and demand nothing. . . .

[B]ut in spite of all this, we made a creditable showing and the result obtained by such a demonstration will go down in history as one of the most effective demonstrations of organized labor ever held on the South Side. Who else but a hypocrite would attempt to prevent people that compose our different communities coming together and discussing things that effect them directly? . . . This great meeting was composed of formerly oppressed stockyards workers who had so obediently observed the mandates of the packing house barons for the past 14 years. At the play ground everybody seemed to be interested in what was being said for their benefit by the different speakers, showing that the true spirit of unity prevailed. . . .

T. Arnold Hill, Executive Secretary of the Urban League . . . outlined the purpose for which the Urban League was established and why they had just cause to understand the benefits that are to be derived through organization. He charged those present with their responsibility inasmuch as it was necessary for them to give the colored men a square deal after admitting them into the organization. He mentioned the fact that people had come to him with stories, some of them possibly false, regarding different situations that confronted them in industry. Some employers use excuses that they are unable to furnish employment to colored men who might apply for work, and in commenting on this situation, he related an incident that came to his attention just recently when a number of colored men were sent by his office to plant for employment and upon applying for the job were told that it would be necessary for them to get a permit from the Union. This they did and when they returned with the permit ready to work, another condition confronted them and this was that they would have to provide themselves with picks and shovels. They did this too, which shows that in many instances where the unions are fair and will deal on the square with colored men, the bosses themselves are directly responsible for some of the discriminations. . . .

In conclusion he charged those present that if he and his colleagues were expected to advise the colored workers to join the union, they expected the union men themselves to be fair toward colored workers.

Source: John Riley, "Big Parade by Stockyards Workers Features Big Drive for Members," *Chicago Whip,* July 19, 1919.

Organizing the Pullman Porters

After A. Philip Randolph became president of the Brotherhood of Sleeping Car Porters (BSCP) in 1925, he used the pages of his monthly magazine, The Messenger, *to educate the black working class on the virtues of unionism. In the following*

A. Philip Randolph, Frank Crosswaith, Wallace Thurman, and the staff of *The Messenger* in the 1920s. After becoming president of the Brotherhood of Sleeping Car Porters in 1925, Randolph used the pages of *The Messenger* to advocate for the union's cause. Photographs and Prints Division, Schomburg Center for Research in Black Culture, The New York Public Library, Astor, Lenox and Tilden Foundations.

editorial, Randolph defines the new, assertive persona that unionized porters must adopt in order to eliminate the workplace culture of servility demanded by employers and reinforced by practices such as tipping.

A. Philip Randolph, "The New Pullman Porter," 1926

A new Pullman porter is born. He breathes a new spirit. He has caught a new vision. His creed is independence without insolence; courtesy without fawning; service without servility. His slogan is: "Opportunity not alms." For a fair day's work, he demands a fair day's wage. He reasons that if it is just and fair and advantageous for the Pullman Company to organize in order to sell service to the traveling public, that it is also just and fair and advantageous for the porters to organize in order to sell their service to the Pullman Company. . . .

The new Pullman porter is a rebel against all that the "Uncle Tom idea" suggests. The former possesses the psychology of let well enough alone." The latter that of progressive improvement. The former relies upon charity and pity; the latter upon his intelligence, initiative and thrift. The old time porter is afflicted with an inferiority complex; the new porter logically takes the position that a man's worth in society is not the result of race, color, creed or nationality; but that a man's worth is based upon the quality of his service to society. The old time porter assumed that a clownal grin or a "buck and wing" was a necessary part of the service in order to extract a dime tip from an amused and ofttimes a disgusted passenger; whereas, the new porter believes that intelligence and dignity and industry are the chief factors in service of quality and value. As a service agent, the new porter seeks to anticipate the desires of his passengers with a view to making their travel ideal. He realizes that his service is a representative form of salesmanship for the Company to the public, and for himself to the Company and the public. His work is not alone regulated by the mechanical requirements of the service, but out of his rich and full experience, he is ever formulating new and higher forms of service. Many constructive and practical ideas lie in the heads of porters who are reluctant to reveal them because they feel that they neither get the proper appreciation or reward from the Company for them. A just wage stimulates the employees to give their best to their employer; it develops a larger interest in the job and a joy in performing a high type of workmanship.

The new porter is not amenable to the old slavedriving methods, his best service is secured through an appeal to his intelligence. Just as he demands fairer treatment than the old time porter, for the same reason, he gives a higher type of service. Just as he rejects charity and pity on the grounds that he is a man, and doesn't need such, so he refuses to make excuses, but performs his duties in accordance with the requirements of efficient service.

His object is not only to get more wages, better hours of work and improved working conditions, but to do his bit in order to raise and progressively improve the standard of Pullman service. The new Pullman porter takes the position that his ability to render the Company increased productive efficiency can only result from his increased physical, moral and mental efficiency, which rest directly upon a higher standard of living, which in turn, can only be secured by a higher, regular income. His insistence upon a regular, living wage is based upon the fact that not only is the tipping system morally unjustifiable, but because tips fluctuate violently in amounts, from month to month, and a porter is for ever uncertain as to how to regulate his household affairs, since he cannot definitely plan on how much money he can spend above his meager wage of $67.50 a month, on his wife's clothing, furniture for his home, or his children's education. No other group of workers are required to work under such distracting uncertainty. Of course, the reason is that they are organized. . . .

The new porter is not flattered by the claim that he has a monopoly on a job which does not yield him a decent living. He maintains that a fuller consideration of the relation of wages to production costs will show wage rates accompanied efficient management, lower production costs, higher production efficiency and a higher type of workmanship. Higher production efficiency is reflected in lower selling prices which makes possible service to a larger group of consumers, and a consequent larger volume of trade. The new Pullman porter contends that low wages encourages indolence, irresponsibility and dishonesty, and hence it is not an economical wage.

The new porter thinks hard but says little.

Source: A. Philip Randolph, "The New Pullman Porter," *Messenger* (April 1926), 109.

The Great Depression and Black Domestic Servants

In 1935, community activists Ella Baker and Marvel Cooke investigated the many street-corner markets that emerged in the Bronx section of New York City where black women gathered in a desperate search of work. White women visited the markets each day and hired the women to do household chores for pitifully low wages. In the following article, which appeared in the NAACP's monthly magazine, The Crisis, *Baker and Cooke explain how these open-air labor markets functioned like antebellum slave markets.*

Ella Baker and Marvel Cooke, "The Bronx Slave Market," 1935

The Bronx Slave Market! What is it? Who are its dealers? Who are its victims? What are its causes? How far does its stench spread? What forces are at work to counteract it?. . .

[T]he Simpson avenue block exudes the stench of the slave market at its worst. Not only is human labor bartered and sold for slave wage, but human love also is a marketable commodity. But whether it is labor or love that is sold, economic necessity compels the sale. As early as 8 a.m. they come; as late as 1 p.m. they remain.

Rain or shine, cold or hot, you will find them there—Negro women, old and young—sometimes bedraggled, sometimes neatly dressed—but with the invariable paper bundle, waiting expectantly for Bronx housewives to buy their strength and energy for an hour, two hours, or even for a day at the munificent rate of fifteen, twenty, twentyfive, or, if luck be with them, thirty cents an hour. If not the wives themselves, maybe their husbands, their sons, or their brothers, under the subterfuge of work, offer worldlywise girls higher bids for their time.

Who are these women? What brings them here? Why do they stay? In the boom days before the onslaught of the depression in 1929, many of these women who are now forced to bargain for day's work on street corners, were employed in grand homes . . . at more than adequate wages. Some are former marginal industrial workers, forced by the slack in industry to seek other means of sustenance. In many instances there had been no necessity for work at all. But whatever their standing prior to the depression, none sought employment where they now seek it. They come to the Bronx, not because of what it promises, but largely in desperation. . . .

We became particularly friendly with a girl [who]. . . had had a regular job in the neighborhood. But let her tell you about it.

"Did I have to work? And how! For five bucks and car fare a week. Mrs. Eisenstein had a sixroom apartment lighted by fifteen windows. Each and every week, believe it or not, I had to wash every one of those windows. If that old hag found as much as the teeniest speck on any one of 'em, she'd make me do it over. I guess I would do anything rather than wash windows. On Mondays I washed and did as much of the ironing as I could. The rest waited over for Tuesday. There were two grown sons in the family and her husband. That meant that I would have at least twentyone shirts to do every week. Yeah, and ten sheets and at least two blankets, besides. They all had to be done just so, too. Gosh, she was a particular woman.

"There wasn't a week, either, that I didn't have to wash up every floor in the place and wax it on my hands and knees. And two or three times a week I'd have to beat the mattresses and take all the furniture covers off and shake 'em out. Why, when I finally went home nights, I could hardly move. . . .

"How did I happen to leave her? Well, after I had been working about five weeks, I asked for a Sunday off. My boy friend from Washington was coming up on an excursion to spend the day with me. She told me if I didn't come in on Sunday, I needn't come back at all. Well, I didn't go back. Ever since then I have been trying to find a job. The employment agencies are no good. All the white girls get the good jobs.

"My cousin told me about up here. The other day I didn't have a cent in my pocket and I just had to find work in order to get back home and so I took the first thing that turned up. I went to work about 11 o'clock and I stayed until 5:00—washing windows, scrubbing floors and washing out stinking baby things. I was surprised when she gave me lunch. You know, some of 'em don't even do that. What I got through, she gave me thirtyfive cents. Said she took a quarter out for lunch. Figure it out for yourself. Ten cents an hour! . . .

The exploiters, judged from the districts where this abominable traffic flourishes, are the wives and mothers of artisans and tradesmen who militantly battle against being exploited themselves, but who apparently have no scruples against exploiting others.

The general public, though aroused by stories of these domestics, too often think of the problems of these women as something separate and apart and readily dismisses them with a sigh and a shrug of the shoulders. The women, themselves present a study in contradictions. Largely unaware of their organized power, yet ready to band together for some immediate and personal gain either consciously or unconsciously, they still cling to that American illusion that any one who is determined and persistent can get ahead.

The roots, then of the Bronx Slave Market spring from: (1) the general ignorance of and apathy towards organized labor action; (2) the artificial barriers that separate the interest of the relief administrators and investigators from that of their "case loads," the white collar and professional worker from the laborer and the domestic; and (3) organized labor's limited concept of exploitation, which permits it to fight vigorously to secure itself against evil, yet passively or actively aids and abets the ruthless destruction of Negroes. To abolish the market once and for all, these roots must be torn away from their sustaining soil.

Source: Ella Baker and Marvel Cooke, "The Bronx Slave Market," *Crisis* (November 1935), 330–31, 340. The author wishes to thank the Crisis Publishing Co., Inc., the publisher of the magazine of the National Association for the Advancement of Colored People, for the use of the material first published in the Novemaber 1935 issue of Crisis Magazine.

The Southern Tenant Farmers' Union

In this undated letter, a black sharecropper in Arkansas identified only as J informs STFU organizer and black preacher E. B. McKinney of the challenges that their local chapter confronted. Landlords used violence, eviction, and arrests to intimidate rural blacks from joining the union. A disciple of Marcus Garvey, this dedicated unionist pledged to inspire his neighbors and help them to overcome their fears with his vision of a righteous society.

Letter from a Black Sharecropper, 1937
E. B. McKinney
J.—Ark.

dear Sir and Brothers of The STFU. it is with great pleasure That I write you. I am indeed glad to be in communication with you personly, and hope to be able to See you at an early date. I want to carry out the Instructions That you all Send me as promptly as I can. I carry The letters and every Thing to The meetings as I am advised to do. I even Take Them from house to house and read to those That cant read so good.

I Tried my best to be in cooperation with my members, but They is afread and refuses to follow instructions as I want to do; They tells me That you all is in Memphis, and we cant do altogeather as you all instruct, without hurting our Selves. I believe That we keep our union work to Secretly. I want The Work to go on, I want to See more Union workers and True Union men and women That are not afread to follow all instructions.

We need Some one That is True and know how to give the right advice to come here at once, and advise we peoples. a lot of them is all upSet over one of our members That got beat up last Tuesday a week ago in The person of Albert Rodgers, and Some of Them is afread to meet. I am not afread. I know The union mean much to us if We follow instructions.

I want to wear my button but my members kicked so and said That we was to week, and said That I would get beat up, for me to wait and See what you all was going to do. I tells Them we Must do something ourselves. You all cant do anything unless we do as you all instruct us.

I am in great need and any one can Investigate any Time They wish to and See That I am in a Suffering condition, but yet I am loyal to the Strike call. all of my members have better advantages Then I have, yet Some of Them Trys to get me to break my pledge. but I wont do it. I bolieve in doeing all That I can to be help to any Rightious cause.

I know, I must suffer Some as others have had to do. I have been Suffering a long Time even before the STFU was organized in This Vicinety, carrying *The Negro World* [the newspaper of the Universal Negro Improvement Association] to our peoples to get Them Jnspired for This day, but was Ignored. Just a few would buy and read. I am now an agent of the *Black Man* [a journal published and edited by Marcus Garvey]. it too is hard to Sell. I want to do every Thing That I can do to help better conditions for every one. you can bet on me doeing what I can do mysellf, but out peoples in This Vicinety causes much suffering by being so fearfull.

P,S. to the S.T.F.U.

Warrn Williams, President of the local, told me That J.H. Blount, The owner of This plantation, Told him That he wanted him to move Monday, or else he would have him put in Jail, and Told him That he wanted to See me. The man That is acting boss Told me That he was going to have The high Sharfff to move Williams, he say we must Pay rent, work, or move, and Told me That it wasnt nothing to That Strike mess, and said if you all wanted Them to stop you would come out here and Tell Them.

The majority of The peoples on This place are union members, but havent never obayed order, and That causes me and Mr. Williams to be The Targets. Wesly Jackson The boss is realy a Traitor to This cause and is Trying to Trap me and fraim, but I am yet Sticking to my pledge I made To The union as best That I can and understand, and want to do what is Right, some of These peoples are not Forced to do as Thay are, and Thay are in better Shape Then I am.

but I caught The Vision in 1923 and want to help in The Fight for Right-iousness, I have been ignored and rejected, so much untell it causes me to go hungry many a day, and in need of food and clotheing. today my health also have failed me. looking to hear from you all Soon.

Source: The Disinherited Speak: Letters from Sharecroppers (New York: Work-ers Defense League for the Southern Tenant Farmers Union, 1937), 28–29.

Black Enthusiasm for the CIO

*Thousands of black workers embraced the Congress of Industrial Organizations'
(CIO) campaign to organize the men and women who labored in the nation's
mass-production industries. In following article, which appeared in the* Chicago
Defender *in 1939, black journalist Harold Preece profiles the activities of black
labor organizers for the CIO's Packinghouse Workers Organizing Committee
(PWOC). Preece captures the challenges that labor organizers encountered trying
to organize black workers at Armour and Company, the enthusiasm for the CIO
among Chicago's black packinghouse workers, the stark contrasts that black unionists drew between the CIO and the American Federation of Labor, the enhanced
reputation of labor unions among all African Americans, the critical role that volunteer labor organizers played in building the union, the leadership roles that black
workers assumed within many union locals, the connections that black unionists
drew between the struggle for labor rights and civil rights, and the faith that they had
in the power of industrial unions to defeat racial discrimination.*

Harold Preece, "What Goes On in Packingtown?" 1939

"If Armour and company forces its thousands of workers throughout America to strike for a union contract, Negroes will not enlist themselves as scabs against the great labor organization which members of their race have helped build. Not as long as a single picket marches before any of the huge plants with their profits ground from the backbreaking, highspeed labor of black and white workers alike."

These emphatic statements were made last week by Hank Johnson, Ar-thell Shelton, Kenneth Collins, and other leaders of the CIO Packinghouse

Workers Organizing Committee on what may be the eve of one of the grimmest labor conflicts in American history. The statements are backed by the thousands of CIO buttons worn by colored packinghouse workers at their labor, worn like shields against low wages and poor working conditions.

"The present conflict at Armour &. Co. is more than a battle between a corporation and a labor union," Hank Johnson remarked to this a writer. "It is also another chapter in that long epic of the Negro people—their struggle for work and security. America's 14,000,000 citizens of my color are more than passive observers in this fight which we have sought to avoid by urging Armour and company to obey the National Labor Relations Act and come to terms with us.

"A national contract, signed by Armour and company, will secure the jobs and better the conditions of the thousands of Negroes now employed in the industry, and stir our people from coast to coast into further action for all the rights guaranteed them under the American constitution."

For black workers have learned to raise their heads and to act unitedly for their rights as free men and women since the P.W.O.C. came into that turbulent district known as "the Yards." The story of that three-year-old organization, sweeping across the industry with the strength of a young giant, is also the story of the successful fight waged by its Negro and white members to abolish discrimination and racial terror in Packingtown, to establish seniority rights and the principle of equal employment for the colored group previously regarded as aliens and outcasts.

From Hank Johnson, the powerfully built man who rose from the Brazos bottoms of Texas to become assistant national director of the P.W.O.C. down to the Negro shop steward who may preach at some storefront church on Sunday, the colored members have been the backbone of that continuing fight to organize [the] industry. . . .

Eight out of the 14 P.W.O.C. locals in Chicago have Negro presidents—men elected to these responsible positions partly through the votes of white workers who until recently looked upon Negroes as their natural enemies. . . .

It was no easy task to begin organization work three years ago in that vast district of Packingtown where lean months of poverty sometimes erupted into explosions of violent hate. Each drawing slim pay envelopes, each subject to the prolonged agony of layoffs, black and white slaved side by side in mutual fear and distrust. It was almost worth a Negro's life if he asked for service at a Packingtown tavern or restaurant, and that antagonism was expressed in what had come to be a proverb of the Yards:

"No Negro had better show his face west of Ashland avenue after dark."

Today, because the P.W.O.C. planted the seed of unity in the stony soil of Packingtown, Negroes walk freely and in safety. Any public place which refused them service would be quickly put out of business by a boycott of the white union members. On the very streets where danger once lurked at every corner for Negroes, colored men stop for long chats about baseball with Polish or Irish workers.

Men of less caliber than Hank Johnson and those who worked so devotedly with him would never have tackled that job of bringing together workers divided by hundreds of rankling little quarrels. "Negroes will never join another packinghouse union," declared supposedly informed spokesmen of the Race as they recalled the betrayal of Negro workers by the now dying American Federation of Labor Butcher Workers union after the unsuccessful strike of 1921. Shunted into jimcrow locals, the Negro workers had fought bravely in that battle only to be denied reinstatement by the hundreds after the strike had been lost.

But the loss of a battle by a people does not mean that they have surrendered. Over the whirring of the machines at Armour's, over the bellowing of the animals driven into the slaughter lines. Negro workers still dreamed of job security, of seniority rights, and of equality. For the spirit of a whole people can never be broken by any oppressions or any defeats though they be driven into the streets to starve. . . .

Arthell Shelton, one of the most valued members of the Chicago P.W.O.C. staff is of the same breed as Hank Johnson—courageous, unflinching in his determination to establish security for those men and women with whom he has worked side by side. . . . "I have never regretted that step," said Shelton, the man who remained a confirmed trade unionist even before there was a union to join. "The P.W.O.C. has not only protected Negroes in their rights as workers but in their rights as citizens.

"Since the coming of the P.W.O.C., Negroes entitled to promotion have a better chance of getting it because the union feels that every man has the right to advance according to his ability, whatever his color.

"A man might spend his life drudging at a semi-skilled job in the sheep kill or some other department. If he were colored, he could count on being underpaid and overworked. Maybe, he would lose a hand or a finger working with knives or a machine under a terrific speedup.

"But the P.W.O.C. has been responsible for an upward revision in the wage scale of Negro workers. If the speed-up becomes too terrific, the boys simply slow down the conveyor lines or maybe throw a stoppage for an hour." . . .

The twenty or so Negro preachers who are shop stewards of the Armour local feel "deep down in their hearts," as one or them, Rev. Isaac Ladson, put it that they are "helping to lift up humanity" through their work in the organization. In the same spirit, other preachers down South are helping to close the divided ranks of the Negroes and poor whites for a new day when all shall have land and bread.

But the true test of any organization lies in the actions rather than the words of its members. Recently, this writer attended a dance at the P.W.O.C. headquarters. . . . There was none of the strained courtesy which one often finds at mixed parties of Negroes and whites. Men and women who worked together in the plants, mingled together without the slightest consciousness of color, and the writer was informed that there would be a baseball game between two of the 14 P.W.O.C. mixed teams the next day.

"Isn't this Americanism in the truest sense?" asked Oscar Wilson, Negro recording secretary of the Packinghouse Workers Council as a Negro and white worker sat down to discuss the third term boom for President [Franklin] Roosevelt over cold bottles of pop.

Source: Harold Preece, "What Goes On in Packingtown?" *Chicago Defender*, September 23, 1939. Used with permission of the Chicago Defender.

Fair Employment Practice Committee

Throughout the war years, African Americans filed thousands of complaints with the Fair Employment Practice Committee (FEPC). Their letters to FEPC investigators and to President Franklin Roosevelt and his wife Eleanor Roosevelt document the depths of employment discrimination in defense industries and express a faith in the moral power of the federal government to enforce racial justice in the wartime workplace. In the first letter, Lillian Stevenson of Pittsburg, California, complains to the First Lady that the International Brotherhood of Boilermakers (IBB) prevented her from getting a job in the Kaiser Shipyards even though she went through the trouble and the expense to take job training classes. In the second document, Willie Williams, a journeymen welder at the Bethlehem-Alameda Shipbuilding Corporation, explains how managers consistently overlooked his experience as a skilled machinist and his excellent employment record to promote him to the supervisory position of leaderman. In the final letter, Joseph Clyde La Chappell, a man of mixed-race ancestry, pleads with President Roosevelt to ban the segregated system of auxiliary unions established by the International Brotherhood of Boilermakers. By denying him the right to work and to earn a living, the Boilermakers, claimed La Chappell, had deprived him of his fundamental rights as a citizen.

Lillian Stevenson to Eleanor Roosevelt, November 18, 1942

Dear Mrs. Roosevelt.

I am writing to you to see if you could help me get a job.

Five weeks ago I apply at the United States Employment Office . . . in Richmond California for a job, which is in the same county that I live

[Contra Costa]. I apply for work in one of Mr. Kaiser ship yards. They said they didn't have anything for colored that day, so they sent me out to the National Defense School which is located . . . in Richmond for 60 hours of welding. Which they promise me a job after I get those hours, and I had to pay to come from Pittsburg [about 30 miles away] as they have no training in this town. I also had to buy a welding out fit to start the course. When I got these sixty hours the instructor refuse to give them to me, so I stayed and complete the course then I got my hours and took my hours back [to] the U.S. Employment Office and they sent me out for a test in welding, and I passed the test and came back to the Boiler Makers Union which is located . . . in Richmond and they refuse me because I was a colored woman I am 29 years old.

Mrs. Roosevelt they are hiring every other race that go there and they need welders. I thought that what we are fighting for freedom.

Mrs. Roosevelt I will appreciate if you would try and get in touch with this Mr. Patton of the Boiler Makers Union concerning this matter. I feel so bad over this I don't know what to do, as I want to do my part as the other women of other women of other races are doing. Will you try and help me please.

Yours Truly

Lillian Stevenson

Source: Complaints against the Boilermakers Unions, Fair Employment Practice Committee, *Selected Documents from the Records of the Committee on Fair Employment Practice* (Glen Rock, NJ: Microfilming Corporation of America, 1971), Reel No. 108.

Statement by Willie P. Williams, April 29, 1944
Oakland, California

Mr. Williams believes he should be a leaderman because, "I entered the yard as a journeyman welder and there are lots of fellows that are leadermen that were trainees when I was a journeyman welder. I also proved my ability by not being an absentee. I have not been given full opportunity to do all the welding that I am capable of handling.

"I also have taken the job instructors training and was among the first of the group that took that course and finished it successfully. Also, was among the first to finish [the training course that] is required before a man can be a leaderman. Other leadermen have taken this course after they were given their rating. Supervisors begged these welders to take these jobs as leadermen, although they said (the men promoted) they knew they were not qualified, but the supervisors said they would teach them.

"Maritime Commission man at Bethlehem said that I am doing a job that lots of welders cannot do, he said what I was doing was a specialists job and claimed I was worth more than I was getting.

"I offered several good suggestions to the War Production Committee on how to increase production and one was voted the best suggestion of the month. Because of all of this, I believe I am good enough to be a Leaderman. There is every nationality as Leadermen or Welding Inspector, except colored."

I have never been given a chance to <u>prove</u> my ability.

If an when I am given that chance I will gladly prove it.

"The job that I am doing, they have tried ten different welders, even to one leaderman, to do my job and haven't any of them been able to do it. I asked for a rating, they wouldn't give it to me. I laid off three days. During that time they used three different welders, no one proved successful. Then I was called in by the foreman and was told I had to take the same job or leave the yard, not giving me any consideration on getting the rating, wouldn't discuss that with me at all."

"When I first went to work Mr. Samuel Martin told me that if I ever heard of any case of discrimination to let management know about it. However, I have told them about my own case of discrimination—but they have done nothing about it.

[signed Willie P. Williams]

Source: Bethlehem-Alameda Shipbuilding Incorporated file, 12-BR-250, Fair Employment Practice Committee, *Selected Documents from the Records of the Committee on Fair Employment Practice* (Glen Rock, NJ: Microfilming Corporation of America, 1971), Reel No. 108.

Joseph Clyde La Chappell to President Franklin D. Roosevelt, February 1944

Mr. President

I am writing you, this letter, with all my Respect.

As and American citizen, I am, and a citizen of the State of California.

Dear Sir, My name is Joseph Clyde La Chappell and I am employed, here at Marin Shipyard here in, [Sausalito], California. We are building Tanker for Victory.

And Mr. President I have been employed here at Marin Shipyard for one year.

An now, the Boilermakers Union Local 6, Have set aside a Jim Crow Local A41 Auxilitory for the Negroes alone.

And I happen to be a member of the Negro race. And now, I am being fired, on account I refused to join, this Jim Crow Auxililatory Local A41, set up by the A.F.L. International Brotherhood of Boilermakers.

I feel, I am being Discriminated against Because I am a so Call Negro.

Mr. President, I am asking you to Intervene in this matter Immediately that American Citizens may be given their constitutional rights.

Mr. President I have been fired twice Already, But I was rehired, as soon as these enjuctions was brought against Company. And now I am working, But will be fired at any time.

Mr. President, as I just wrote, saying so Call Negro.

Mr. President, I mean this, I am just as (White) as millions of of People, And I have just as Good brains as million of white people and still, I am call a Negro.

And I am as I would say, partly a member of the White Race. And I have not got no black relative, But I have, as I am told, some stran of Negro blood in me.

But, I am, not trying to denying it. And now certin groops or denying my rights to a job and a living, and my right as an American Citizen.

That Why Mr. President, I am Calling upon you to Protetct my (Constitutional Right) and to see that those Groops, such as the International Brotherhood of Boilermakers Local 6 are doing.

The A.F.L. is demorlizing me, and is doing all they can to keep me from doing my share for Victory.

And they are also denying my right to a job, and also they or keeping me from earning a living as a human and a Citizen of the United States of American.

I am your friend, and also a loyal citizen, and a supporter of the Demorcrat way of life.

And I have Voted in all elections as a Demorcrat.

Joseph Clyde La Chappell

Source: Fair Employment Practice Committee, *Selected Documents from the Records of the Committee on Fair Employment Practice* (Glen Rock, NJ: Microfilming Corporation of America, 1971), Reel No. 111.

Black Steelworkers Remember the CIO

In 1961 the United Steelworkers (USWA) conducted a series of interviews with some of the union's oldest members, which it featured in the union's monthly magazine, Steel Labor. *Among those interviewed were four African American workers—Joe Cook, Eddie Longshore, Bartow Tipper, and Anthony McCann—who emphasized the dramatic change in working conditions since the Congres of Indus-*

trial Organizations (CIO) organized the industry. Not only did they emphasize the material benefits of wages and job security that the union won for all workers, but they stressed how the union enabled ordinary men such as themselves to work in dignity. Their comments underscore the enduring appeal of unions to black industrial workers in the postwar period.

"The Old Members Won't Forget," 1961

Joe Cook, retired member of USWA Local 1029, had more than 42 years service with Valley Mould and Iron Co., Chicago, when he retired last year on a unionwon pension. "Greatest thing the union has done as far as I am concerned," said Cook, "was to get the eighthour day. I believe that it has been the thing that has caused the longer life that working men and women now enjoy."

In his thoughts about the accomplishments of the union, Cook said, "Fifty years ago my wife and I came to Chicago carrying our lunch in a bag and riding in a Jim Crow car. In 1956 we went to the Los Angeles union convention in a Pullman car, slept in a nice clean bed and woke up and ate our breakfast in the dining car. This is what the CIO and the Steelworkers' Union did for me."

Mr. Cook was first and only president of one of the very first USWA locals, up to the time of retirement. He can remember working for 36 cents an hour for a 10hour day, sevenday week. He was a member of the old Amalgamated [Association of Iron, Steel, and Tin Workers] but the company did not recognize his lodge because it was so weak.

* * * * *

Eddie Longshore is 45 years old and works at the Republic Steel [Company] Plant in Massillon, Ohio, where is a member of Local Union 1124. Brother Longshore is a furnace operator helper at the plant and has been an employe for 22 years and a member of the United Steelworkers for that same period.

Brother Longshore said "since the organizing of our union at this plant, we have accomplished very much to elevate the standard of living for the working class people.

"I feel a great sense of satisfaction in being a part of this great organization when I think of the many benefits that have been made available not only to members of our union, but to people generally throughout our great nation and even the world.

"The attainment of human dignity on the job is no small contribution to the American way of live.

"My experience with the Steelworkers Union has been satisfying. Long live the United Steelworkers of America."

* * * * *

Bartow Tipper who is 54 years old lives at 290 Return Street, Aliquippa, Pa., and has been an employe of Jones & Laughlin Steel Corporation for 35 years.

Brother Tipper said "I remember the early days of the SWOC [Steelworkers Organizing Committee] in Alquippa and I often thank God for this great union of ours, the United Steelworkers of America, its leaders and most of all to our President David J. McDonald.

"I have been a member of this union since its inception and one of the most important things this union has attained is human dignity which we all enjoy today. Even the company recognizes that now and they indicate that they are going to try to communicate with us.

"Just to think before we had this great union of ours, the foreman could send you home for a day or a week or fire you outright for no reason at all. Even those people who were fortunate enough to have steady work had to bear the most horrible working conditions.

"We needed a union and we got a strong union as a result of many struggles. Let's do everything to keep our union strong."

* * * * *

Anthony McCann, 64, started at General American's steel car department in 1920 and despite a layoff at one time, still boasts 26 years' seniority. His 1936 wages of 45 cents hourly have moved to $2.20 per hour. "The greatest thing that ever was—that's our union," says Anthony. "Used to be that a man didn't know when he had a job. Now we have protection and security. The union still continues to prosper. When it doesn't, the working man is finished."

Source: "The Old Members Won't Forget! . . . The New Members Shouldn't Forget!" *Steel Labor* (June 1961), 20–22.

The Montgomery Bus Boycott, 1956

In June of 1956, African American journalist Ted Poston traveled to Montgomery, Alabama, and reported on the bus boycott in a twelve-part series of articles that appeared in the New York Post. *Poston profiled many of the ordinary black people of Montgomery, those whom he called the "real backbone and rulers of the protest movement." In the following article, he relates the story of a confrontation between a black domestic servant, whose identity he protects, and her white employer over her support of the boycott.*

Ted Poston, "The Negroes of Montgomery," 1956

She was an unlettered woman of about 45, and she had been working as a domestic since her early teens. But she displayed an amazing grasp of economics which should have shamed Mayor W. A. (Tacky) Gayle and Montgomery's other two City Commissioners.

She was the only Negro to whom you had talked who had actually been fired for refusing to ride the Montgomery City Lines buses during the protracted boycott.

"But they hired me back that same night they fired me," she explained. "They had to."

"Because I'm helping them buy that new house they got out in the Mount Meigs section. Because, without me, they couldn't keep that 1955 Buick the Mister insisted on trading the old car in for."

The other six women in the bright red station wagon, which was taking them to their domestic jobs at 6 a.m., chuckled appreciatively. But you found the answer a bit complicated, so you asked her to start at the beginning.

"Well," she said, adjusting her plump body to a more comfortable position, "the Mister ain't such a bad man as white folks go. And until this White Citizens Council thing came along, all of my dealings was with the Missus. . . .

"So he comes back home from one of them [White Citizens Council] meetings where they had made him a sergeant or usher or something the night before. And he walks into my kitchen just as I'm getting ready to put dinner on the table.

"'Sarah,' he said to me (that is not her name), 'Sarah,' he said, 'you ain't one of them fools that have stopped riding the buses, is you?' And I said, 'Yessuh, I is.'

"And he say: 'I ain't gonna have none of this Communist foolishness in my house, Sarah. Now you're coming to work on that bus tomorrow morning.' And I say: 'No, sir. I don't think so.'

"And he say: 'Now don't talk back to me like that, even if you is been here three years.' And before I could say anything else, the Missus calls him in the dining room, and he says to me: 'You just wait a minute, we'll settle this when I come back.'

"I could hear them arguing out there while I put the stuff on the stove to keep it warm, and I could hear him tell the Missus: 'She'll do what I say or get out—'

"So I got my bag together and walked on out the back door while they still was arguing. And in a few minutes, Mrs. Alberta James (driver of the Hutchinson Baptist Church station wagon) came whissing by, and I got on in and went on about my business."

She paused in her long recital, and one of the other women murmured: "Tell him about what happened that night."

"Well," she took up again, "I'm setting home about 10 that night and getting ready to go to bed and there came this knock on the door. I guessed who it was right away, and I went there, and sure enough it was the Mister.

"And before I could even open the screen, he says: 'Sarah, you coming to work tomorrow morning ain't you?' And I said: 'No, sir, I don't guess so; you fired me."

"And he say: 'Look, ain't no need us losing our heads like this; you come on back to work now.' And I said: 'No, sir; you fired me, and another lady wants me to come to her tomorrow. She said she'd pay me $15 instead of the $12 the Missus pays me.

"Well that sort of hit him and he don't say nothing for a minute and I don't say nothing neither. And finally he say: 'If it don't be for the children liking you so much, I wouldn't do it. But you come on back and I'll give you the $15 if I got to.'

"And I say: 'Well, I promised this other lady—' and he said: 'Sarah, you know the children like you; now you come on back to work tomorrow morning.' I don't say nothing and he keeps on talking. He wants to apologize but he can't make himself do it.

"So finally I say: 'I got to ride the bus?' And he say: 'I don't give a damn; you just get there the best way you can. But get there, Sarah; you hear me?'"

The other women couldn't contain their bubbling laughter any longer.

But you ask: "But what is this about you paying for their house and car?"

And the laughter subsides as she answers rather caustically:

"It's just this. I get there at 6:30 every morning. I dress and feed the children and get all three of them off to school while the Mister and Missus both rush out to their work.

"I clean up the upstairs and fix the lunch for the children when they come home for lunch. Then I clean the rest of the house and fix the dinner for the children and the Missus and the Mister. They come home and ain't got nothing to do but set down and eat.

"I admit that she washes up the dinner dishes, for I go home after I serve it, but that is all she does do."

She paused and then continued in a soft, bitter voice:

"Now if I wasn't there to do it, she'd have to do all that herself. And she couldn't do it and go to business to.

"Well she pays me $12 a week so she can go out and make $52 a week in her job. I know that's what she make, for I seen her payroll stub.

"Now if it wasn't for that $40 a week she makes on me, they couldn't meet the mortgage or the payment on that new car neither. They couldn't make it on his check alone."

"It's the God's truth," one of the other women seconded from the jump seat in the station wagon. "And they ain't the only ones. Practically every one of them young couples and plenty old ones, too, in these new subdivisions can't make it if the women don't work too."

"And if we all was to quit work," another put in, "and the womens had to stay at home, there'd be more dispossessing than you could shake a stick at, and the instalment people would be taking back everything they owned."

But the original narrator was not through. She was smiling when she concluded her story.

"You know," she said, "I hadn't promised no other lady nothing. And nobody offered me no $15, although I probably could get it somewhere else if I tried.

"But I heard the Missus tell the Mister just that week before that she was getting a $6 raise. And I felt some of that raise belonged to me."

And the general laughter was unrestrained.

The Economics of Civil Rights

In the spring and summer of 1963, Gloria Richardson spearheaded the civil rights movement in Cambridge, Maryland. Uncompromising and confrontational in her approach to protest politics, Richardson quickly gained a national reputation. In the following speech that she delivered at the Salem Methodist Church in New York City just two weeks before the 1963 March on Washington for Jobs and Freedom, Richardson explains that the problems that confronted African Americans were fundamentally economic. Consequently, they demanded more than the integration of public accommodations. For without key resources—housing, education, and employment—African Americans would remain excluded from full participation in the promise of American life.

Gloria Richardson, "Cambridge, Maryland, 'City of Progress' for Rich," 1963

The situation in Cambridge is easy to understand. If the white leaders are able to ensure us the right to eat in the town we help to support, to receive adequate education for the future we will commonly share, to provide us with employment that will improve the economic standing of the entire town, then we can work harmoniously for the good of every citizen in Cambridge.

But the question is now—as it has been all along—whether the white leaders, politicians, and business men can bring themselves to understand that we are absolutely serious in all of our demands; whether they can comprehend what we mean when we insist that "we want freedom, and we want it now." If, finally, they can grasp these things, then life in Cambridge will be better for black and for white. But if they continue to regard us as their passive servants—the fleshly embodiments of their statuettes of Negro footmen—then there may truly be fire next time. . . .

What the town's leaders will have to realize is that our problems, and theirs, go far deeper than the desire of a few Negroes to eat at previously segregated restaurants, or sit where they want in a movie theater. For public accommodations is just a symbol of indignities so profoundly a part of Cambridge life that they cannot be spotlighted during one march or one protest.

To remedy the inequities of housing or employment or education in Cambridge, the white people really will have to examine their way of life—and much more profoundly than if I happen to sit next to one of them at a lunch counter. They will have to accept the risk of an uncertain future, where the white masses as well as the Negroes begin to question the pattern of jobs and schooling that has so long constricted them. They will, ultimately, have to accept the basic premise of democracy: that the people as a whole really do have more intelligence than a few of their leaders, and that they know what is best for themselves.

The problem in Cambridge is principally an economic one, and this means that when we plan for the future we must keep economics in mind. Desegregated schools are irrelevant to families who cannot afford to buy their children school books, or provide them with enough space at home to study. An opening of public places is irrelevant to people who cannot spend money in them. Federal housing projects are irrelevant if the rest of the ghetto conditions—faulty education and lack of employment—are maintained.

The only way to break this vicious circle is to ensure better jobs. To ensure better jobs, the entire community must work together harmoniously; each race must learn to trust the other, and more important, both races must learn to trust their common future. . . .

We demand, as ever, full and fair employment, better housing, access to restaurants and recreation facilities, truly integrated schools, and the release of the freedom fighters still in reform school or facing sentences. . . .

The choice that Cambridge and the rest of the nation faces is, finally, between progress and anarchy, between witnessing change and experiencing destruction. The status quo is now intolerable to the majority of Negroes and will soon be intolerable to the majority of whites. People have called our movement the Negro Revolution. They are right; the changes for America that will flow from what Negroes throughout the country are doing shall be truly revolutionary. And we can only hope and work, and work some more, to make that revolution creative—and not spattered with blood. . . .

Source: Gloria Richardson, "Cambridge, Maryland, 'City of Progress' for Rich," *New America*, August 31, 1963.

The Memphis Garbage Workers' Strike, 1968

Within weeks of the beginning of the 1968 sanitation workers' strike in Memphis, the Reverend James Lawson, a local minister and nonviolent strategist in the civil rights movement, organized the black community in support of the strikers. Organizers for Community on the Move for Equality (C.O.M.E.) distributed volunteer pledge cards that asked black residents to commit to supporting daily marches, nightly rallies, boycotts of downtown businesses and enterprises owned by Memphis mayor Henry Loeb, and contributions to a strikers' relief fund. Through these well-coordinated activities, African Americans in Memphis converted the local labor dispute into a social movement that linked the workers' cause with the broader struggle of all African Americans to expand the meaning of equality.

Have Sanitation Workers A Future?
Yes If You Will Help to Build It!
How? That's Simple—
WE NEED YOU!

1. Do not shop downtown, or with the downtown branch stores anywhere in the city or any enterprise named Loeb.
2. Stop your subscriptions to the daily newspapers. Get news about the Movement from the radio or television or by joining the mass meetings. Be sure to pay your newspaper carrier his commission.
3. Do not buy new things for Easter. Let our Lent be one of sacrifices. What better way to remember Jesus' work for us and the world?
4. Support the workers with the letters and telegrams to the Mayor and the City Council.
5. Join in the daily marches downtown.
6. Call others each day and remind them of the movement.
7. Attend the nightly mass meetings Monday through Friday.
8. Do not place your garbage at the curb. Handle it the best way you can without helping the city and the Mayor's effort to break the strike.

9. Whenever you associate with white people, let them know what the issues are and why your support the cause.

10. Support the relief efforts for the workers and their families with gifts of money and food. Checks can be out to "C.O.M.E" and food taken to Clayborn Temple A.M.E. Church, 280 Hernando.

Community On the Move for Equality
Work Card
Name _____ Phone _____
Address _____
I will march _____ I will picket _____
I can answer phone or do clerical work _____
I can serve on a committee:
Work Committee

_____

Telephone Committee

_____

Transportation Committee

_____

Hours I can best serve:
9:00 am–11:00 am_____
11:00 am–1:00 pm_____
1:00 pm–3:00 pm_____
3:00pm–6:00pm_____
6:00pm–8:00pm_____
8:00pm–10:00pm_____
10:00pm–12:00pm_____
Signature_____

Source: Exhibit 2, *City of Memphis vs. Martin Luther King, Jr.*, 1968, Records of the United States District Court, 1685–2004, Record Group 21, Western District of Tennessee, Western (Memphis) Division, National Archives and Records Administration Southeast Region, Atlanta, GA [Online version, available through the Archival Research Catalog (ARC identifier 279326) at www.archives.gov, April 1, 2012].

Employment Discrimination at Shoney's, 1984

In 1985, Sharon Johnson became one of thousands of African American employees of Shoney's who filed a complaint with the Equal Employment Opportunity Commission (EEOC) against the restaurant chain. Johnson had worked for years as a waitress at one of the company's restaurants in Montgomery, Alabama, but she had been repeatedly denied promotions and had trained many white waitresses who later became her supervisors. In the following deposition that she gave in her civil suit against Shoney's, Johnson describes an incident in 1984 when two white supervisors verbally abused her and the white store manager disciplined her when she appealed to him for help. Johnson requested a meeting with the white store manager, a man named Glenn, whose last name she did not remember. She explains what happened when she went into his office to inform him about how she had been verbally abused by the kitchen manager and the dining room supervisor. In December 1985, Shoney's settled with Johnson and other black waitresses who had been denied promotions to managerial positions.

Deposition of Sharon Johnson

Q.

What happened? What led to the three reprimands?

A.

I had a breakfast order. It was a number two, eggs poached with toast. I think it was bacon or whatever. And when I called the order in, the [white] kitchen manager [Ellen Nix], she said—there was a lot of cursing involved in that. Well she cursed me out because of the way I called it in.

Q.

Tell me what she said.

A.

She said let me see how you got this shit spelled. If you have got this shit spelled the way you pronounce it, this is some ignorant ass shit you have got down here. . . .

And I looked at her, I said I'm sorry if I pronounced it wrong. I am quite sure that you know what I want. I may have pronounced it wrong. It might be misspelled, but you really know—you understand what I am trying to say. I walked off from her to go and take care of another customer. When I came back, Ellen Nix and the [white] dining room supervisor [Monterey Johnston] was standing on the cook's line close to the waitress line. Ellen Nix was cursing. . . . She was discussing me with Monterey. She was telling about how I misspelled this and all that, and they was discussing what I had done wrong. And I said—and so I approached them, and I asked then, is there anything wrong. She said—she said you God damn straight something is wrong, you know. And I told her, I said you don't talk to me that way. If I made a mistake, you can correct me, but other than that—so Monterey said, Sharon, you hush. I said okay. I said but don't let her talk to me that way. Ellen kept on cursing. Okay. I walked away from both of them. . . . .

A.

I knocked on Glenn's office door, and I told him what was going on. He said before you get started, let me get the dining room supervisor in here and the kitchen manager. We will begin to start talking about what has happened.

Ellen said that she was playing with me. And I said—you know, I told her, if you were playing with me, why was the cursing all necessary to correct my problem. You know, she said—oh, what did she say. What did she say? When she said that she was just playing with me, and Glenn made a statement like—this is what he said—he made a statement, I don't care—he said you still do not—what did he say—he said overlook your superiors. When Monterey told you to hush, you did not hush. When Ellen told you that you had made a mistake on your ticket, you talked back to her. I said Glenn, I talked back to Ellen when she started cursing at me because I told her if I had made a mistake, did not pronounce it or spell it right, I'm sorry. But I am quite sure that you know what I want. This is what I said to Ellen. And about Monterey, I said in a way I did not talk back to her. When she told me to hush, I said will you make Ellen stop cursing me and I will hush. That is what I told her. And I said another thing, you are not my superiors. You are over me as a manager, but you are not my superiors. And he said well, what I am saying is that you still don't talk back. I said I was not talking back. I was trying to make them understand what I was saying and, you know, understand what I was saying. Then he said—he started to writing me up, and I said what are you writing me up for. And he said for talking back. . . . I said what you are saying to me is what Ellen did was right to curse me like that? He said I am not saying that she was right and I am not saying that she was wrong. But ever way—whatever way I handle Ellen as a manager, that is my business. You ain't got nothing to do with that. And so I walked out of the office.

So Monterey called me back in the office, you know, and told me that, you know, I called this meeting and that I had better stay here and listen to everything that they have got to say. And so what I told her and him, I said I understand what you are saying, I was not supposed to talk back. But management or no management, if they stand there and curse me without me saying something, and all of the time I was talking to Ellen, and I never did curse her. I just told her please do not talk to me like that, I do not appreciate it. Because if I made a mistake, you correct me, but other than that—and so I went back to work. I got written up three times that day for talking back to management, for walking out of a meeting that I had called, and for threatening the manager.

Q.

Threatening the manager?

A.

Yes.

Q.

How did you do that?

A.

What did I say? I said Ellen,—this what I said, I said Ellen, you are lying on me. And I walked out the door. I said Ellen, you are lying on me, and when you curse me, curse me in all kind of language and you said everything to me. And I said what you did was wrong, and one day you will pay for it. That is what I told her.

Q.

What did you have in mind when you said that?

A.

I don't—when I said that, I didn't think violence or anything like that by me touching her, because one way she is going to pay for it—God will make her pay for it on her suffering bed. I meant it that way. It wasn't that I was going to hit her or touch her or have anybody else jump on her. I figured that, you know, the Lord was going to take care of her some way.

Source: Deposition of Sharon W. Johnson, November 11, 1985, *Sharon W. Johnson, et al., v. Bill Long, et al.,* U.S. District Court for the Middle District of Alabama, Case No. 85-H-1183-N. *Haynes et al. v. Shoney's, Inc.* Papers, courtesy of the Florida State University Libraries, Special Collections and Archives.

~

Selected Bibliography

The earliest surveys of black workers in the United States tended to be written by labor economists and were principally concerned with the relationship between black workers and the labor movement. They remain valuable, in many cases, essential reading on black labor history. They include Horace R. Cayton and George S. Mitchell, *Black Workers and the New Unions* (1939); Lorenzo Greene and Carter Woodson, *The Negro Wage Earner* (1930); F. Ray Marshall, *The Negro and Organized Labor* (1965) and *The Negro Worker* (1967); Herbert Northrup, *Organized Labor and the Negro* (1944); Sterling Spero and Abram L. Harris, *The Black Worker* (1931); Robert Weaver, *Negro Labor: A National Problem* (1946); and Charles H. Wesley, *Negro Labor in the United States, 1850–1925* (1927). In 1966, the Ford Foundation awarded a major grant to the Industrial Research Unit of the Wharton School that funded a study entitled Racial Policies of American Industry. Under the direction of Herbert R. Northrup, scholars produced a number of reports on the history of black employment for various industries. These included Darold T. Barnum, *The Negro in the Bituminous Coal Mining Industry* (1970); Walter A. Fogel, *The Negro in the Meat Industry* (1970); John C. Howard, *The Negro in the Lumber Industry* (1970); Herbert R. Northrup, *The Negro in Automobile Industry* (1968); Howard W. Risher Jr., *The Negro in the Railroad Industry* (1971); Richard L. Rowan, *The Negro in the Steel Industry* (1968); Lester Rubin, *The Negro in the Shipbuilding Industry* (1970); and Lester Rubin and William S. Swift, *The Negro in the Longshore Industry* (1974).

More recent surveys of black workers by labor historians include Philip S. Foner, *Organized Labor and the Black Worker, 1619–1973* (1974); William H. Harris, *The Harder We Run: Black Workers since the Civil War* (1982); Jacqueline Jones, *American Work: Four Centuries of Black and White Labor* (1998); and Robert H. Zieger, *For Jobs and Freedom: Race and Labor in America since 1865* (2007). For libertarian critiques of organized labor, see David E. Bernstein, *Only One Place of Redress: African Americans, Labor Regulations, and the Courts from Reconstruction to the New Deal* (2001); and Paul D. Moreno, *Black Americans and Organized Labor: A New History* (2006). Important collections of essays on black workers include Eric Arnesen, ed., *The Black Worker: Race, Labor, and Civil Rights since Emancipation* (2007); John H. Bracey Jr., August Meier, and Elliot Rudwick, *Black Workers and Organized Labor* (1971); and Milton Cantor, comp., *Black Labor in America* (1969). Three collections of essays on southern labor history edited by Robert H. Zieger include important articles on black labor history; these are *Organized Labor in the Twentieth-Century South* (1991); *Southern Labor in Transition, 1940–1995* (1997); and *Life and Labor in the New New South* (2012). Philp S. Foner and Ronald L. Lewis, eds., *The Black Worker: A Documentary History from Colonial Times to the Present* (1978) is an invaluable eight-volume collection of primary sources in black labor history.

W. E. B. Du Bois's landmark book *Black Reconstruction in America, 1860–1880* (1935) portrayed Reconstruction as the story of working people in which he emphasized not only the class conflict central to the transition from slavery to freedom but also the activism of black workers in their struggle to define the meaning of freedom after slavery. Eric Foner's *Reconstruction: America's Unfinished Revolution* (1988) built upon and updated Du Bois's interpretation and likewise emphasizes African American activism and agency in defining the boundaries of freedom in the aftermath of the Civil War as well as questions of class and class conflict. Heather Cox Richardson, *The Death of Reconstruction: Race, Labor, and Politics in the Post–Civil War North, 1865–1901* (2001), examines the connections between labor politics and the broader political retreat from Reconstruction.

A number of case studies feature the role of black workers in the transition from slavery to freedom. On southwest Georgia, see Susan Eva O'Donovan, *Becoming Free in the Cotton South* (2007); on Louisiana, see John Rodrigue, *Reconstruction in the Cane Fields: From Slavery to Free Labor in Louisiana's Sugar Parishes, 1862–1880* (2001) and Rebecca Scott, *Degrees of Freedom: Louisiana and Cuba after Slavery* (2008); on the 1876 rice strikes in South Carolina, see Brian Kelly, "Black Laborers, the Republican Party, and the Crisis of Reconstruction in Lowcountry South Carolina," *International Review of Social History* 51 (2006): 375–414 and "Labour and Place: The Contours of Freedpeoples' Mobilization in Reconstruction South Carolina," *Journal of Peasant Studies* 35, no. 4 (October 2008): 653–87; and Eric Foner, *Nothing but Freedom: Emancipation and Its Legacy* (1983); other important studies of the transition from slavery to freedom include Julie Saville, *The Work of Reconstruction: From Slave to Wage Laborer in South Carolina, 1860–1870* (1994); and Leslie Schwalm, *A Hard Fight for We: Women's Transition from Slavery to Freedom in South Carolina* (1997).

All of these scholars have drawn upon the Freedmen and Southern Society Project (FSSP), a collaborative research effort centered at the University of Maryland under the direction of Ira Berlin and Leslie S. Rowland. These scholars have mined the National Archives of the United States to publish *Freedom: A Documentary History of Emancipation, 1861–1867*, a massive multivolume collection of primary sources. Each volume contains extended interpretive essays that place the documents in their historical context. While all of the volumes uncover the importance of labor in the transition from slavery to freedom, four in particular are noteworthy; they are Ira Berlin et al., eds., *The Destruction of Slavery*, ser. 1, vol. 1 (1985), *The Wartime Genesis of Free Labor: The Upper South*, ser. 1, vol. 2 (1993) and *The Wartime Genesis of Free Labor: The Lower South*, ser. 1, vol. 3 (1990); and Steven Hahn et al., eds., *Land and Labor, 1865*, ser. 3, vol. 1 (2008). The FSSP inspired many studies of transition from slavery to freedom during Reconstruction.

FSSP also influenced studies on the emergence of sharecropping and postwar rural labor relations; these include Jonathan M. Bryant, *How Curious a Land: Conflict and Change in Greene County Georgia, 1850–1885* (1996); Barbara Fields, *Slavery and Freedom on the Middle Ground: Maryland during the Nineteenth Century* (1985); Lynda Morgan, *Emancipation in Virginia's Tobacco Belt, 1850–1870* (1992); and Joseph P. Reidy, *From Slavery to Agrarian Capitalism in the Cotton Plantation South: Central Georgia, 1800–1880* (1992). Alex Lichtenstein has written a series of articles that challenges the interpretation that emancipation transformed slaves into wage laborers. He instead argues that black sharecroppers and tenant farmers were more like peasants with important ties to the land that wage laborers did not have; see "Was the Emancipated Slave a Proletarian?" *Reviews in American History* 26 (1998): 124–45; and "Proletarians or Peasants?: Sharecroppers and the Politics of Protest in the Rural South, 1880–1940," *Plantation Society in the Americas* 5 (1998): 297–331.

Among the many studies of black workers in the rural South between emancipation and the Great Depression are William Cohen, *At Freedom's Edge: Black Mobility and the Southern White Quest for Racial Control,*

1861–1915 (1991); Pete Daniel, The Shadow of Slavery: Peonage in the South, 1901–1969 (1972); Steven Hahn, A Nation under Our Feet: Black Political Struggles in the Rural South from Slavery to the Great Migration (2003); Robert Higgs, Competition and Coercion: Blacks in the American Economy, 1865–1914 (1977); Sharon Ann Holt, Making Freedom Pay: North Carolina Freedpeople Working for Themselves, 1865–1900 (2003); Gerald Jaynes, Branches without Roots: Genesis of the Black Working Class in the American South, 1862–1882 (1989); Robin Kelley, Hammer and Hoe: Alabama Communists during the Great Depression (1990); Jeffrey Kerr-Ritchie, Freedpeople in the Tobacco South: Virginia, 1860–1900 (1999); Jay R. Mandle, The Roots of Black Poverty: The Southern Plantation Economy after the Civil War (1978); Roger L. Ransom and Richard Sutch, One Kind of Freedom: The Economic Consequences of Emancipation (1977); Jarod Roll, Spirit of Rebellion: Labor and Religion in the New Cotton South (2010); Susan Mann, "Slavery, Sharecropping, and Sexual Inequality," Signs: Journal of Women in Culture and Society 14, no. 4 (1989): 774–98; Mark Schultz, The Rural Face of White Supremacy: Beyond Jim Crow (2005); Jonathan M. Wiener, "Class Structure and Economic Development in the American South, 1865–1955," 84, no. 4 (October 1979): 970–92; Jeannie Whayne, A New Plantation South: Land, Labor, and Federal Favor in Twentieth-Century Arkansas (1996); and Nan Woodruff, American Congo: The African American Freedom Struggle in the Delta (2003). A number of works investigate black workers and the southern system of convict labor and convict leasing; these include Douglas A. Blackmon, Slavery by Another Name: The Re-Enslavement of Black Americans from the Civil War to World War II (2009); Alex Lichtenstein, Twice the Work of Free Labor: The Political Economy of Convict Labor in the New South (1996); Matthew Mancini, One Dies, Get Another: Convict Leasing in the American South, 1866–1928 (1996); and David M. Oshinsky, Worse Than Slavery: Parchman Farm and the Ordeal of Jim Crow Justice (1997).

A number of other studies focus on the experiences of black workers in the New South; these include, Tera W. Hunter, To 'Joy My Freedom: Southern Black Women's Lives and Labors after the Civil War (1997); Dolores Janiewski, Sisterhood Denied: Race, Gender, and Class in a New South Community (1985); Paul Ortiz, Emancipation Betrayed: The Hidden History of Black Organizing and White Violence in Florida from Reconstruction to the Bloody Election of 1920 (2005); Peter Rachleff, Black Labor in the South: Richmond, Virginia, 1865–1890 (1984); and Paul B. Worthman and James R. Green, "Black Workers in the New South, 1865–1915," in Nathan Huggins, Martin Kilson, and Daniel Fox, Key Issues in the Afro-American Experience (1971). Both Warren Whatley, "African-American Strikebreaking from the Civil War to the New Deal," *Social Science History* 17, no. 4 (Winter 1993): 525–58; and Eric Arnesen, "The Specter of the Black Strikebreaker: Race, Employment, and Labor Activism in the Industrial Era," *Labor History* 44, no. 3 (2003): 319–35, provide valuable insights on black workers who crossed the picket lines of labor strikes. Brian Kelly, "Sentinels for New South Industry: Booker T. Washington, Industrial Accommodation and Black Workers in the Jim Crow South," *Labor History* 44, no. 3 (August 2003): 337–58, examines the class tensions between black workers and black elites. Brian Kelly, "Policing the 'Negro Eden': Racial Paternalism in the Alabama Coalfields, 1908–1921," *Alabama Review* 51 (1998): 163–83 and 243–65, investigates mine operators' experiments with welfare capitalism.

One of the most contentious historiographical debates in African American labor history has been over whether black workers made substantive and meaningful gains, politically and economically, through the labor movement, or whether organized labor used unions to subordinate and suppress the aspirations of black workers. Herbert Gutman's famous essay "The Negro and the United Mine Workers of America: The Career and Letters of Richard L. Davis and Something of Their Meaning: 1890–1900," in Julius Jacobsen, ed., *The Negro and the American Labor Movement* (1968), suggested black and white workers, at times and under certain conditions, achieved an uneasy labor solidarity. Herbert Hill, the former labor secretary of the NAACP, published an expansive critique of Gutman's argument and the work of his disciples in 1988, shortly after Gutman's death. See, "Myth-Making as Labor History: Herbert Gutman and the United Mine Workers of America," *International Journal of Politics, Culture, and Society* 2 (1988): 132–200; several scholars published rejoinders to Hill's essay in *International Journal of Politics, Culture, and Society* 2 (1989): 361–403. Many of the works cited below on black workers in various industries and communities engage the so-called Gutman-Hill debate. Studies that investigate the central questions in the controversy include Eric Arnesen, "Following the Color Line of Labor: Black Workers and the Labor Movement Before 1930," *Radical History Review* 53 (1993): 53–87, and "Passion and Politics: Race and the Writing of Working-Class History," *Journal of the Historical Society* 6, no. 3 (2006): 323–56; Rick Halpern, "Organized Labor, Black Workers, and the Twentieth-Century South: The Emerging Revision," in Melvyn Stokes and Rick Halpern, eds., *Race and Class in the American South Since 1890* (1994); Michael Goldfield, "Race and the CIO: The Possibilities for Racial Egalitarianism during the 1930s and 1940s," *International Labor and Working-Class History* 44 (1993), 1–32; a number of scholars wrote rejoinders in ibid., 33–63; Goldfield replied to his critics in "Race and the CIO: Reply to Critics," *International Labor and Working-Class History* 46 (1994): 142–60.

Works that explore black workers and their unions in the steel industry include Dennis Dickerson, *Out of the Crucible: Black Steelworkers in Western Pennsylvania, 1875–1980* (1986); John Hinshaw, *Steel and Steelworkers: Race and Class Struggle in Twentieth-Century Pittsburg* (2002); Ruth Needleman, *Black Freedom Fighters in Steel: The Struggle for Democratic Unionism* (2003); Bruce Nelson, *Divided We Stand: Americans Workers and the Struggle for Black Equality* (2001); Robert J. Norrell, "Caste in Steel: Jim Crow Careers in Birmingham, Alabama," *Journal of American History* 80 (1993): 952–88; Henry McKiven, *Iron and Steel: Class, Race, and Community in Birmingham, Alabama, 1875–1920* (1995); Judith Stein, "Southern Workers in National Unions: Birmingham Steelworkers, 1936–1951," in Robert Zieger, ed., *Organized Labor in the Twentieth-Century South* (1991) and *Running Steel, Running America: Race, Economic Policy, and the Decline of Liberalism* (1999).

Studies of black workers in forest industries include William P. Jones, *The Tribe of Black Ulysses: African American Lumber Workers in the Jim Crow South* (2005); Robert Outland, *Tapping the Pines: The Naval Stores Industry in the American South* (2004); Stephen H. Norwood, "Bogalusa Burning: The War against Biracial Unionism the Deep South, 1919," *Journal of Southern History* 63, no. 3 (1997): 591–628; Mark Fannin, *Labor's Promised Land: Radical Visions of Gender, Race, and Religion in the South* (2003) explores the Brotherhood of Timber Workers as does David Roediger, "Gaining a Hearing for Black-White Unity: Covington Hall and the Complexities of Race, Gender, and Class," in Roediger, *Toward the Abolition of Whiteness: Essays on Race, Politics, and Working Class History* (1994).

Black workers and their unions in the meatpacking industry receive extensive coverage in James Barrett, *Work and Community in the Jungle: Chicago's Packinghouse Workers, 1894–1922* (1987); Horace R. Cayton and George S. Mitchell, *Black Workers and the New Unions* (1939); Rick Halpern, "Interracial Unionism in the Southwest: Fort Worth Packinghouse Workers, 1937–1954," in Robert H. Zieger, ed., *Organized Labor in the Twentieth-Century South* (1991) and *Down on the Killing Floor: Black and White Workers in Chicago's Packinghouses, 1904–1954* (1997); Roger Horowitz, "*Negro and White, Unite and Fight!*" *A Social History of Industrial Unionism in Meatpacking, 1930–1990* (1997); Paul Street, "The Logic and Limits of 'Plant Loyalty': Black Workers, White Labor, and Corporate Racial Paternalism in Chicago's Stockyards, 1916–1940," *Journal of Social History* 29, no. 3 (1996): 659–81, and "The 'Best Union Members': Class, Race, Culture, and Black Worker Militancy in Chicago's Stockyards during the 1930s," *Journal of American Ethnic History* 20, no. 1 (2000): 18–49. For an excellent film that dramatizes the struggle to build an interracial union in the Chicago stockyards during World War I, see *The Killing Floor* (1985) directed by Bill Duke.

Studies that trace black workers and their unions in the coal mining industry include Stephen Brier, "Interracial Organizing in the West Virginia Coal Industry: The Participation of Black Miner Workers in the Knights of Labor and the United Mine Workers, 1880–1894," in Gary Fink and Merl E. Reed, eds., *Essays in Southern Labor History* (1977); Edwin L. Brown and Colin J. Davis, eds., *It Is Union and Liberty: Alabama Coal Miners, 1898–1998* (1999); David Alan Corbin, *Life, Work, and Rebellion in the Coal Fields: The Southern West Virginia Miners, 1880–1922* (1981); Brian Kelly, *Race, Class, and Power in the Alabama Coalfields, 1908–21* (2001); Ronald Lewis, *Black Coal Miners in America: Race, Class, and Community Conflict, 1780–1980* (1987); Daniel Letwin, *The Challenge of Interracial Unionism: Alabama Coal Miners, 1878–1921* (1998); Karin Shapiro, *A New South Rebellion: The Battle against Convict Labor in the Tennessee Coalfields, 1871–1896*, and "William R. Riley: Limits of Interracial Unionism in the Late-Nineteenth-South," in Eric Arnesen, ed., *The Human Tradition in American Labor History* (2004); and Joe William Trotter, *Coal, Class, and Color: Blacks in Southern West Virginia, 1915–1932* (1991).

The black Pullman Porters and the Brotherhood of Sleeping Car Porters are the subject of Beth Tompkins Bates, *Pullman Porters and the Rise of Protest Politics in Black America, 1925–1945* (2001); William H. Harris, *Keeping the Faith: A. Philip Randolph, Milton P. Webster, and the Brotherhood of Sleeping Car Porters, 1925–37* (1977); Jack Santino, *Miles of Smiles, Years of Struggle: Stories of Black Pullman Porters* (1991); and Larry Tye, *Rising from the Rails: Pullman Porters and the Making of the Black Middle Class* (2005). For biographical treatments of A. Philip Randolph, see Eric Arnesen, "A. Philip Randolph: Labor and the New Black Politics," in Eric Arnesen, *The Human Tradition in American Labor History* (2004); Jervis Anderson, *A. Philip Randolph: A Biographical Portrait* (1986); Andrew Kersten, *A. Philip Randolph: A Life in the Vanguard* (2006); and Paula F. Pfeffer, *A. Philip Randolph, Pioneer of the Civil Rights Movement* (1996). Black railroad workers are the subject of Eric Arnesen, "'Like Banquo's Ghost, It Will Not Down': The Race Question and the American Railroad Brotherhoods, 1880–1920," *American Historical Review* (1994): 1601–33, and *Brotherhoods of Color: Black Railroad Workers and the Struggle for Equality* (2001); Theodore Kornweibel Jr., *Railroads in the African American Experience: A Photographic Journey* (2010); and John Michael Matthews, "The Georgia 'Race Strike' of 1909," *Journal of Southern History* 40, no. 4 (1974): 613–30.

A number of studies investigate the working lives of black workers in the automobile manufacturing industry and their relationship with the United Automobile Workers; these include Beth Tompkins Bates, *The Making of Black Detroit in the Age of Henry Ford* (2012); Kevin Boyle, "'There Are No Union Sorrows That the Union Can't Heal': The Struggle for Racial Equality in the United Automobile Workers, 1940–1960," *Labor History* 36 (1995): 5–23, and *The UAW and the Heyday of American Liberalism, 1945–1968* (1998); Dan Georgakas and Marvin Surkin, *Detroit, I Do Mind Dying: A Study in Urban Revolution* (1975); James A. Geschwender, *Class, Race, and Worker Insurgency: The League of Revolutionary Black Workers* (1977); David M. Lewis-Colman, *Race against Liberalism: Black Workers and the UAW in Detroit* (2008); August Meier and Elliot Rudwick, *Black Detroit and the Rise of the UAW* (1979); Kieran Taylor, "American Petrograd: Detroit and the League of Revolutionary Black Workers," in Aaron Brenner, Robert Brenner, and Cal Winslow, eds., *Rebel Rank and File: Labor Militancy and Revolt from Below in the Long 1970s* (2010); and Heather Ann Thompson, *Whose Detroit? Politics, Labor, and Race in a Modern American City* (2004). Thomas N. Maloney and Warren C. Whatley, "Making the Effort: The Contours of Racial Discrimination in Detroit's Labor Markets, 1920–1940," *Journal of Economic History* 55, no. 3 (September 1995): 465–93; and Christopher L. Foote, Warren C. Whatley, and Gavin Wright, "Arbitraging a Discriminatory Labor Market: Black Workers at the Ford Motor Company, 1918–1947," *Journal of Labor Economics* 21, no. 3 (2003): 493–531, investigate racial discrimination in Detroit-area labor markets and its impact on black autoworkers.

Studies of black public employees include Jane Berger, "'A Lot Closer to What It Ought to Be': Black Women and Public-Sector Employment in Baltimore, 1950–1975," in Robert H. Zieger, ed., *Life and Labor in the New South* (2012); Samuel Krislov, *The Negro in Federal Employment: The Quest for Equal Opportunity* (1967); Joseph McCartin, "'Fire the Hell out of Them': Sanitation Workers' Struggles and the Normalization of the Striker Replacement Strategy in the 1970s," *Labor: Studies in Working-Class History of the Americas* 2, no. 3 (2005): 67–92; Philip F. Rubio, *There's Always Work at the Post Office: African American Postal Workers and the Fight for Jobs, Justice, and Equality* (2010); and Francis Ryan, *AFSCME's Philadelphia Story: Municipal Workers and Urban Power in the Twentieth Century* (2011).

A number of scholars have examined the lives of black longshoremen and their unions; these include Eric Arnesen, *Waterfront Workers of New Orleans: Race, Class, and Politics, 1863–1923* (1991); Peter Cole, *Wobblies on the Waterfront: Interracial Unionism in Progressive-Era Philadelphia* (2007); Howard Kimeldorf and Robert Penney, "'Excluded' by Choice: Dynamics of Interracial Unionism on the Philadelphia Waterfront, 1910–1930," *International Labor and Working-Class History* 51 (Spring 1997): 50–71; Bruce Nelson, *Divided We Stand: Americans Workers and the Struggle for Black Equality* (2001); Daniel Rosenberg, *New Orleans Dockworkers: Race, Labor, and Unionism, 1892–1923* (1988); and Calvin Winslow, ed., *Waterfront Workers: New Perspectives on Race and Class* (1998).

Studies of black domestic servants include Elizabeth Clark-Lewis, *Living In, Living Out: African American Domestics and the Great Migration* (1994); Elizabeth Ross Haynes, "Negroes in Domestic Service in the United States," *Journal of Negro History* 8 (1923): 384–442; Tera W. Hunter, *To 'Joy My Freedom: Southern Black Women's Lives and Labors after the Civil War* (1997); Vanessa H. May, *Unprotected Labor: Household Workers, Politics, and Middle-Class Reform in New York, 1870–1940* (2011); Rebecca Sharpless, *Cooking in Other Women's Kitchens: Domestic Workers in the South, 1865–1960* (2010); and Katherine Van Wormer, David W. Jackson III, are Charletta Sudduth, *The Maid Narratives: Black Domestics and White Families in the Jim Crow South* (2012). Other studies of black women workers include Karen Tucker Anderson, "Last Hired, First Fired: Black Women Workers during World War II," *Journal of American History* 69, no. 1 (June 1982): 82–97; Venus Green, *Race on the Line: Gender, Labor, and Technology in the Bell System, 1880–1980* (2001); Jacqueline Jones, *Labor of Love, Labor of Sorrow: Black Women, Work, and the Family, from Slavery to the Present* (1985); Xiomara Santamarina, *Belabored Professions: Narratives of African American Working Womanhood* (2005); and Bette Woody, *Black Women in the Workplace: Impacts of Structural Change in the Economy* (1992).

Studies of African American workers in shipyards include Katherine Archibald, *Wartime Shipyard: A Study in Social Disunity* with a new introduction by Eric Arnesen and Alex Lichtenstein (1947; 2006); Marilynn S. Johnson, *The Second Gold Rush: Oakland and the East Bay in World War II* (1993); Alex Lichtenstein, "Exclusion, Fair Employment, or Interracial Unionism: Race Relations in Florida's Shipyards during World War II" in Glenn T. Eskew, ed., *Labor in the Modern South* (2001); Bruce Nelson, "Organized Labor and the Struggle for Black Equality in Mobile during World War II," *Journal of American History* 80 no. 3 (1993): 952–88; and Charles Wollenberg, "*James v. Marinship*: Trouble on the New Black Frontier" in Daniel Cornford, ed., *Working People of California* (1995).

Among the many works on the Great Migration that emphasize the role of black workers are Abraham Epstein, *The Negro Migrant in Pittsburgh* (1918); Peter Gottlieb, *Making Their Own Way: Southern Blacks' Migration to Pittsburgh, 1916–1930* (1987); James R. Grossman, *Land of Hope: Black*

Southerners and the Great Migration (1991); George E. Haynes, *The Negro at Work during the World War and during Reconstruction* (1921); Gretchen Lemke-Santangelo, *Abiding Courage: African American Migrant Women and the East Bay Community* (1996); Carole Marks, *Farewell—We're Good and Gone: The Great Black Migration* (1989); Shirley Ann Wilson Moore, *To Place Our Deeds: The African American Community in Richmond, California, 1910–1963* (2000); Kimberly L. Phillips, *AlabamaNorth: African-American Migrants, Community, and Working-Class Activism in Cleveland, 1915–45* (1999); Joe William Trotter, *Black Milwaukee: The Making of an Industrial Proletariat* (1985), and Joe William Trotter, ed., *The Great Migration in Historical Perspective: New Dimension of Race, Class, and Gender* (1991); see also Nell Irvin Painter, *Exodusters: Black Migration to Kansas after Reconstruction* (1976).

The relationship between black workers, labor politics, and civil rights organizations are the subject of Beth Tompkins Bates, "New Crowd Challenges the Agenda of the Old Guard in the NAACP, 1933–1941," *American Historical Review* 102, no. 2 (April 1997): 340–77; Erik S. Gellman, *Death Blow to Jim Crow: The National Negro Congress and the Rise of Militant Civil Rights* (2012); Risa Lauren Goluboff, *The Lost Promise of Civil Rights* (2010); Dona Cooper Hamilton and Charles V. Hamilton, *The Dual Agenda: Race and Social Welfare Policies of Civil Rights Organizations* (1997); Steven A. Reich, "Soldiers of Democracy: Black Texans and the Fight for Citizenship, 1917–1921," *Journal of American History* 82, no. 4 (March 1996): 1478–1504, and "The Great War, Black Workers, and the Rise and Fall of the NAACP in the South," in Eric Arnesen, *The Black Worker: A Reader* (2007); Mary G. Rolinson, *Grassroots Garveyism: The Universal Negro Improvement Association in the Rural South, 1920–1927* (2007); and Raymond Wolters, *Negroes and the Great Depression: The Problem of Economic Recovery* (1970), which describes in detail the emergence of the National Negro Congress.

A number of scholars of black labor have emphasized the emergence of a black-labor alliance in the 1930s and 1940s that contained within it many of the seeds of the postwar civil rights movement; Jacquelyn Dowd Hall, "The Long Civil Rights Movement and the Political Uses of the Past," *Journal of American History* 91, no. 4 (2005): 1233–63; Rick Halpern, "The CIO and the Limits of Labor-Based Civil Rights Activism: The Case of Louisiana Sugar Workers, 1947–1966" in Robert H. Zieger, ed., *Southern Labor in Transition, 1940–1955* (1997); Michael K. Honey, *Southern Labor and Black Civil Rights: Organizing Memphis Workers* (1993); Robert Rogers Korstad, *Civil Rights Unionism: Tobacco Workers and the Struggle for Democracy* (2007); Robert Korstad and Nelson Lichtenstein, "Opportunities Found and Lost: Labor,

Radicals, and the Early Civil Rights Movement," *Journal of American History* 75, no. 3 (1988): 786–811; Thomas Sugrue, *Sweet Land of Liberty: The Forgotten Struggle for Civil Rights in the North* (2008). This "long civil rights" thesis is not without its critics; see for example, Eric Arnesen, "Reconsidering the 'Long Civil Rights Movement'," *Historically Speaking* 10, no. 2 (April 2009): 31–34; and Alan Draper, "The New Southern Labor History Revisited: The Success of the Mine, Mill and Smelter Workers Union in Birmingham, 1934–1938," *Journal of Southern History* 62 (1996): 87–108.

On the Fair Employment Practice Committee, see Eileen Boris, "'The Right to Work Is the Right to Live!' Fair Employment and the Quest for Social Citizenship," in Manfred Berg, ed., *Two Cultures of Rights: The Quest for Inclusion and Participation in Modern America and Germany* (2002); Andrew Edmund Kersten, *Race, Jobs, and the War: The FEPC in the Midwest, 1941–46* (2007); and Merl E. Reed, *Seedtime for the Modern Civil Rights Movement: The Presidents Committee on Fair Employment, 1941–1946* (1991). Charles D. Chamberlain, *Victory at Home: Manpower and Race in the American South during World War II* (2003) investigates the way that the expansion of the federal government, especially the War Manpower Commission, reshaped the lives of black workers in the South during World War II.

Scholars that emphasize the relationship between the labor movement and the civil rights movement as well as the civil rights movement's demand for economic justice include Greta De Jong, *A Different Day: African American Struggles for Justice in Rural Louisiana, 1900–1970* (2002); Alan Draper, *Conflicts of Interest: Organized Labor and the Civil Rights Movement in the South, 1954–1968*; Laurie B. Green, *Battling the Plantation Mentality: Memphis and the Black Freedom Struggle* (2007); Michael K. Honey, *Going Down Jericho Road: The Memphis Strike, Martin Luther King's Last Campaign* (2007); Thomas F. Jackson, *From Civil Rights to Human Rights: Martin Luther King, Jr., and the Struggle for Economic Justice* (2007); William P. Jones, *The March on Washington: Jobs, Freedom, and the Forgotten History of Civil Rights*; Max Krochmal, "An Unmistakably Working-Class Vision: Birmingham's Foot Soldiers and Their Civil Rights Movement," *Journal of Southern History* 4 (2010): 923–60; Peter B. Levy, *Civil War on Race Street: The Civil Rights Movement in Cambridge, Maryland* (2003); Charles Payne, *I've Got the Light of Freedom: The Organizing Tradition and the Mississippi Freedom Struggle* (1995); and Jerald E. Podair, *Bayard Rustin: American Dreamer* (2009).

Studies that investigate the impact of Title VII of the Civil Rights Act of 1964 on black workers include Paul Frymer, *Black and Blue: African Americans, the Labor Movement, and the Decline of the Democratic Party* (2008); Nancy MacLean, *Freedom Is Not Enough: The Opening of the American*

Workplace (2006); Timothy Minchin, *Hiring the Black Worker: The Racial Integration of the Southern Textile Industry, 1960–1980* (1999), *The Color of Work: The Struggle for Civil Rights in the Southern Paper Industry, 1945–1980* (2001), *Don't Sleep with Stevens!: The J. P. Steven Campaign and the Struggle to Organize the South, 1963–1980* (2005), and *From Rights to Economics: New Perspectives on the History of the South* (2007). On black workers and the case against Shoney's, see Steve Watkins, *The Black O: Racism and Redemption in an American Corporate Empire* (1997). On contemporary black workers, the work of Steven Pitts at the University of California Labor Center is invaluable; see http://laborcenter.berkeley.edu/index.shtml.

Excellent collections of oral histories of black workers in various industries and workplaces include Rick Halpern and Roger Horowitz, *Meatpackers: An Oral History of Black Packinghouse Workers and Their Struggle for Racial and Economic Equality* (1996); Michael K. Honey, *Black Workers Remember: An Oral History of Segregation, Unionism, and the Freedom Struggle* (2002); Horace Huntley and David Montgomery, *Black Workers' Struggle for Equality in Birmingham* (2004); David D. Perata, *Those Pullman Blues: An Oral History of the African American Railroad Attendant* (1996); and Harvey Schwartz, *Solidarity Stories: An Oral History of the ILWU* (2009). Important memoirs of black workers include, Charles Denby, *Indignant Heart: A Black Worker's Journal* (1989); Nell Irvin Painter, *The Narrative of Hosea Hudson: His Life as a Negro Communist in the South* (1979); Theodore Rosengarten, *All God's Dangers: The Life of Nate Shaw* (1974); and Robert E. Turner, *Memories of a Retired Pullman Porter* (1954).

Index

Abbott, Robert, 65
affirmative action, 153–54, 157–58
African American workers: in
   agriculture, 10–15, 22, 24–27,
   26, 28–30, 33–40, 63, 69, 82, 87,
   92–94,; 121, 176–78, 190–91 (see
   also sharecropping; Southern Tenant
   Farmers Union); ascendency;
   into the middle class, 158–60; in
   automobile industry, 69, 100–103,
   103, 120, 149–52,; 163–64; in
   building trades, 74, 135–36, 136;
   in coal-mining industry, 49,
   52–54, 120; in; cotton-textile
   manufacturing, 154–56, 161; in
   defense industries, 106–7, 107,
   194–98; in domestic service, 45–47,
   46, 64, 69, 72, 90, 187–89, 200–2;
   general conditions of, 40–44, 61–62,
   64–65, 68–74, 87–88, 116–18, 117,
   118, 158–66, 162, 163; in longshoring,
   56, 57, 83, 100; in lumber industry,
   40, 41, 41, 42, 43, 44, 47–48, 49,
   52, 123; in meatpacking industry,
   68, 69, 72, 76–79, 98, 120, 191–94;
   mobility of, 40–41, 47–48, 63–65
   (see also Great Migration; in
   paper manufacturing, 154–56);
   professional, 158–59; in public
   employment, 116, 118, 144–45,
   147–49, 164–65; in railroad industry,
   43–44, 83–84, 84, 94–95, 176–78;
   in sanitation, 141–44, 145–47; in
   service-sector employment, 156–58,
   162–63, 206–8; in shipbuilding, 104,
   105, 194–98; in steel industry, 43,
   68, 69, 71, 71–72, 73, 74–76, 98, 99,
   118–20, 154, 161–62, 198–200; in
   turpentine industry, 48; women, 35,
   45–47, 46, 64, 68–69, 72, 90, 107,
   108, 116, 117, 125, 145, 158, 160,
   163, 187–89, 200–2, 206–8
Alabama, 33, 49, 58, 65
Alabama Dry Dock and Shipbuilding
   Company, 108–9
Agricultural Adjustment Act (1933), 92
Agricultural Adjustment
   Administration (AAA), 92–93
Amalgamated Association of Iron,
   Steel, and Tin Workers, 74–75, 199

~

About the Author

Steven A. Reich is associate professor of history at James Madison University in Harrisonburg, Virginia. He teaches courses in labor, African American, and Southern history as well as in historical research methods. He served as the Department of History's graduate program director from 2007 to 2012. He is the editor of the three-volume *Encyclopedia of the Great Black Migration* (2006) and has written articles on Southern labor history, the Great Migration, racial violence, and black political activism in the Jim Crow South in journals such as *The Journal of American History* and *The Journal of the Historical Society*.